SIGHTED SUB, SANK SAME

The United States Navy's Air Campaign against the U-Boat

ALAN C. CAREY

CASEMATE

Philadelphia & Oxford

Published in the United States of America and Great Britain in 2019 by
CASEMATE PUBLISHERS
1950 Lawrence Road, Havertown, PA 19083, USA
and
The Old Music Hall, 106–108 Cowley Road, Oxford OX4 1JE, UK

Copyright 2019 © Alan C. Carey

Hardback Edition: ISBN 978-1-61200-783-0
Digital Edition: ISBN 978-1-61200-784-7

A CIP record for this book is available from the British Library

Printed and bound in the United States of America

Typeset in India for Casemate Publishing Services. www.casematepublishingservices.com

For a complete list of Casemate titles, please contact:

CASEMATE PUBLISHERS (US)
Telephone (610) 853-9131
Fax (610) 853-9146
Email: casemate@casematepublishers.com
www.casematepublishers.com

CASEMATE PUBLISHERS (UK)
Telephone (01865) 241249
Email: casemate-uk@casematepublishers.co.uk
www.casematepublishers.co.uk

Contents

Acknowledgements

"Older men start wars, but younger men fight them."

ALBERT EINSTEIN

I dedicate this work to those who survived and those who perished on both side of the U-boat War. I want to thank Mark Aldrich of the Tailhook Association for providing photographs, particularly of the Martin PBM Mariner, the U-boat Archive developed by Captain Jerry Mason USN (Ret), the National Archives at College Park, Maryland, the Naval History and Heritage Center, and the National Naval Aviation Museum's Emil Buehler Library. I especially want to thank the veterans of U.S.N. patrol squadrons who I interviewed and corresponded with over the years. Finally, I give special tribute to Mike Jarrett and the Bernard Stevens, both Dunkeswell natives, who kept the history of Dunkeswell Airbase alive.

Alan C. Carey
March 15, 2019

Maps

The North Atlantic. Primary areas of operations by U.S. Naval air forces from September 1939 to May 1945. Land-based operations focused on areas in range of patrol aircraft, while escort carrier groups covered areas in the mid-North and South Atlantic.

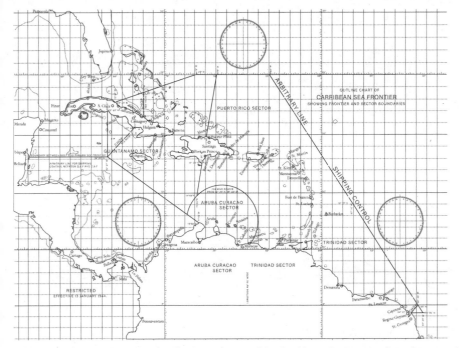

Caribbean Sea frontier. An updated and enhanced view of the Caribbean Sea Frontier from the original found in the official history of that command located in the National Archives. (See Chapter 3)

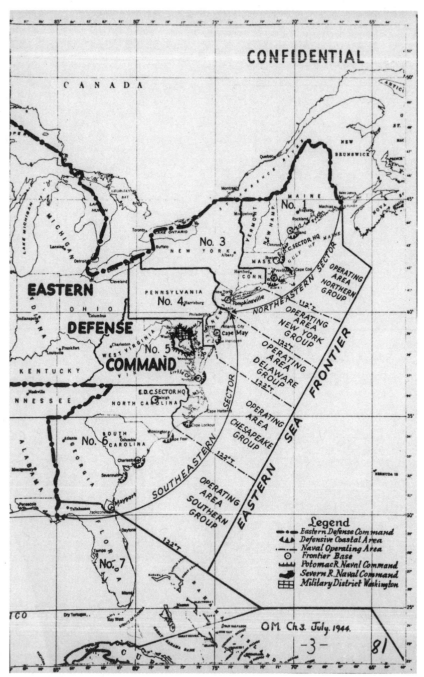

Eastern Sea frontier search sectors. Original map found in the History of the Eastern Sea Fronter, U.S. Atlantic Fleet. It shows the Eastern Sea Frontier divided by operational control areas for land and sea-based naval units. (See Chapters 2 and 3)

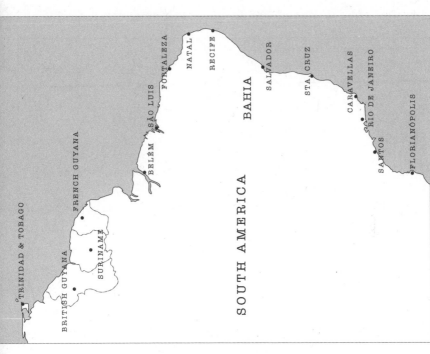

U-boat blitz off Brazil July 1943. Original map, located in the official history of Fleet Air Wing 16, showing merchant shipping attacked by U-boats and attacks conducted by the command's land-based air units. (See Chapter 5)

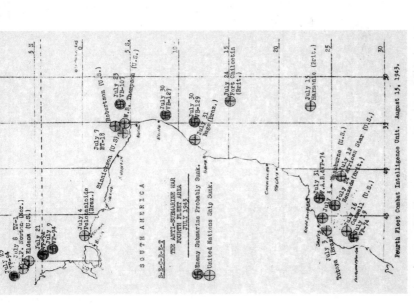

Fleet Air Wing 16 operations (1943–45). Land-based units of Fleet Air Wing 16 primarily operated from airfields located at Belém, Fortaleza, Natal, and Recife between 1943 and 1945. (See Chapters 4 and 5)

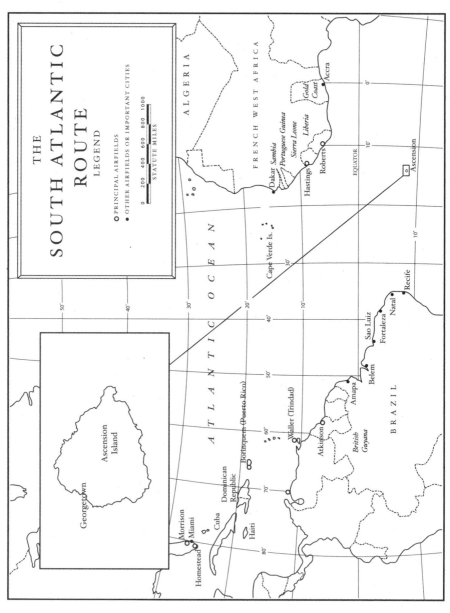

The South Atlantic route. Area search sectors conducted by U.S. air and surface units, along with an inset view of Ascension Island, where a detachment

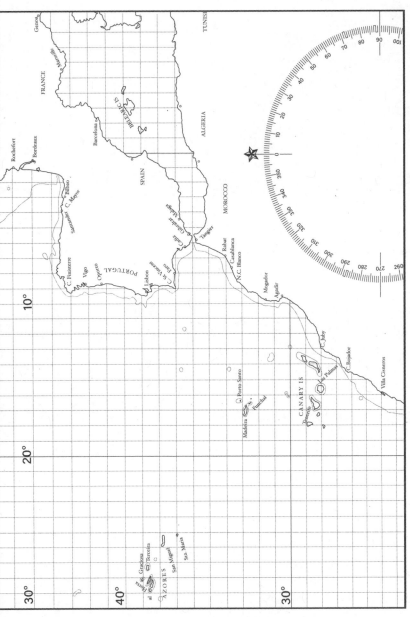

Mediterranean and Atlantic operational areas. Fleet Air Wing 15 operated from Port Lyautey, French Morocco (now Kenitra, Morocco), located just north of Rabat on the Mediterranean coast. Search sectors were in a line stretching from waters off Algeria southward to Agadir, Morocco. Escort Carrier Groups conducted operations in the waters beyond the ranges of land-based aircraft. (See Chapters 7, 9 and 10)

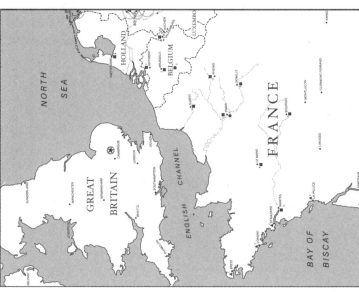

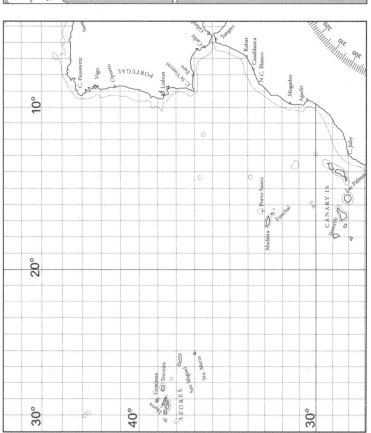

North-central Atlantic area of operations by U.S. Escort Carrier groups. ASW patrols by air units assigned to escort carriers operating in the Atlantic began in February 1943. The first successful sinking of a German submarine in areas shown in this map occurred on 5 June 1943. (See Chapters 9 and 10)

Fleet Air Wing Seven operational area. Naval air units based in England primarily operated out of St. Eval, North Cornwall, and Dunkeswell, East Devon. Primary search sectors covered the English Channel to the Bay of Biscay. (See Chapter 8)

Introduction

"The only thing that ever really frightened me during the war was the U-boat peril."

WINSTON CHURCHILL

This is the story of the United States Navy's air campaign against German submarines in World War II. It was a far-ranging conflict encompassing the entire Atlantic, from Iceland to South America, across to the English Channel, Bay of Biscay, and Mediterranean. German U-boats sank or damaged approximately 3,500 Allied and neutral ships including 175 warships in the Atlantic (with a total gross tonnage of more than 15 million gross tons). Yet, those numbers are meaningless compared to some 72,000 sailors, merchant seamen, and passengers who were lost when their ships went down.[1]

Nazi Germany's efforts to keep supplies from reaching Europe came at a high price, losing 783 U-boats and approximately 30,000 men between 1939 and 1945. This struggle for mastery over the sea-lanes began on September 3, 1939, when the German submarine *U-30*, commanded by Kapitänleutnant Fritz-Ludwig Lemp, sank the 13,500-ton British ocean liner S.S. *Athenia* off the Irish Coast, with a total of 128 passengers, including 28 Americans. Lemp, acting against orders targeting a civilian ship, signaled the Battle of the Atlantic. The mastermind behind the U-boat war Admiral Karl Dönitz, Befehlshaber der U-Boote (BdU—Commander-in-Chief of U-boats), and later Oberbefehlshaber der Marine (ObdM—Commander-in-Chief of the German Navy). His plan was to conduct an all-out campaign, designed to sink the maximum number of ship tonnage per submarine per day. Yet, at the outset, he was limited in what his fleet could accomplish due to its size and logistics.

In September 1939, the German Navy had at its disposal only 46 operational U-boats, based in German ports, which wasn't nearly enough to take a significant toll on Allied shipping. Logistically, their fleet had limited ability to remain in operational areas for extended periods due to the long distances required to travel from their primary bases at Hamburg, Wilhelmshaven, and Kiel. To make his plan work, Dönitz needed more U-boats and bases closer to the Atlantic convoy routes.

With the fall of France in June 1940, Britain stood alone against the might of Germany's air and sea power. Hitler's ultimate goal was to starve Britain into submission by mounting a naval blockade to stop war materials and food supplies

Rear Admiral (Konteradmiral) later Grand Admiral (Großadmiral) Karl Dönitz as the commander of Germany's U-boat fleet was the mastermind his nation's submarine campaign. (National Archives)

from reaching the island nation. Germany's primary weapon, the U-boat, operating in Wolf-packs of up to a dozen or more vessels, hunted merchant ships trying to make their way across the Atlantic from North and South America. For mutual protection the ships formed convoys protected by a screen of British destroyers. Yet, this could not stop the U-boat unrelenting attacks, and losses mounted to the point it became very doubtful Britain could survive.

U-boat operations during the first seven months of the war targeted shipping off to the west and northwestern approaches to Great Britain, the English Channel, North Sea, waters of Norway and Sweden and the Bay of Biscay. Germany's ability to extend U-boat operations into the mid and South Atlantic was enhanced with the occupation of France in June 1940 allowing Dönitz to base his combat *frontflottille* (flotilla) of U-boats. Submarine bases were established at the French ports of Brest (1st Flotilla), Bordeaux (12th Flotilla), the deep-water port of La Pallice at La Rochelle (3rd Flotilla), Lorient (10th Flotilla), and St Nazaire (6th Flotilla).

The establishment of bases in France and the increase in submarine production allowed Dönitz to launch his strategy of *Die Rudeltaktik* (wolf pack), where packs of U-boats, numbering between 8 and 20, fanned out across the Atlantic. The first U-boat to make an initial contact would radio back the convoy's course, speed, and disposition to the BdU at Lorient, France, so the rest of the pack would form up and intercept shipping. Dönitz first put the tactic into practice in October 1939, when the Hartmann Group, composed of three U-boats, intercepted Convoy HG-3 and sank three vessels. However, the first three wolf packs sent out between June 12, and August 19, 1940 were unsuccessful. The fourth, composed of five submarines, on the other hand, intercepted the 53-ship Convoy SC-2 during the first week of September sinking five vessels totaling nearly 21,000 tons. It was the beginning of "The Happy Time" for the U-*Bootwaffe*, a period between May and December 1940, when Allied and neutral merchant ships felt defenseless against Germany's U-boat juggernaut.

Responding to this menace, Allied forces waged a combined air and sea campaign that ranged from the Arctic Circle to the southern tip of Africa in this combined effort to protect the Atlantic lifeline. American air forces played a significant role in the war against the U-boat with U.S. aircraft destroying 159 with land-based and career-based naval planes accounting for half of that total between 1942 and 1945. However, through 1942 and into the first half of 1943, the naval air arm had very limited means of conducting effective anti-submarine warfare. It lacked sufficient numbers of patrol aircraft, had no very-long range aircraft in its inventory, such as the Boeing

-17 Fortress or Consolidated B-24 Liberator, and suffered from poor operational rocedures. Compounding those deficiencies was the attitude held by those at the highest evels of the U.S. military and those of the British in terms of strategy, tactics, and the fficient use of American air forces in the Battle of the Atlantic, especially during 1942. he British viewed their maritime patrol aircraft as an offensive platform to conduct nti-submarine warfare (ASW) operations, while the Americans viewed such aircraft s defensive weapons needed to protect transatlantic convoys. The American view of ntisubmarine warfare and the role of aircraft would evolve as the Arsenal of Democracy vent into full war production as the inventory naval aircraft increased, technological nnovations blossomed, and the methods for conducting ASW operations matured.

The U.S. Navy's air arm during 1941 and 1942 was far too inadequate to serve s an effective anti-submarine force, lacking aircraft capable of long-range patrols radius of 400–600 miles/644–965 kilometers) or very long-range (radius up to ,000 miles/1,609 kilometers). Such assets would be in high demand in the Pacific nd for convoy duty in the North Atlantic. The U.S. Navy sent out every available ircraft and blimps to hunt U-boats along the east coast, with the Army Air Force ontributing to the First Bomber Command under operational control of the Navy. he Civil Air Patrol (CAP) contributed to the effort. The U.S. Navy operated a ariety of aircraft for convoy coverage and ASW from single engine floatplanes, o four-engine heavy bombers, and lighter-than-air blimps. For overwater patrol weeps, the Navy acquired the Consolidated PBY-5A Catalina, Martin PBM Mariner models 1, 3, 3C, 3D, 3S), Consolidated PB4Y-1 (B-24) Liberator, Lockheed PBO Hudson, and the Lockheed PV-1 Ventura. The deployment of escort carriers with omposite squadrons operating the Grumman TBF/M Avenger torpedo bomber nd Grumman 4F4 Wildcat fighter expanded operations far beyond the range of patrol aircraft with the ability to operate across the entire Atlantic Ocean. U.S. Naval ircraft proved to be useful tools in the Allied effort to destroy the effectiveness of J-boat operations.

A Consolidated PBY-5A comes in for a landing on field at Argentia, Newfoundland returning from one f the constant anti-submarine patrols maintained over the North Atlantic. The Consolidated PBY-5A Catalina flying boat saw extensive service with the United States Navy and several Allied nations during he war. (National Archives)

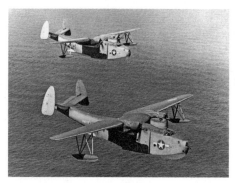

Several variants of the Martin PBM Mariner saw U.S. Naval service during the pre-war years, through World War II and beyond beginning with the PBM-1. Picture here is a C-series with radar dome. (Mark Aldrich)

Designated as the Model 37-21-01 Ventura, th aircraft would evolve as requirements for it change with versions designated as the British Ventura I IIA and GR. Mk. V, and the American B-34, PV-1 PV-2, and PV-3. (National Archives)

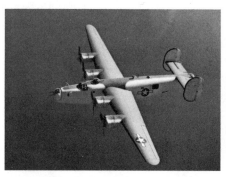

The first B-24 Liberator heavy bombers operated by the Navy varied little from the U.S. Army Air Force (U.S.A.A.F) B-24D with the distinctive Plexiglas nose. The distinctive Navy version of the Liberator had the ERCO bow turret that extended the length of the aircraft by approximately three feet. (National Archives)

U.S. Navy Composite Squadrons (VC) based aboar escort carriers operating in the Atlantic operated th Grumman TBF/TBM Avenger torpedo bomber Seen here are TBF-1Cs of VC-69 with *Horribl Homer* in the foreground. The aircraft could carr depth bombs/charges and a Mk-24 acoustic torped in the bomb bay as well as 3 and 5-inch rocket under the wings. (Tailhook Association).

The Grumman F4F/FM-2 Wildcat fighte operated in the Atlantic Theater well afte replaced by the Grumman F6F Hellcat in the Pacific. Wildcat pilots provided suppressing fir with wing-mounted .50 caliber machine gun while Avengers went in for a bombing run (Tailhook Association)

Submarine Detection Equipment

American airborne submarine detection equipment evolved from scanning the water with binoculars during neutrality patrols to air and land-based high-frequency direction finders by early 1942, to air-to-surface radar, the acoustic sonobuoy and an acoustical homing torpedo by mid-1943.

HF/HD pronounced "Huff-Duff," would pick up the radio transmissions from U-boats, giving the Allies the ability to track their course. Shore-based intercept operations were set up in Iceland, Greenland, down the United States Eastern Seaboard, along the Gulf of Mexico, the Caribbean to South America.[2]

The introduction of radar-equipped aircraft became instrumental in the effectiveness of locating a surfaced submarine far beyond that of binoculars. A handful of U.S. naval patrol aircraft late in 1941, possessed primitive air to surface radar (ASV) courtesy of the British Government. Yet, sufficient numbers of such aircraft would not become available until the middle of 1942.

The interest in airborne radar was rooted in a memorandum issued on August 5, 1940 by the Chief of Naval Operations, Admiral Harold Rainsford Stark, who established general rules for exchange of scientific and technical information between the United States and Britain. This cooperation known as the Tizard Mission, named after the senior British member, Sir Henry Tizard, consisted of a series of conferences with the first starting on August 29.

Equipment for locating the source of high frequency radio transmissions played a major role in defeating the German submarine menace. Direction finders at coastal stations and onboard ships proved themselves capable of pinpointing the exact location of any submarine using high frequency transmissions. (National Archives)

Naval Lieutenant John A. Moreno, of the U.S. Navy's Bureau of Aeronautics, discussed shipboard and airborne radar with the British. He disclosed the development of the cavity magnetron vacuum tube, capable of generating high power radio waves and making centimeter-band radar possible, allowing for smaller antennae arrangements and reducing the size of radar sets for aircraft usage. The result was the British Mk II ASV radar developed by the Royal Aircraft Establishment at Farnborough, England, in the early 1940s.

Rear Admiral Harold G. Brown proposed the U.S. Navy's own radar development program on October 3, 1940, with the first general meeting by the National Defense Research Committee's (NDRC) Radiation Laboratory as the principal agency

The first operational radar installation on a Navy plane was this PBY-2 Bureau Number 0454 from VP-54 shown here on 9 June 1941 at Naval Air Station, Anacostia, Washington, D.C. NAS Norfolk is also cited as the location. (National Archives)

assignment to radar development, meeting on November 11 at the Massachusetts Institute of Technology (MIT).

A week later, on the 18th, Admiral Stark issued a directive authorizing the official use of the abbreviation RADAR for Radio Detection and Ranging Equipment. The Navy established Project Roger on May 3, 1941, at the Naval Aircraft Factory located at the Philadelphia Naval Shipyard for manufacturing and testing of airborne radar, with Captain Wilson P. Cogswell, USNA 1922, in command.[3]

Rear Admiral John H. Towers, USNA 1906, Chief of the Bureau of Aeronautics, having the distinction of being Naval Aviator Number 3, issued a preliminary plan on August 7, 1941 to fit a handful of naval aircraft with radar with long-range search radar installed on patrol planes. The Grumman TBF (TBM) Avenger torpedo bomber would have short-range radar. The first available British Mk II ASV radar followed in June 1941, with technicians installing it aboard PBY-2 Catalina 54-P-10 of VP-54 at Naval Air Station Anacostia in November—thus becoming the first naval aircraft fitted with ASV radar, with forward-looking antennae located below the nose turret and sideways-looking aerials installed on the aircraft's port and starboard side. By the fall of 1941, one Catalina PBY-5A of VP-71, VP-72, and VP-73 along with two VP-74 PBM-1 Mariners were equipped with IFF (Identify Friend of Foe (IFF) and ASV sets.

The Radiation Laboratory developed its own microwave AI-10 radar with Planned Position Indicator (PPI), with flight-testing aboard a Lockheed XJO-3 (Lockheed Electra Junior) beginning on August 1 and ending on October 16, 1941. The 360-degree scan AN/APS-2 radar (nicknamed George), for K-Class blimps and patrol aircraft, went into production at the beginning of 1942. This radar, lighter than the AI-10, featured smaller antennae dimensions, allowing for the transmitter, receiver, and antennae to be housed in under-wing pods or in wing fairings. The AN/APS-3, produced by the Philco Corporation, followed in 1943. Installed aboard medium

Close up view of the interior of the bomb bay of a Grumman TBM Avenger showing sonobuoys positioned for dropping in the event of an encounter with a German U-boat. (National Archives)

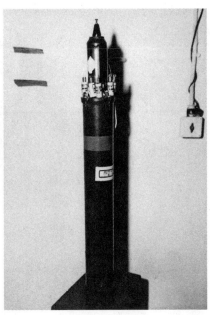

Close view of a sonobuoy used for under water detection onboard. The pilot of an Avenger aircraft would release clusters of the buoys and the crew would listen to pinpoint a submarine's position. (National Archives)

patrol planes such as the Ventura PV-1 and the Grumman TBF torpedo bomber, the radar could detect surface ships up to 30 miles away and surfaced submarines at 15 miles. The Western Electric AN/APS-4, a lighter version of the AN/APS-3, appeared in 1944. The AN/APS-6, in turn, replaced the AN/APS-4.

Since airborne radar could not detect a submerged submarine, the Navy Underwater Sound Laboratory in New London introduced the sonobuoy in the fall of 1943. About five inches in diameter and four feet long, the AN/CRT-1 held a hydrophone attached to a 30-foot wire, which released upon impact with the water. A radio operator on board a patrol plane would then listen for sounds emanating from a submarine's screws. However, it had one major flaw: a single buoy could not give a precise location of a target. Therefore, the aircraft would drop a pattern of buoys into the water in an effort to pinpoint the submarine's location. They were code-named purple, orange, blue, red, and yellow (POBRY).

Weaponry

Naval patrols in the early days of the war carried AN-Mk-17 aerial depth charges weighing a total of 325 pounds, with 234 pounds of TNT. The AN-Mk-44 and AN-Mk-47 replaced the Mk-17, weighing approximately the same as the Mk-17,

The Mk-24 acoustic torpedo in the bomb bay of a TBF/M Avenger aboard USS *Card* (CVE-11) on 16 August 1943. Avengers and PB4Y-1 Liberators were armed with the weapon for ASW work. (National Archives)

Arming an Avenger torpedo bomber with five-inch rockets aboard the USS *Card*. The rockets were first used in the Atlantic on an attack against *U-758* in January 1944. (National Archives)

but filled with Torpex. The Mk-53 was a later development and saw limited use in the war. Occasionally, patrol aircraft used a 650-pound-depth charge. Escort carrier based TBF/M Avengers carried the same depth charges and, by late 1943, carried the 3.5-inch Forward Firing Aircraft Rocket (FFAR) beginning in June 1943, and the 5-inch FFAR in December 1943.

The Mk-24 *Proctor* Aerial Mine, known as either *Zombie Fido* or *Proctor*, was an aerial torpedo, with the capability to detect and home in on the cavitation noise of a submarine's screws. In the fall of 1941, the U.S. Navy asked the Office of Scientific Research and Development (OSRD) for a feasibility study for developing an acoustic, air-launched, anti-submarine torpedo. On December 10, 1941, the OSRD held a meeting at Harvard University to study the proposal with General Electric, David Taylor Model Basin, the Harvard University Underwater Sound Laboratory, and Bell Laboratories. By March 1943, 15 months after conception, the Mark-24 went into production.

German Detection Equipment

Equipping U-boats with radar and receivers to detect enemy surface forces and aircraft seemed relatively taxing and unsuccessful for German technicians who needed to construct systems small enough to fit inside a submarine. The Berlin-based company Gesellschaft für Elektroakustische und Mechanische Apparate (GEMA)

The Type VII series was considered as the workhorse of the German submarine force. The Type VIIC had a displacement of 769 tons, a length of 220 feet (67.10m), a surface speed of 17.7 knots, a submerged speed of 7.6 knots and carried a crew of 44–52. Offensively, the VIIC had five torpedo tubes (four bow and one stern) and could carry a maximum load of 14 torpedoes. Its maximum diving depth was 721 feet (220m). (National Archives via Tom Gates)

The Type IX series were long-range submarines. IXC was a 1,120-ton vessel with a length of 249 feet (76m) with a maximum surface speed of 18 knots and a maximum diving depth of 755 feet (230m) and carried a crew of 48–56. It could carry a maximum of 22 torpedoes, fired from four torpedo tubes forward and two tubes aft. The IXC/40 class was a slight modification of the Type IXC boat with a slightly increased range, somewhat higher surface speed, and a bit heavier at 1,545 tons fully loaded and submerged. (National Archives via Tom Gates)

U-873 Type IXD-2 and *U-234* (left) Type XB in dock at Portsmouth, New Hampshire after surrendering in May 1945. The Type IXD was more than 500 tons heavier and almost 32 feet (10m) longer than the IXC/40. It was armed with a maximum of 24 torpedoes in six tubes, four at the bow and two at the stern. (National Archives via Tom Gates)

first developed the FMG 41G and FuMo 29 Seekat with a range of 4.3 miles (7 kilometers).[4] This set was installed on the Type IXC U-boat. The FuMo 61U FuMo 65U1 Hohentwiel radar systems, developed by the corporation C. Lorenz AG, began appearing on U-boats in August 1943, and could detect ships up to 6.2 miles (10 kilometers) and aircraft 12.4 miles (20 kilometers). Apparently, U-boat commanders distrusted the system because of its radiation emissions, believing the

Allies would pinpoint the location of a U-boat using the system through direction finding gear. However, the -61U was installed on many Type VII, Type IX, and Type XXI while the -65U1 was fitted on a few Type XXI.

U-boat commanders were initially supportive of installing radar detectors, and three major models were developed. The FuMB-1 (Funkmessbeobachtungsgeräts) Metox 600A ground search radar (GSR), developed by the French company Metox-Grandin & Sadir, detected the emissions from the British Mk II airborne interception. However, in August 1943, the Germans believed Metox was compromised, allowing the Allies to home in on the radar's emissions and increase the number of attacks on U-boats, and thus banned its use. Metox hadn't been compromised, British Intelligence was deciphering messages encrypted by the Enigma Machine. The Germans were so confident in Enigma they jumped to the conclusion that Metox was the reason for the uptick in attacks from aircraft.[5] Telefunken developed the FuG 350 Naxos-I, followed by the FuG 3501a Naxos, radar-warning receiver in September 1943, which could detect the British H2S radar, with a detecting range of 4.97 miles (8 kilometers). The Wanz G-1 Hagenuk, updated to the G-2, replaced the Metox and radiated far less emissions. However, U-boat commanders, in general, remained skeptical of such equipment believing radiation emissions were to blame for the Allies' vastly improved ability to track submarines. Such equipment was capable of detecting aircraft at a range of 30–60 miles (18.6–37 kilometers). However, in cases, when Allied aircraft detected a surfaced U-boat, it appeared the submarine's crew were unaware of approaching aircraft until visually sighted either suggesting the radar detection gear was non-functioning or monitored.[6]

CHAPTER I

Neutrality
(September 1939–December 1941)

"The aeroplane can no more eliminate the submarine than a crow can fight a mole."
ADMIRAL DÖNITZ, AUGUST 1942

Since the end of World War I, the American public, with a majority of politicians in Washington, held strong isolationist sentiments, particularly about keeping the country from becoming embroiled in the affairs of Europe. This sentiment intensified with the outbreak of a new conflict in September 1939. Publicly, President Franklin D. Roosevelt expressed a similar view to avoid American involvement, but privately his sympathy lay with the British and French since he saw the United States involvement in the war as unavoidable. Supplying those countries would allow additional time for the United States to strengthen its military capability. The Roosevelt Administration formulated American foreign policy aimed at securing the nation's own interests and security in the Western Hemisphere by issuing the Neutrality Act on September 5, 1939. This authorized the United States Navy to establish surface and air neutrality patrols and providing American military aid beginning in November 1939, when Congress amended the Neutrality Act of 1935, which allowed private American businesses to sell arms and materials to belligerent nations. However, only the vessels of the recipient or neutral countries could transport such materials, while United States-flagged vessels were prohibited from carrying the goods into combat zones. Furthermore, to limit the prospect of American casualties, the amendment banned its citizens from sailing on belligerent passenger or merchant vessels.

Neutrality Patrols (September 1939–December 1941)

The U.S. Atlantic Fleet, with Admiral James O. Richardson as Commander in Chief of the Fleet, formed the nucleus of early neutrality patrols, which would eventually extend from Iceland to South America. Naval shore-based patrol aircraft units, based at naval air stations along the east coast during September 1939, consisted of Patrol Wing (PatWing-3) with VP-33 (12 PBY-3), PatWing-5 with squadrons VP-51 (12 PBY-1s), VP-52 (6 P2Y-2s), (12 P2Ys), and VP-54 (12 PBY-2s). Naval shore establishments in the Caribbean at the outbreak of the war consisted of Guantanamo

Navy Patrol Squadron Fifty-Six (VP-56) of Patrol Wing Five (PatWing-5) at NAS Norfolk, Virginia received its first Martin PBM-1 in December 1940 and by March 1941 it had 10 PBM-1s including this one Mariner 56-P-6. The squadron flew neutrality patrols until September 1941 when it was redesignated as a training squadron. (Mark Aldrich)

Bay, Cuba, Panama Canal Zone, and Culebra Island between Puerto Rico and St. Thomas, Virgin Islands, with the latter having Marine Bourne Airfield established in 1935. In September 1940, to enhance military power in the Americas, and to aid Britain's ASW campaign, the Americans and British entered into an agreement known as the Destroyer-Naval Base Deal. The British received 50 World War I-era "four-stack" destroyers in exchange for 99-year leases to build military installations in the Caribbean, consisting of Antigua, Bahamas, British Guiana, Jamaica, St Lucia, and Trinidad.

By early 1941, Great Britain was losing the Battle of the Atlantic and, with the real prospect of the United States being drawn into the conflict, the U.S. Navy began devising a plan to protect the Atlantic sea-lanes. In March 1941, out of this necessity to conduct proper aerial and surface observation of the waters off the eastern seaboard, the U.S. Navy organized Patrol Wing, Support Force Atlantic Fleet. The function of the Patrol Wing was to provide anti-submarine, anti-raider, and shipping protection from Cape Hatteras to Newfoundland (patrols were later extended to Iceland and Greenland). For the next nine months, U.S. Navy Patrol Squadrons (VP) 51, 52, 53, 55, and 56 (equipped with such aircraft as the Consolidated PBY-5 Catalina and Martin PBM-1 flying boat) conducted aerial surveillance, and mapping

VP-55 was established at NAS Norfolk as part of PayWing-5 on 1 August 1940 and had twelve Martin PBM-1s by March 1941 with 55-P-8 seen here in October 1940 as one of the squadron's first Mariners. (Mark Aldrich)

from Quonset Point, Rhode Island, Norfolk, Virginia and, by the end 1941, from Argentia, Newfoundland.

CINCLANT (Commander-in-Chief Atlantic Fleet Vice Admiral Royal E. Ingersoll) Operational Order 2-41 established Support Force Atlantic Fleet under the command of fifty-five-year-old Rear Admiral Arthur L. Bristol, Annapolis Class of 1908, and former Commander Patrol Wings U.S. Fleet. The force consisted of Destroyer Squadrons 7, 30, and 31 and Patrol Wing Support Force with squadrons VP-51, -52, -53, -55, and -56 with tenders *Albemarle* (AV-5), *Belknap* (APD-34), and *George E. Badger* (APD-3), while the force turned in their early model Consolidated PBYs for PBY5As. Bristol maintained his aboard the destroyer tender *Prairie* (AD-15), while overseeing the establishment of Naval Air Station (NAS) Argentia, which in 1941 was a small, isolated fishing village located on the rocky coast of Newfoundland, 85 miles west of St. John's, separated from the mainland by Placentia Bay. In January 1941, under the American Bases Act, the British Government granted the United States a 99-year lease to build a naval base at Argentia.

Commander-in-Chief Atlantic Fleet Vice Admiral Royal E. Ingersoll served as CINCLANT from January 1942 until November 1944 when he took command of the Western Sea Frontier (Official United State Navy Photograph)

VP-55 Consolidated PBM-1 55-P-1 being hoisted aboard the Seaplane *Albemarle* (AV-5) on 1 May 1941 at Argentia, Newfoundland from where the squadron conducted neutrality patrols. On 1 July 1941, the squadron was redesignated as VP-74. (Steve Ginter via Mark Aldrich)

A pre-war VP-52 Consolidated PBY-5 Catalina 52-P-8 at NAS Norfolk in 1941. The squadron conducted neutrality patrols from Argentia, Newfoundland from February 1941 to November 1941 and from bases in Bermuda, the Caribbean, and Brazil from December 1941 to April 1943. (Bill Swisher Collection via Bill Scarborough and Mark Aldrich)

Four crewmen of this pre-war Catalina, one atop the wing and three on the aircraft's bow, watch as naval personnel bring the PBY into position for refueling. (National Archives)

VP-72 PBY-5 Catalina 72-P-12 in late 1941. The squadron served with PatWing-7 and PatWing-8 flying neutrality patrols until transferring to the Pacific in January 1942. (Mark Aldrich)

For the United States, Argentia would provide a year-round deep-sea port, free of ice, for patrolling the North Atlantic shipping lanes. The Navy promoted Bristol to Vice Admiral in February 1942, and he continued to serve as the support force commanding officer until his death two months later from a heart attack.[1]

On May 17, 1941, Fleet Admiral Ernest J. King, Chief of Naval Operations, issued Confidential Serial 023438 to the commanding officers of the Atlantic and Pacific Fleets, which ordered a reorganization of Patrol Plane Wings. This reorganization split the Support Force into two Wings: Patrol Wing 7 and Patrol Wing 8, with the mission clarified on September 12, 1941 when Captain Henry M. Mullinnix, Commanding Officer of the Argentia Air Detachment, received from Bristol Operation Plan No. 1-41 (revised on October 23, 1941) which dictated that Wing aircraft would operate in the Western Atlantic Area. This area would be:

> Bounded on the east by a line from the north along 10 degrees west as far south as latitude 53 degrees north. Thence by rhumb line to latitude 53 degrees north, longitude 26 degrees west. Thence south, and extending as far west as the continental land areas but excluding Naval Coastal Frontier, Naval District land and waters areas, Canadian coastal zones, and the territorial waters of Latin American countries.[2]

The Wing's mission within the area would:

Protect United States and foreign flag shipping other than German and Italian against hostile attack by

1. Escorting, covering, and patrolling for the defense of convoys, and, by destroying
2. German and Italian naval, land, and air forces encountered.
3. Insure the safety of sea communications with United States strategic outposts.
4. Support the defense of United States territory and bases, Iceland and Greenland.
5. Trail merchant vessels suspected of supplying, or otherwise assisting the operations of German or Italian naval vessels or aircraft.

The operations plan stressed that Wing aircraft were to:

> MAINTAIN CONSTANT AND IMMEDIATE READINESS TO REPEL HOSTILE ATTACK. OPERATE AS UNDER WAR CONDITION, INCLUDING COMPLETE DARKENING OF PLANES WHEN ON ESCORT DUTY DURING DARKNESS, VARYING PLANE ALTITUDES AS NECESSARY.[3]

On July 1, 1941, PatWing-7 squadron designations changed from VP-52 to VP-72 and VP-53 to VP-73 with VP-56's PBMs absorbed into VP-74 (VP-55) or were transferred to PatWing-5. The Eastern Sea Frontier grew during 1942 to include PatWing-9, PatWing-11, and PatWing 12. Those organizations changed to Fleet Air Wings in early 1942 as FAW-7, FAW-8, FAW-9, FAW-11, and FAW-12. Neutrality Patrols in the Icelandic area continued with aircraft stationed with tenders *Goldsbourgh* (AVD-3) and *Ganett* (AVP-8). PatWing 7 and 8, with the latter transferring to the Pacific on 15 December 1941, conducted patrols from NAS Argentia, Newfoundland with detachments operating from Iceland. Each of the Eastern Sea Frontier Patrol Wings consisted of four squadrons of 12 amphibious PBY-5A Catalina or PBM Mariners supported by seaplane tenders. PatWing-5 was composed of PBY-5A Catalina VP-81, VP-82, and VP-83. Severe

A PBY-5 taxiing along wind-swept waves somewhere along the Eastern Sea Frontier was typical of the conditions often faced by naval patrol squadrons. (National Archives)

An unidentified U.S. Navy patrol plane covers a transatlantic convoy while patrolling the Eastern Sea Frontier during 1941. (National Archives)

Admiral Ernest J. King Commander in Chief, U.S. Atlantic Fleet from February 1941 to March 1942 and Chief of Naval Operations March 1942 to December 1945. (National Archives)

winter weather conditions hampered flights to such an extent that the Navy acquired 20 lend-lease Lockheed Hudson Mk IIIA (USAAF A-29) twin-engine light bombers destined for the RAF with PatWing-8 at Norfolk, receiving VP-82 equipped with 15 of the PBO-1 Hudson. Twenty-two aircrews arrived for duty on November 18, becoming the first naval squadron to operate a land-based bomber.

In September 1941, U.S. warships began the dangerous game of escorting convoys on their journey to Britain, which put American lives in harm's way. On September 4, *U-652* launched an unsuccessful torpedo attack against the destroyer *Greer* (DD-145) sailing towards Iceland. This lone incident sparked the beginning of a *de facto* war between the United States and Nazi Germany. It was only a matter of time before American military personnel became casualties of an undeclared war. On the night of October 15–16, *U-568* torpedoed the American destroyer *Kearny* (DD-432), escorting a

On 17 October 1941, German submarine *U-568* torpedoed and damaged the American destroyer *Kearny* (DD-432), as seen in this image, near Iceland, resulting in 11 killed and 22 injured. In May 1942, *U-568* was sunk by depth charges dropped by British destroyer HMS *Hero* and destroyer escorts HMS *Eridge* and HMS *Hurworth*. (National Archives)

On 31 October 1941, Korvettenkapitän Erich Topp's *U-552* torpedoed and sank the American destroyer *Reuben James* (DD-245), resulting in 100 killed and 44 survivors. *U-552* was scuttled on 5 May at Wilhelmshaven, Germany. (National Archives)

50-ship convoy (SC-48), the destroyer stayed afloat but 11 American sailors died. A few weeks later, *U-552* sank the destroyer *Reuben James* (DD-245) off Iceland, while it escorted convoy HX-156, and only 45 enlisted ratings and no officers of 144 aboard survived.

U-boat operations during the fall of 1941 were primarily against merchant shipping crossing back and forth from Canada and the United Kingdom, and operations extending south along the East Coast of the United States after Germany and Italy declared war against the United States on December 11, 1941.

U-boat operations off North America began with *U-84*, one of seven boats comprising Wolfpack Seydlitz, which departed St Nazaire on December 27, 1941 and conducted an unsuccessful patrol southeast of Newfoundland. Wolfpack Ziethen followed with 12 boats targeting merchant shipping outbound from Canada between January 6 and 17. Kapitänleutnant Horst Degen, commanding *U-701*, operating 360 miles east-southeast of Egger Island, Greenland, struck first on the sixth sinking the British merchant ship *Baron Erskine*, a straggler from convoy SC-62. The U-boat surfaced after the attack and questioned survivors aboard a lifeboat, 34 of the 41-man crew, before resuming patrol. The ship's crew disappeared, among them, galley boy William Elder, the youngest member at 16. The carnage continued as ten more merchantmen, including three tankers of 8,000 tons, slipped under the cold waters of the North Atlantic while the human cost numbered more than 300 merchant seamen.

The 6,768-ton tanker *Coimbra* flying the flag of a foreign ally, sliding beneath the waves after falling victim to a submarine off Long Island about 100 miles east of New York, January 1942. (National Archives)

CHAPTER 2

Eastern Sea Frontier Operations (January 1942–August 1943)

"Hold what you've got and hit them where you can."

ADMIRAL ERNEST J. KING

U-66, 109, 123, 125, and *130* arrived off the eastern seaboard of the United States on January 13, 1942 to begin the U-boat campaign called Operation *Paukenschlag* (*Drumbeat*), planned by Admiral Dönitz to substantially increase Allied shipping losses and score a propaganda coup by conducting submarine operations with relative immunity in sight of the United States mainland. The Wolfpack first struck shipping off Newfoundland and Nova Scotia with *U-123,* commanded by Kapitänleutnant Reinhard Hardegen, sinking the 9,000-ton British merchantman *Cyclops* off Nova Scotia on the 12th just after 0100 hours. Two torpedoes broke the ship in two and it sank within five minutes, killing 87 crew and passengers out of the 182 aboard. Korvettenkapitän Ernst Kals, commanding *U-130,* followed the day after by sinking the Argentia-bound 1,500-ton Norwegian steamer *Frisco,* which carried lumber. The ship's master, two deck officers, and an able seaman were killed from two torpedo hits, while the remaining 15 members of the *Frisco* abandoned ship in two lifeboats—six were rescued. Kals scored a second kill eight hours after sinking the *Frisco,* when *U-130* sank the 5,400-ton Panamanian steamer *Friar Rock,* a straggler from Convoy SC-64, 110 miles off Newfoundland. Six of the 37-man crew survived. The U-boats continued southward towards the eastern seaboard where the lights of American coastal towns and cities continued to blaze, oblivious that enemy submarines were about to bring the war in full view. The Germans High Command became quickly aware of the Americans lacking sufficient numbers of surface and air forces to protect coastal shipping.

Drumbeat arrived off the United States coast at 0834 hours, 60 miles off Montauk Point, Long Island, when the first of three torpedoes from *U-123* struck the Panamanian tanker *Norness,* which carried 12,000 tons of fuel oil. Thirty-nine of the ship's crew abandoned ship before two more torpedoes completed the vessel's destruction. *U-123* proceeded to sink another five ships, two off New York and three off North Carolina, one some 12 miles offshore. Hardegen ran out of torpedoes and began the trek home

A U.S. Navy PBY-5A patrolling the Atlantic seaboard during 1941–1942 covering four merchant ships during their outline patrol as the convoy heads towards Britain. (National Archives)

only to encounter more merchantmen on January 25 and 27; the U-boat's deck gun finished off three, bringing the U-boat's total to nine ships sunk, totaling 53,000 tons. Total Allied losses for January and February were 65 ships lost totaling 389,218 tons.[1]

Admiral King began employing effective command and control measures, beginning with the establishment of individual sea frontiers that extended outward from North America. The primary duty of each frontier command was to defend shipping by providing air coverage for transatlantic convoys and to conduct ASW operations within their zone of responsibility.

All military forces in each frontier fell under the complete operational control of the respective Commander Sea Frontier. The Navy established five frontiers composed of the Eastern Sea Frontier, Canadian Coastal Zone, Gulf Sea Frontier, the Panama Sea Frontier, and the Caribbean Sea Frontier. Additionally, the vastness of the Atlantic required the establishment of the Bermuda, Azores, Brazil, Freetown, the Southwest Atlantic, and the Southeast Atlantic Frontiers. The Eastern Sea Frontier extended from the Canadian border to northern Florida. The Gulf Sea Frontier encompassed the Gulf of Mexico as far south as the border between Mexico and Guatemala, most of the Florida Coast, the northern half of the Bahamas, and the eastern half of Cuba. The Panama Sea Frontier covered the Pacific and Atlantic coasts of Central America and Colombia, and the Caribbean Sea Frontier included the rest of the Caribbean and the northeast coast of South America.[2]

Commander Daniel V. Gallery and other officers at the commissioning of the Fleet Air Base, Iceland, on 20 January 1942. He would later command the escort carrier *Guadalcanal* (CVE-60) during the capture of German submarine *U-505*. (National Archives)

Sighted Sub, Sank Same

The only interception and attack on an enemy submarine during January 1942 by an American patrol plane, occurred on the 28th when VP-82 PBO-1 Hudson 82-P-9, piloted by 28-year-old Aviation Machinist Mate First Class Donald Francis Mason, AMM1c (NAP), engaged Oberleutnant Eberhand Greger's Type VIIB *U-85* off Newfoundland, while covering Convoy HX-172. The attack would be heralded by the Navy and provide positive news to the American people in the darkest days of World War II, but the event is marked as creating one of the greatest quotes in history. The four-man enlisted crew aboard the PBO left Argentia at 1310 hours for an anti-submarine sweep astern of convoy HX-172. Radioman Charles Darwin Mellinger, two hours into the flight, was looking through a pair of binoculars in the navigator's position in the bow, when he spotted a flash of reflected light of a periscope. *U-85*, some 800 feet (244 meters) below, cruised in the rough, wind-driven sea on an opposite course of the patrol plane, 18 miles (29 kilometers) east of Nags Head, North Carolina. The U-boat had successfully sunk the 4,900-ton Norwegian merchantman *Chr. Knudesen* that had left New York harbor four days before, in which the crew of 33 perished.

Mason turned the aircraft and began losing altitude for a run astern and across the U-boat's course using the still visible periscope as the aiming point. Two 325-pounds (147 kilograms) Mk XVII depth bombs left the Hudson's belly, as the aircraft crossed the target at 25 feet (7.6 meters) and 165 knots. Plumes of the explosions spread one on each side of the periscope, estimated distance being ten feet abreast of the scope, causing the U-boat to lift out of the water and exposing the conning tower. The crew observed the *U-85* to take a vertical plunge and was sure in its destruction, especially when bubbly oil began to spread across the surface. Mason did not stay in the area and, as he pointed the Hudson towards base, he called to base and reported, "Sighted sub, sank same."[3]

The Navy promoted Mason to Aviation Chief Machinist Mate and awarded him the Distinguished Flying Cross (DFC). However, the celebration of the *U-85*'s demise was somewhat premature, as the U-boat reportedly suffered no damage or injuries to the crew and continued on patrol, sinking the 5,400-ton British steamer *Empire Fusilier* off St John's, Newfoundland, on the night of February 9, killing nine of the ship's complement. The *U-85*'s luck finally ran out on April 14, 1942, when it became the first U-boat sunk off the United States, and the first by a U.S. warship during a night surface engagement with the U.S. destroyer *Roper* (DD-147). Hit by the warship's three-inch gun, the submarine began to sink, and Oberleutnant zur See Greger ordered abandon ship. Approximately half of the crew made it into the water, as the destroyer delivered the *coup de grace* by dropping 11 depth charges amongst the survivors, killing every one of them. The *Roper*'s captain, Lieutenant Commander

The graves of 29 crewmembers from *U-85* at Hampton National Cemetery in Hampton, Virginia. They abandoned their submarine after the U.S. destroyer *Roper* (DD-147) heavily damaged the boat on 13 April 1942. They were killed when the destroyer dropped depth charges amongst them believing another U-boat had been located. (National Archives)

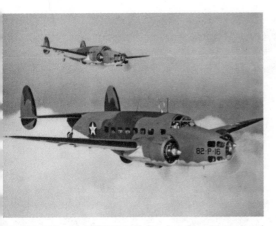

Two VP-82 Lockheed PBO-1 Hudson bombers, 82-P-16 and -17 in original British camouflage based in Newfoundland early 1942. Two aircrews from VP-82 scored the first two submarine kills for the fledgling Atlantic-based Navy patrol squadrons. (Tailhook Association)

Hamilton W. Howe, assumed, based on a false radar contact, that another U-boat had been located and thus gave orders to resume depth charging. The destroyer's crew began retrieving the bodies beginning at 0717 hours and completed the recovery at 0932 hours, when the 29th body was hauled aboard. The U.S. military took the bodies ashore and buried them at Hampton National Cemetery.[4]

U-boat operations extended further south to Florida during February, with two American and one Dutch tankers falling victim to Korvettenkapitän Hans-Georg Friedrich Poske's *U-504*, between 22nd and 26th, while *U-128* commanded by Kapitänleutnant Ulrich Heyse sank the American tankers *Pan Massachusetts* on the 19th, and *Cities Service Empire* three days later. An area extending from North Carolina, Bermuda, and New York became the watery grave of 24 merchant ships and many of their crews between February 3 and 28, by nine U-boats (*U-103, 106, 107, 108, 109, 432, 564, 578,* and *653*), while off Newfoundland and Nova Scotia, merchant losses totaled 15. The losses represented over 200,000 tons of shipping sunk during the month without a single loss of a U-boat. Merchant shipping losses increased during March 1942, as the Eastern Sea Frontier continued to be the center point of U-boat operations, with some 40 ships totaling150,000 tons. Nine of those ships fell to Kapitänleutnant Johann Mohr and *U-124* between March 14 and 23. Such operations, conducted with relative impunity, ended when *U-656* and *U-503* became the first Axis submarines sunk by American land-based naval patrol planes.

Type VIIC *U-656* left the submarine base at Kiel on February 4, 1942 for its second patrol under the command of thirty-seven-year-old Korvettenkapitän Ernst Kröning. The boat, commissioned the previous September, embarked on its first patrol on January 15 as part of Wolfpack Schlei, operating off the British Isles, but, after 14 days, the vessel returned home with its virginity still intact. The second patrol was in its fourth week and *U-656* had yet to score as Kröning stationed his vessel off the southeastern tip of Newfoundland. The U-boat surfaced, in sight of Cape Race on Avalon Peninsula, and in range of enemy patrol aircraft, during the early afternoon of March 1. Radioman L. E. Griffith, looking through binoculars aboard PBO Hudson P-8 of VP-82, spotted *U-656* traveling easterly through small white caps created by a 15-knot northwesterly wind. Pilot Griffin informed his

The 7,451-ton tanker *R. P. Resor* burning to wreckage off the New Jersey coast on 27 February 1942, near Asbury Park. She was torpedoed by *U-578* shortly after midnight. Only two of the 43 crew members aboard survived. (National Archives)

pilot Ensign William Tepuni who turned and saw the vessel as the plane flew at an altitude of 600 feet. There appeared to be nobody topside, no watch as required to spot enemy aircraft or ships as two Mk-17 depth bombs fell from the bomber's belly as Tepuni aimed the PBO across *U-656's* axis from 50 feet (15.2 meters). The explosives detonated close to the vessel's starboard bow while *U-656* submerged. Five minutes later, a large oil slick formed ahead of the U-boat's suspected track. The pilot sent a contact report before leaving for base, at 1440 hours an hour and ten minutes after making contact. The U-boat may have survived the initial attack as a trail of oil continued to flow on an easterly heading. VP-82 Hudsons (82-P-5, 82-P-8, and 82-P-10) returned three hours later, dropping depth bombs ahead of the slick. *U-656*, with 45 souls aboard, did not return to Kiel.[5]

Donald F. Mason, promoted to Chief Petty Officer, scored VP-82's second kill the following month on the 15th, southeast of Newfoundland, while providing air coverage of a merchant convoy. *U-503*, commanded by 33-year-old Kapitänleutnant Otto Gericke, left Lorient on February 1, for its first patrol, and had yet to engage enemy shipping when the American plane spotted the surfaced U-boat at 1411 hours. The detonation of four depth bombs spread across 30 feet (9.1 meters) from the now submerging vessel's stern, followed by wood splinters, cork, and oil spreading across the surface, marked the final resting place of *U-503* and its 51-man crew.

The three submarine attacks conducted by VP-82, ending in the destruction of two vessels, were the result of visual sightings of surfaced U-boats off Newfoundland,

PBO-1 Hudson 82-P-? of VP-82 based in Newfoundland in early 1942. Two PBO-1s flown by patrol plane commanders (pilots) Ensign William Tepuni sank *U-656* while Chief Petty Officer Donald F. Mason sank *U-503* during February 1942. (Thomas Doll via Mark Aldrich)

and in range of American and Canadian patrol aircraft. This was a deadly mistake for two inexperienced submarine crews on their first and ultimately last voyage. Four months would pass before Eastern Sea Frontier naval patrol aircraft encountered and successfully destroyed an enemy submarine.

The development of effective airborne anti-submarine equipment and tactics by the Allies began to take form in the late spring of 1942, along with increasing availability of naval surface vessels to institute convoying along the eastern seaboard. By July 1942, the convoy system, with armed escorts, extended along the eastern seaboard to Newfoundland, along with increased air patrols, resulting in a reduction of merchant shipping losses. The number of U.S. naval surface vessels for escort and ASW increased from 68 to 134 between April and July while the number of available patrol aircraft increased from 350 to 580 during the same period.

The first successful tracking of a U-boat through HF/DF and airborne radar from a U.S. land-based naval aircraft occurred when PBM-3C Mariner P-1 of VP-74 sank Type IXC *U-158*, under the command of Knight's Cross recipient Kapitänleutnant Erwin Rostin, west of Bermuda on June 30. *U-158* departed Lorient on May 4 for a third patrol, most likely anticipating to either match or surpass the first patrol in which five merchantmen were sunk and two damaged, three of them part of Convoy ONS-67, outward bound from Nova Scotia. The previous two patrols accounted for 17 ships sunk, with a total tonnage of over 100,000 tons. The first ship sighted on the latest patrol, and sunk 500 miles southeast of Bermuda, was the British-registered *Darina*, an 8100-ton motor tanker. The *Darina* became the first of 12 ships sunk by torpedoes or shellfire between May 20 and June 29, 1942. The Latvian-registered cargo ship *Everalda* became Rostin's last kill, 360 (579 kilometers) miles southwest of Bermuda. The *U-158* surfaced, the deck gun manned, and proceeded to fire 15 shells into the ship. The U-boat commander halted the attack long enough for the

Everalda's crew to abandon ship and board two lifeboats, except for the ship's captain and another crewmember taken aboard the submarine as prisoners. The cannon fire failed to sink the ship and a boarding party went aboard to open the seacocks, causing the ship to sink two hours after the attack began at 1745 hours. Before the ship went down, the boarding party retrieved secret codes and other confidential paperwork.

Rostin sent lengthy reports regarding the captured documents to BdU that British and American direction finders detected, allowing for an accurate pinpointing of *U-158*'s location. Aviation Radioman Third Class Wrencie Victors aboard a PBM piloted by Lieutenant Richard E. Schreder obtained a fix on the submarine and the plane conducted a longitudinal attack, dropping two depth bombs. The first exploded directly under the U-boat's stern, the second struck the deck, apparently lodging in place, and exploded as the submarine submerged for the last time with 54 men and the two prisoners.[6]

July 1942 saw a significant increase in losses of U-boats operating off North America with seven sunk in the U.S. Strategic Area, two in the North Atlantic Frontier, two in the Eastern Frontier, two in the Panama Frontier, and one in the Gulf of Mexico. Army and Naval aircraft sank two *U-154* by a USAAF A-20 Havoc of the 59th Bombardment Squadron on July 6, and one *U-576* by two naval floatplanes providing cover for an outward-bound convoy. Kapitänleutnant Hans Dieter Heinicke, aboard Type VIIC *U-576* on its fifth patrol, spotted Convoy KS-20 off North Carolina on July 15, 1942, and torpedoed U.S. bulk carrier *Chilore*, Panamanian tanker *J. A. Mowinckel* and the Nicaraguan merchantman *Bluefields*, sinking the latter, while *Chilore* later sank in the mouth of Chesapeake Bay. *Mowinckel* stayed afloat. The submarine then surfaced amidst the convoy off Cape Hatteras, North Carolina, whereupon two Navy Vought OS2U Kingfisher floatplanes from Scouting Squadron Nine (VS-9) dropped depth bombs within the explosive's kill radius. While the armed merchantman provided cannon fire, *U-576* sank taking the 45-man crew with it.[7]

Two VP-74 Martin PBM-1 Mariners, 74-P-2 in the background and 74-P-4 in the foreground, at Bermuda Airport in March 1942. Both have red and white rudder stripes. (Bill Swisher via Mark Aldrich)

EASTERN SEA FRONTIER OPERATIONS (JANUARY 1942–AUGUST 1943) • 19

An early Martin PBM of VP-74 (74-P-8) in foreground with camouflaged ammunition dump in background at NAS Bermuda. At the back (left) in front of the sign that reads, "Danger, High Explosives, KEEP OUT" are depth bombs and torpedoes. (Tailhook Association)

Martin PBM-1 of VP-74 being towed up the seaplane ramp at Navy Air Station (NAS) Bermuda on 27 April 1942. A Vought OS2U Kingfisher floatplane is flying overhead while a U.S. Marine guards a .50-caliber machine gun. (Tailhook Association)

"Sank sub, open club"

August 1942 saw the loss of four U-boats off Labrador and Iceland in the North Atlantic including the 1600-ton, Type XIV, Milch Cow *U-464*, a supply and refueling submarine, sunk off Iceland by a PBY-5A Catalina from VP-73. *U-464* spent the night of August 19–20 proceeding at slow speed on the surface, on a course of approximately 150 miles (241 kilometers) south of Iceland. The BdU warned the boat's skipper, Kapitänleutnant Otto Harms of patrolling Allied aircraft, yet he felt confident to remain on the surface and continued to do so when dawn approached. The Catalina 73-P-9, piloted by Lieutenant (jg) Robert Brown Hopgood, departed Reykjavik to cover a British task force to the southeast. Co-pilot Ensign Bradford Dyer tapped Hopgood's shoulder and pointed towards an object a mile-and-a-half away. The pilot reported, "As we closed within a mile, it was apparent that the object was a submarine fully surfaced doing less than four knots. At the time, we were flying at about 500 feet [152 kilometers]."[8] Dawn had just arrived, the sky complexly overcast, the sea churning from a 3-knot wind, as the Catalina flew through rainsqualls towards the U-boat. Hopgood rang battle stations and set the plane into a glide. The U-boat set off a yellow-white recognition flare. Three men stationed in the conning tower waived at the approaching plane as five Mark 17 depth bombs, mounted on the wings, fell towards *U-464* from a height of 100 feet (30.4 meters). Hopgood recounted,

> Immediately after releasing our depth bombs, I kicked left rudder, pulling into a climbing turn, and looked aft. Two columns of water between seventy-five and one hundred feet high were visible on either side of the submarine and just aft of her conning tower.[9]

Survivors of the U-boat said one of the bombs exploded to starboard, one to port and three fell on the upper deck forward. The starboard bomb did the most damage, blowing in diving tanks and causing the U-Boat tolist. The Catalina circled to port and his port and bow gunners opened fire, hitting the submarine, but doubtful fire from .30 and .50 caliber machine guns would cause a lot of damage to the steel-hulled U-boat. The depth bombs had their work as a large amount of oil flowed from the vessel, while compressed air and water blew from a point just aft of the conning tower and from the port side. A heavy squall developed and Hopgood lost contact on the sub after making an additional strafing attack.

By this time, *U-464*'s 20-millimeter and 3.7-centimeter guns began returning fire. However, after firing two magazines, a faulty round jammed the larger gun. The PBY encountered light, meager and inaccurate return fire during both strafing runs. During the aircraft's second attack, its crew described the fire from *U-464* as quite accurate, and, as the range had become too great for effective tracer aiming from the aircraft, Hopgood decided to call headquarters for help on the wireless transmitter, meanwhile remaining out of range in the clouds. For the next three-quarters of an hour, the aircraft employed these tactics, the U-Boat opening fire whenever it came within range. At about 0600 hours, a squall settled over the boat and contact was lost.

PBY-5A Catalina patrol planes from VP-73 returning from patrol head for U.S. Navy Fleet Air Base, Iceland on 23 March 1942. Lieutenant (jg) Robert B. Hopgood's crew aboard 73-P-9 sank *U-464* off Iceland in August 1942. (National Archives)

Hopgood provided convoy coverage for the next two hours before breaking away to relocate *U-464*. 12 miles astern of the task force there appeared a large pool of oil and, upon closer inspection, most of the boat's crew were in the water swimming towards the Icelandic fishing vessel *Skaftfellingur* stationed some 30 yards alongside the submarine. The PBY, flying low over the *U-464*, received intense machine gun and cannon fire causing Hopgood to break away from conducting another attack. He then pointed his aircraft towards a pair of British destroyers to guide them to *U-464*.

Free from further attacks by the American plane, Harm's men looked unsuccessfully for two men who washed overboard while operating the 3.7-centimeter gun. Harms then ordered increased speed, while ascertaining whether the boat was capable of submerging. Despite the damage, it managed to attain 8 or 9 knots. After a short while, the Engineer Officer reported that the boat was incapable of diving, and Harms then decided to abandon ship at the earliest opportunity. At this point, the U-boat sighted the Icelandic fishing vessel, earlier the same morning by the Catalina. Harms ordered, "Abandon ship."

Meanwhile, U-boat commander ordered the scuttling of the submarine and with a few remaining crewmembers abandoned ship and swam to the trawler. Once aboard, apparently, the Germans subdued the boat's crew and made plans to sail the vessel back to friendly waters, but cannon fire from approaching British destroyers,

PBY-5A P-8 Catalina Bureau Number 2458 of VP-73 based in Iceland during April 1942 when the squadron was tagged with conducting convoy coverage. Note the depth bombs mounted under the wing. (National Archives)

HMS Castleton and *Newark,* halted that plan. Harms and his crew surrendered to the Icelandic crew as a second destroyer arrived.[10]

The crew transferred over to the destroyers to become prisoners of war. When the British had taken the last German off the *Skaftfellingur*, Hopgood radioed base, "Sank sub, open club." A reference to the Officers' Club closed at the orders of Fleet Air Base, Reykjavik Commander Captain Daniel V. Gallery, who had ordered the club closed until VP-73, sank a U-boat (the squadron had seven unsuccessful attacks prior to *U-464*).[11]

Two U-boats patrolling off Iceland fell to attacks from VP-73 and VP-84, Type VIIC *U-582* in October, and *U-408* in November, the latter being the last sunk by land-based naval patrol planes in 1942. PBY-5As of VP-73 made contact with five or six surfaced U-boats between 0800 hours and 1745 hours, while providing convoy coverage southwest of Iceland on October 6, 1942. The submarines were part of the 19-boat Wolfpack Luchs (Lynx), and VP-73 sank one of the *U-582* commanded by Kapitänleutnant Werber Schulte, which had previously sunken seven merchant ships in earlier patrols.

Korvettenkapitän Reinhard von Hymmen's *U-408* sailed from Narvik, Norway, on October 31, probably hoping to have a successful second patrol as the first, when

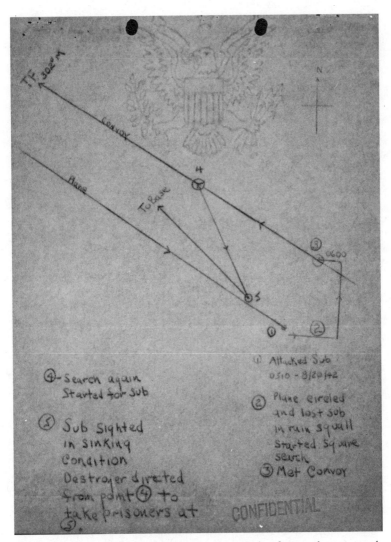

There were a considerable number of instances where photographs of an attack were not taken due to weather, darkness, malfunctioning camera, or having no camera on board. A drawing from the after action report of Lieutenant (jg) Hopgood's attack on *U-464*. (National Archives)

the submarine's torpedoes and gunfire sank three merchantmen of convoy PQ-18 off Iceland in September. Hymmen stationed his boat in the waters between Northern Iceland and Greenland looking for an unfortunate enemy vessel to cross his path on the morning of November 5. VP-84's Lieutenant R. C. Millard, piloting PBY5-A 84-P-8 on patrol in the Greenland Sea north of Iceland, after initially picking up a contact by radar, visually spotted *U-408* on the surface at 1122 hours. Between eight and nine men on the conning tower were swept or jumped into the sea as Millard

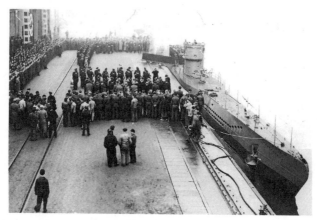

Type VIIC *U-408* at commissioning on 19 November 1941, commanded by Kapitänleutnant Reinhard von Hymmen, was on its third patrol when it was sunk by a PBY-5A from VP-84 on 5 November 1942. (Author's Collection)

released four depth bombs. Wood splinters, oil, and unidentified debris, along with the men, were all that remained on the surface after the explosions. The PBY circled the area for nearly an hour, the crew looking down as the U-boat survivors died one by one from hypothermia. The rest of the crew inside *U-408* who hadn't been killed by the explosions drowned or died when the vessel imploded as it reached crush depth.

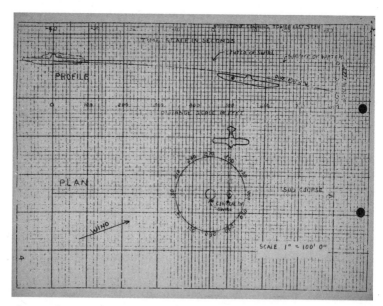

A drawing showing the attack on *U-408* found as part of the after action report filed after the submarine's destruction by VP-84's Lieutenant R.C. Millard piloting PBY-5A 84-P-8. (National Archives)

Eastern Sea Frontier (January–August 1943)

From December 1942 through March 1943, Eastern Sea Frontier and Icelandic based naval patrol squadrons were unsuccessful in the destruction of enemy submarines. By spring 1943, Allied shipping losses through U-boat attacks in the Atlantic and Artic regions had reached an alarming number of 359 (1,500,000 gross tons) between January and May 1943. However, Allied shipping losses in the North Atlantic began decreasing as the BdU began shifting submarine operations into the South Atlantic, and Allied ASW weaponry and tactics evolved.

Largest Merchant Shipping Losses in the North and South East Atlantic February–May 1943

Month	Ships	Gross Tons
Feb	36	227,109
March	60	376,772
Apr	21	130,026
May	24	129,040

Samuel Eliot Morison, *The Atlantic Battle Won* (2001)

Meanwhile, the Atlantic Fleet continued to address organizational issues. The Navy established Air Forces Atlantic Fleet at Quonset Point on January 1, 1943. Operation Plan 1–43 assigned control of units under the command of Rear Admiral Alva D. Bernhard, formerly Commander of Fleet Air Wings Atlantic Fleet, as Commander Air Force, Atlantic Fleet (COMAIRLANT). The reasoning for the move was to streamline operational control that was haphazard at best. From the beginning of the war there were problems with air organization between air units operating from sea frontiers and those of fleet air units assigned to the Pacific Theater. Particularly frontier units suffered chronic deficiencies of aircraft and equipment with personnel having to beg, borrow, and rely on the Army for long-range patrol duty. The previous organizational spider web made procurement of aircraft, equipment and unit assignment of aircraft involve different commands: COMINCH, CINCLANT, and Commander Eastern Sea Frontier. The establishment of COMAIRLANT streamlined the organizational chaos. All administrative air commands, including that of carriers, carrier replacement squadrons, fleet air wings, naval aircraft and lighter-than-air based on the Atlantic Coast were reassigned to COMAIRLANT. In this reorganization, there was a need for closer coordination between air commands of the Frontier and the Fleet, illustrated by assigning Fleet Air Wing Commanders as task group commanders. To develop new anti-submarine weapons and tactics, Rear Admiral Francis S. Low ordered the commissioning on April 1, 1943, of the Aircraft Anti-Submarine Development Detachment under the administration of

Commander Air Force, Atlantic Fleet and under the direct command of Captain (then Commander) Aurelius B. Vosseller, former commanding officer of VP-74. Here for the first-time naval pilots and crewmen, technicians, and men of science worked side by side in the same detail with the one purpose of improving the air aspects of anti-submarine warfare. The products of scientific warfare combined with naval air tactics would form into an efficient means of hunting enemy submarines.[12]

"Its mission was to: conduct experiments on airborne anti-submarine equipment in order to determine the practical value of that equipment and to recommend improvements thereto; to develop the best tactical uses of the accepted equipment including attack procedures for search planes, convoy escorts, and night tactics for aircraft units assigned to anti-submarine warfare."[13]

VB-125 became the first Atlantic-based Lockheed PV-1 Ventura squadron to sink an enemy submarine, the new designation for VP-82 after reforming. The squadron began as VP-82 flying the PBO Hudson until reforming at Quonset Point on September 27, 1942 to begin transitioning to the PV-3 Ventura, the Navy designation for the Ventura Mk. II, until PV-1s were available in December. Based at Argentia, Newfoundland and operating under FAW-12, the squadron began ASW and Convoy coverage. On April 27, 1943, PV-1 125-B-6, piloted by Lieutenant Thomas Kinaszczuk, attacked the surfaced Type IXC *U-174*, under the command of twenty-six-year-old Oberleutnant zur See Wolfgang Grandefeld, off Cape Race, Newfoundland. This was the U-boat's third cruise; previously it had

VP-82 reorganized as VB-125 and transitioned from the PBO-1 Hudson to the Lockheed PV-1 Ventura. PV-1 Ventura 125-B-6 was the aircraft responsible for *U-174*'s destruction. The early version of the PV-1 retained the bombardier's station in the nose. Visible are the two fixed 0.50-caliber machine guns, which were supplemented in later models with a chin package of three additional 0.50 guns. (National Archives)

sunk five merchant ships between October 31 and December 5, 1942. It had also survived three Allied attacks the previous year. It survived a shelling and depth charge attack from the Royal Norwegian Corvette *HNoMs Potentilla* on August 25, with damage to the deck and conning tower, and escaped unscathed from two depth bomb attacks from VP-83 on December 15. Approaching the submarine, the bomber came under intense anti-aircraft fire with the Ventura sustaining heavy damage, but not before Kinaszczuk dropped a string of depth charges sinking the U-boat, leaving no survivors of its 53-man crew.

Between May 14 and June 24, 1943, VP-84 sent the crews of four U-boats to their deaths off Iceland, beginning with Type VIIC *U-640* on May 14, setting a record for number of enemy submarines sunk by a single American patrol squadron, which earned it the Presidential Unit Citation. Three of the four boats were conducting their first patrols. *U-640*, a part of Wolfpack Iller, under the command of Oberleutnant zur See Karl-Heniz Nagal, was two weeks out from Kiel on its maiden patrol. Lieutenant P. A. Bodinet flying east of Cape Farewll, Greenland spotted and sank Nagal's boat on May 14, leaving no survivors. Lieutenant Millard, who previously found and sank *U-408*, dropped a Mk-24 acoustic torpedo Proctor homing torpedo, sinking the Type VIIC *U-467* southeast of Iceland on the 25th. This was the first documented sinking of a U-boat using the new weapon. June saw the loss of Type VIIC *U-388* and type IXC/40 *U-194* from successful attacks by PBY5-As of VP-84. Lieutenant E. W. Wood spotted and sank *U-388* commanded by Oberleutnant zur See Peter Sues on the surface southeast of Cape Farewell on the 20th, becoming the first Type IXC/40 second U-boat lost to a Proctor. Oberleutnant zur See Sues and his crew had only been at sea on their first cruise for 12 days. Kapitänleutnant Hermann Hesse, previously commander of *U-133*, took *U-194* out for its first patrol on Kiel on June 12, and was discovered by Lieutenant J. W. Beach's crew on the 24th, southwest of Iceland and became the third U-boat sunk by a Mk-24 Torpedo.

Most patrol squadrons suffered operational accidents resulting in the deaths of combat aircrews. VP-84 was no different. The squadron suffered two fatal accidents in Iceland with the first occurring on December 27, 1942 when a PBY flown by Lieutenant H. H. Luce crashed not long after takeoff on Keflkavik Peninsula, killing him and seven men aboard. On June 11, 1943, Lieutenant (jg) Douglas Vientra and all but one of his crew died while attempting to rescue the crew of an RAF B-17 Flying Fortress that had ditched. The PBY hit a high wave and sank, leaving its crew of nine floating in two lift rafts. Five days later rescuers found only Lionel Pelletier Aviation Radioman First Class alive the others having died of exposure.

A patrol plane earlier on August 7, reported an enemy submarine 300 miles (482 kilometers) east of Norfolk, Virginia. A PV-1 Ventura from VB-128, piloted by Lieutenant (jg) Frederick C. Cross, departed Floyd Bennett, New York, to look for it. The bomber's radar picked up Type VIIC *U-566*, commanded by Kapitänleutnant Hans Hornkohl, at 1322 hours 300 miles (483 kilometers) east of Cape Charles,

Ventura 125-B-6 piloted by Lieutenant (jg) Thomas Kinaszczuk attacking *U-174* southwest of Newfoundland on 27 April 1943. The submarine's bow reappears on surface moments before disappearing into the North Atlantic. (National Archives)

The crew of 125-B-6 pose in front of their PV-1 Ventura after the sinking of *U-174*. Above and to the right of "B-6" is a U-boat victory marking. Lieutenant (jg) Thomas Kinaszczuk (far left) was the patrol plane commander (National Archives). Shown (left to right): Lieutenant Junior Grade Thomas Kinaszczuk, USNR, pilot; Lieutenant Robert J. Slagle, USN, co-pilot; Aviation Machinist's Mate Third Class Joseph A. Holt, USNR, gunner; and Radioman Second Class Robert W. Berg, USNR. (National Archives)

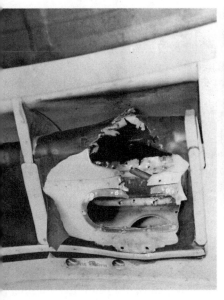

Two images showing damage to PV-1 125-B-6 caused by anti-aircraft fire from *U-174*'s 20mm guns. The plane, although badly damaged, made it safely back to base at Argentia. (National Archives)

Virginia. The U-boat's antiaircraft hit the PV-1 as it came out of a cloud, knocking out one engine and mortally wounding Cross. Although wounded, he continued the attack and dropped his depth charges, which were near misses. The heavily damaged plane could not stay in the air and Lieutenant Cross conducted a successful ditching allowing him, the co-pilot Lt. (jg) Thomas J. Aylward Jr., and radioman James A. Welch to exit the sinking plane. The turret gunner, however, went down with the plane and Cross later succumbed to his wounds before a PBM arrived on the scene. The Ventura's pilot received the Navy Cross, posthumously. Back at base, the squadron's executive officer, Lieutenant Joseph M. George, heard about Cross' ditching and headed out with his crew in another Ventura. Base communications picked up a radio report from Lieutenant George saying, "Approaching scene of action." He and his crew disappeared, brought down by the submarine's fire while the patrol plane attacked with depth bombs. A third squadron PV-1 arrived piloted by Lieutenant J. R. Smith along with a PBM Mariner from VP-211, flown by Lieutenant E. C. Scully. The Ventura dropped four depth charges as the U-boat submerged. A malfunctioning diving tank forced the submarine to resurface; the anti-aircraft guns resumed aggressive action to bring down a third American plane, scoring minor damage to both aircraft. The submarine then submerged again leaving Hornkohl and the anti-aircraft gunners topside. The commander clung to the periscope while waves swept the gunners overboard. The patrol planes departed assuming the submarine sank; however, *U-566* resurfaced 20 minutes later. The U-boat made its escape after bringing aboard the captain and gunners. VB-128 lost two aircraft and all but two crewmen while another squadron plane and a VP-211 PBM suffered battle damage. Admiral Dönitz's Battle Standing War Order 483 ordering U-boats to remain surfaced and engage enemy aircraft proved successful this time, but Allied pilots would adapt tactics to counter this aggressiveness by launching coordinated attacks with one or more aircraft sweeping a U-boat's deck with machinegun fire and rockets while others conducted depth charge or torpedo attacks. *U-566* survived another two months until its scuttling on October 24, 1943 in the North Atlantic after suffering damage from six depth charges from a British Wellington aircraft.[1]

On October 4, 1943, Commander Charles Westhofen of VB-128 avenged the deaths of two aircrews by spotting Type VIIC *U-279* southwest of Iceland, but, before he could attack, the submarine submerged. Westhofen decided to leave and come back later to see if the boat surfaced. An hour later, the pilot spotted the U-boat on the surface and the PV-1 went down for an attack. Despite heavy anti-aircraft fire the Ventura pilot made a low-level attack and dropped three depth charges across the length of the hall. The submarine disappeared, leaving survivors in the water. Westhofen came back around and machine-gunned the survivors struggling in the water. During the flight back to base, he turned to his co-pilot, Lieutenant (jg) John Luther, and explained that a quick death by gunfire would be better than a slow one freezing. The 48-man crew died from the machine gun fire or from hypothermia in the freezing waters of the North Atlantic.[15]

On May 20, 1943, Admiral King established the Tenth U.S. Fleet with a centralized anti-submarine command, Commanded by Admiral King himself with Rear Admiral Low as chief-of-staff. His mission consisted of coordinating and directing naval forces in the Battle of the Atlantic by:

1. The destruction of enemy submarines.
2. The protection of Allied shipping in the Eastern, Gulf, and Caribbean Sea Frontiers.

Two images show the sinking of *U-279* commanded by Oberleutnant Otto Finke. It was caught on the surface and sunk by depth bombs from a Ventura flown by Lieutenant Charles L. Westhofen of VB-128. None of the 48 crewmen aboard the vessel survived. (National Archives)

3. The exercise of convoy shipping that are United States responsibilities.
4. The correlation of United States antisubmarine training and material development training.[16]

Liberators to the Navy

The establishment of the Tenth Fleet did not include the Army's anti-submarine squadrons based along the Eastern Sea Frontier, thereby excluding them from a centralized command structure in which General Hap Arnold desired that Navy planes conduct ASW operations jointly with Army planes under the command of an Air Force general and to operate under Air Force tactics. Admiral King strongly disagreed on operational policy arguing that naval aircraft function as that of British Coastal Command, escorting convoys and attacking submarines operating near the shipping. The Air Force labeled that as being defensive in nature while its policy was offensive with the slogan, "Search, Strike, Sink!"[17]

The disagreement reached the boiling point when King asked Arnold to furnish B-24 for duty in Newfoundland during the first week of June 1943. The general acquiesced, but ordered the squadron's commanding officer to conduct offensive ASW operations and not engage in convoy escort duty. Before the United States officially went to war and through 1943, both U.S. Army Air Force conducted ASW operations in the North and South Atlantic with land-based aircraft. Caribbean-based Air Force units, operating the B-18 Bolo and A-20 Havoc, sank three U-boats between July and October 1942 (*U-153, 654*, and *512*). The Air Force also established B-24 units in late 1942 and early 1943: the 479th and 480th Anti-submarine Groups.

King after appraised of the situation in Newfoundland declared the Army bombers useless if the planes could not perform escort duty. A conference held on 10 June by Arnold General Joseph T. McNarmey, Rear Admiral John S. McCain, and Captain M. B. Gardner, the two generals stated the Air Force no longer wanted to participate in ASW and full control of the endeavor granting naval aviation with such operations. The Air Force agreed to turnover anti-submarine operations to the Navy with the provision that the Navy would not participate in strategic bombing. The Navy's desire to operate very long patrol aircraft in the Pacific resulted in the Air Force turning over 700 B-24 Liberators for the former's use during the war. The Navy established over a dozen B-24 bomber squadrons in the Pacific, while VB-103, 105, 107, 110, 111, 112, 113, and 114 operated from bases along the eastern seaboard, Azores, Brazil, French Morocco, or England.

Lieutenant Commander William Thomas Eaton commissioned one of the earliest of such units, Navy Bombing Squadron 103 (VB-103), on March 15, 1943, at U.S. Naval Auxiliary Air Station Camp Kearney in San Diego. Easton and a majority of squadron officers and enlisted personnel present that day had previously served with PBY-5A Patrol Squadrons 11 and 23, which had returned from action in the South

Gene McIntyre began his military career before the entry of the United States in World War II when he joined the Royal Canadian Air Force as a pilot trainee. He left flight training before completion after the U.S. declared war on Japan. (Gene McIntyre)

Pacific. Arriving at Camp Kearney, some of the enlisted men, such as Gene McIntyre and Carlton Lillie, were somewhat surprised to find themselves training in a B-24. Gene McIntyre began his Navy flying career in February 1943 as an enlisted Ordnanceman in PBY and said of his transfer: "We couldn't visualize why we were going to B-24s."[18]

In May 1943, VB-103 became the first U.S. Navy B-24 squadron to begin anti-submarine operation in the Atlantic Theater. The employment of the B-24 Liberator in Argentia, along with PV-1 Ventura squadrons stationed in Greenland and Iceland permitted continuous air cover for transatlantic convoys. The introduction of long-range aircraft effectively closed down an area known as the "black hole" of the mid-North Atlantic, which was previously beyond the range of Allied aircraft and where U-boats reigned freely.

Flight operations, as part of FAW-7, were conducted from Bristol Field, named in Honor of Vice Admiral Arthur L. Bristol, commanding officer of Task Force 24, who died of pneumonia aboard his flagship tender *Prairie* (AD-14), at Argentia on April 20, 1942. Bristol Field cost 9 million U.S. Dollars to build and consisted of three 5,000-foot concrete runways, extended to 6,000 feet (1829 meters) before the end of the war. Heavy fog and snow forced the cancellation of flight operations or returning aircraft were diverted; the airfield had to be shut down due to heavy snow or thick fog. At times, it was necessary to divert to Greenland, Iceland, or Northern Ireland. Consequently, crews carried a toothbrush and a razor.

Long patrols, necessary to reach the mid-Atlantic, required a heavy gas load as aircraft were required to return from missions with a minimum of three hours fuel supply, due to the uncertain weather conditions. Therefore, to extend range and flying time, personnel removed the armor plating, some of the guns, oxygen equipment, and one of the bomb bay fuel tanks, which reduced the weight from 67,000 (30391 kilograms) to approximately 63,000 pounds (28576 kilograms).

Once in the air, flying conditions were extremely difficult for pilots who often encountered fog, rain, sleet, and snow. Poor visibility required the use of the APS-15 radar to search for enemy submarines, but even pilots could not rely on the instrument all the time. On several occasions, after a radar contact was made pilots aborted attack runs when they realized they were about to bomb an iceberg. Gene McIntyre recalled, "A lot of times when you were going in on radar you didn't know what it was."[19]

Charles P. "Muck" Muckenthaler, a survivor of Pearl Harbor, and a veteran of patrol squadron VP-11, remembered making a memorable low visibility run in his plane *Muck's Mauler* B-5 "E" (BurAer 32035), after his radar operator picked up a blip. While the Liberator's pilot homed in on the target, Joe Powell, an Aviation Pilot (AP), manned one of the free-swinging .50 caliber machine guns in the nose. As the PB4Y-1 closed in, Muckenthaler realized it was a Newfoundland fishing vessel and ordered his gunners to hold fire but, in the nose, Powell's headphones had fallen off and he did not hear the order and began blasting away. Muckenthaler aborted the run, but not before Powell fired a few rounds at the boat. The boat was unharmed but, from then on, Powell was nicknamed "Trigger."[20]

VB-103's prime duty of sub-hunting was limited by the time they arrived, as U-boats had moved out of the routine patrol areas of American and Canadian aircraft. However, Lieutenant (jg) Theodore S. "Swede" Thueson, in the PB4Y-1 *Impatient Virgin* B-7 "G" (Bureau Number 32022), conducted the squadron's only submarine attack from Argentia on August 12, 1943. Thueson, a VP-23 veteran of the Solomon Islands Campaign in the South Pacific, spotted Oberleutnant zur See Otto Erich Bluhm's Type VIIC *U-760* fully surfaced and, approaching from the submarine's stern, he and his crew began a 22-minute battle with the vessel. On the U-boat's deck, a couple of the crew ran towards their anti-aircraft gun and began firing as the Liberator came in for a depth charge run.

While the plane's bow and top turret gunners laid down heavy fire, Thueson pickled off three depth charges but his aim was a little off and the nearest explosion occurred 50 feet off the U-boat's starboard bow. However, the blast was close enough to wash one of the U-boat's men over the side and lift the submarine out of the water. As the bomber came around for another run, the U-boat slowly submerged beneath the waves so Thueson aborted the run. In the U-boat, the crew inspected the damage and found the explosion had bent the forward torpedo tubes. This reduced the vessel's diving speed but the *U-760* managed to evade further attacks and slowly made its way to the Spanish port of Vigo on September 8, 1943 where the crew was interned at El Ferrol for the duration.[21]

During VB-103's three-month stay at Argentia, the squadron flew 268 missions totaling 2,003 operational hours. During this period, the squadron suffered the loss of 21 men. VB-103's first loss occurred on June 24, 1943, when Lieutenant Herbert K. Reese Jr., in the Liberator *Elmundo the Great* (Bureau Number 32046), failed to return while on convoy escort, 700 miles northeast of Argentia. A message intercepted later from *U-271* operating near the convoy reported they shot down the bomber. The Navy soon formed two additional PB4Y-1 squadrons, or ASW operations, VB-105 for the Eastern Sea Frontier and VP-83, later designated VB-107, for the Brazilian Area. Although a third, VB-113 was established it became a replacement squadron for personnel and aircraft for FAW-7. Lieutenant Commander Francis E. Nuessle's VB-105 began operational life as VP-31, a PBY-5 Catalina squadron, which served in the Caribbean, Quonset Point, and Argentia between December

1941 and March 1943. In April 1943, the squadron designator changed to VB-10⁵ and traded in the PBY-5A for the PB4Y-1.

Commander Nuessle, a combat-hardened veteran, was no stranger to the danger of lurking U-boats, as the former commanding officer of the *Gannet*, a small seaplane tender sank on June 2, 1942. The *Gannett*, with the British ship HMS *Sumar* departed Bermuda to search for the torpedoed merchant ship *Westmoreland*. The search proved unsuccessful and the ships were ordered back to base in the afternoon four days later. However, during the night, the two ships separated and, during the predawn hours of the seventh, German torpedoes hit the *Gannet* and it went down within five minutes, taking 14 of its crew with it. Lieutenant Nuessle joined some 60 survivors on life rafts after fighting free of the sinking ship's suction. He ordered the rafts lashed together, and the wounded brought aboard. Later that day two Mariners from VP-74 flown Lieutenant Commander John W. Gannon and Lieutenant Winslow L. Pettingell rafts and landed with each plane taking aboard 11 survivors. An American destroyer arrived on the scene and picked up the remaining survivors. Five months later, on November 1, 1942, Nuessle became commanding officer of VP-31. Beginning on May 15, 1943 the squadron began transitioning to the PB4Y-1 and, after a few months familiarization with the Liberator, VB-10⁵ transferred to Kindley Field, Bermuda in June 1943 for ASW operations. Squadron aircraft conducted two attacks against U-boats, one on July 3 and August 7. The first resulted in no apparent damage to the unidentified submarine, but Type VIIE *U-84* commanded by Kapitänleutnant Horst Uphoff, Iron Cross First Class, was lost on the return home from its eighth patrol off Bermuda. Previous patrols had netted the submarine six merchantmen sunk and one damaged off the Eastern Sea Frontier and in the Gulf of Mexico. At 1045 hours, Liberator B-4 piloted by Lieutenant Thomas R. Evert spotted the submarine while cruising at 7,000 feet (2134 meters) approximately 355 (571 kilometers) miles southwest of Bermuda and put the bomber into steep dive. Some of Uphoff's men topside enjoying the sun and fresh air quickly manned the antiaircraft guns as the bomber bore down bomb bay doors open and its gunners firing attempting to clear the U-boat's deck. Those left standing on the deck ran for cover behind the conning tower as Evert pickled off four depth charges.

The Liberator climbed up to 1,200 feet (366 meters) as the charges exploded sending up thick plumes of water, temporarily obscuring *U-84*. The boat then submerged as the plane circled for a second run and dropped a Mk-24 Fido. The official damage assessment listed the submarine as damaged, but German records after the war showed Uphoff and his crew were lost. Lieutenant Evert and his crew perished two months later on an ASW mission from St. Eval, England.

U-84 was the last enemy submarine lost in the North Atlantic to a land-based naval patrol plane based along the Eastern Sea Frontier during the war. U-boat losses continued to increase with the heaviest, at the time, occurring in July with

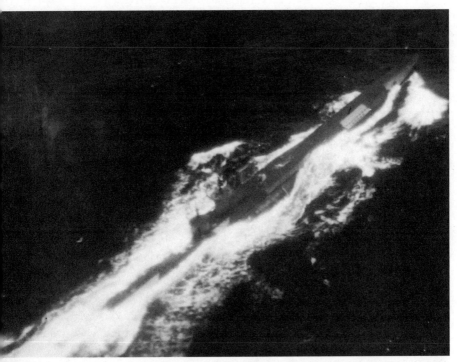

U-84 damaged by plane from the escort carrier *Core* (CVE 13). The submarine escaped but was later sunk on 7 August 1943 by a Mk-24 torpedo released from a VB-105 PB4Y-1 Liberator flown by Lieutenant Thomas R. Evert. He and his crew were lost while based in England. (National Archives)

46 U-boats destroyed, 37 sunk in the North Atlantic with other Allied land-based aircraft accounting for 28. August brought very little to U-boats with only four ships sunk in the South Atlantic, while worldwide losses of submarines reached 22, 18 by aircraft. The losses of July and August forced U-boats to remain submerged until nighttime, and that held to a minimum, to recharge batteries. As will be seen, U-boat commanders often ignored this tactic. BdU attempted to regain the initiative in September by targeting North Atlantic convoys once again. This resumption of the battle accounted for six ships sunk, but the "good times" of 1940–42 did not rematerialize. However, U-boats had reverted to surfacing at night for the minimum time necessary for the charging of batteries and only six submarines were lost to the Allies.

The availability of long-range aircraft, combined with the widespread use of new anti-submarine technology by the Allies, saw a remarkable increase in the number of U-boats lost and a sharp decrease in the latter's score of shipping sunk. Only three merchant ships were lost in October in the North Atlantic, while not a single vessel was lost in November 1943; 40 submarines were lost during those months. December fared no better as U-boats failed to sink a single ship in the North Atlantic.

CHAPTER 3

Caribbean Sea Frontier
(February 1942–August 1943)

"The enemy holds every trump card, covering all areas with long-range air patrols and using location methods which we still have no warning."

KARL DÖNITZ

Before Pearl Harbor, the United States held a strong military presence in the Caribbean with naval facilities in Panama, Cuba, and Puerto Rico with successful negotiations allowing the use of Britain's oversea territories of Antigua, Barbados, British Guyana, Jamaica, and Trinidad. Negotiations with the French would bring Martinique, while the Dutch allowed the use of their territories in the West Indies. The thought of the war spreading to Central and South America fostered cooperation between those regions and the United States soon after Pearl Harbor with Nicaragua allowing American military forces the use of its land and territorial waters for the duration. Cuba and El Salvador soon followed. Naval air stations by the end of 1942 would also include Barranquilla, Columbia, Curacao, Puerto Castilla, Honduras and Corinto, Nicaragua.[1]

The Caribbean Defense Command, established in early 1941, preceded the Caribbean Sea Frontier (CARIBSEAFRON) with the mission of defending the Caribbean, Central America, Venezuela, Columbia, Ecuador, and French Guinea. The establishment of the Caribbean Naval Frontier, renamed the Caribbean Sea Frontier followed in late 1941 and consisted of the Guantanamo Sector, Puerto Rico Sector and Trinidad Sector under the command of the Tenth Naval District. The Caribbean Sea Frontier encompassed an area of two and a half million square miles; from its northwest corner to the southwest and northward, the area covered approximately 3,500 miles. Although the Navy exercised control of anti-submarine operations in the region, it lacked aircraft and relied on the Army Air Force to perform the air aspect of ASW operations. The air force began operations in mid-January 1942 with A-20 Havocs of the 59th Bombardment Squadron flying out of Aruba and Curacao.

Increasing Allied air and naval surface forces successfully detecting and sinking U-boats in the North Atlantic forced the BdU to begin shifting patrols to target transatlantic convoys sailing out of range of land-based aircraft and south of the Caribbean, where American ASW assets were weak. U-boat operations shifted from

The pilot of a PBM-3C scanning the waters of the Atlantic or Caribbean through binoculars to locate a German U-boat reportedly in the area on 13 January 1943. (Official U.S. Navy Photograph, now in the collections of the National Archives)

the North Atlantic to the Caribbean, Gulf of Mexico, and South Atlantic upon the realization that targets were plentiful and sailed relatively undefended in southern waters. Operation *Neuland* (*New Ground*) in the Caribbean followed a blitz in the Gulf of Mexico. *Neuland* operations were concentrated around Trinidad, owing its proximity to Venezuela's oil fields, the bauxite mines in Dutch Guiana, and petroleum manufacturing facilities on the Dutch islands of Curacao and Aruba. Between February and July 1942, 114 vessels were lost to U-boat attacks in that area. Yet, the U-boat war in the region was relatively short, beginning in February 1942, peaking during that summer, and practically ending the following August.

The stage was set as *U-156* under the command of Kapitänleutnant Werner Hartenstein arrived outside San Nicholas harbor of Aruba on the evening of February 15, 1942. The well-lit shoreline, marking the behavior of unsuspecting inhabitants of the Dutch colony, outlined several oil-laden tankers. The quiet, carefree night ended as torpedoes slammed into the 4,300-ton British tanker *Pedernales,* followed moments later by the 2,400-ton tanker *Oranjestad* exploding from the impact of two torpedoes. Oil from the torn hauls poured out of the shattered hulls, quickly ignited, and massive flames spread across the water. The 6,400-ton American tanker *Arkansas* became the next victim of *U-156*'s torpedoes with its cargo of crude oil adding to the inferno. Hartenstein then maneuvered the boat offshore of an oil refinery with the intention of using his 105-millimeter cannon. The gun crew loaded a shell and fired; however, the shell detonated inside the barrel as one of the crew failed to remove the barrel's tampion and shrapnel, mortally wounding one man and seriously wounded another. Crewmembers cut off the damaged end of the barrel allowing two rounds to be fired at the refinery. Hartenstein halted further action as 155-millimeter cannon rounds flew over the boat exploding beyond, as the fingers of spotlights illuminated the water in search of the enemy vessel. The air campaign against this menace began the following day when an Army A-20 Havoc of the 59th Bombardment Squadron unsuccessfully attacked *U-67* off the Venezuelan coast and a second A-20 attacked *U-502* later in the afternoon without success, both failing due to inexperienced aircrews and without being equipped with aerial depth charges.

Later that month Kapitänleutnant Nicolai Clausen's *U-129* sank seven merchant-men in a two-week period. His first victim was the Norwegian freighter *Nordvanger* on the 20th, followed by the Canadian freighter *George L. Torain* and the American *West Zeda* two days later. Clausen ended the month by sinking the Panamanian freighter *Bayou* on the 28th. Twenty-four ships, a majority of them tankers, totaling over 118,000 tons, fell to U-boats during the first month of U-boat operations in the Caribbean. Panic may not have swept Allied command in the Caribbean, but it increased the amount of urgency as it became obvious by the end of February that a full assault by enemy submarines had materialized in the Caribbean by not only German U-boats, but Italian submarines as well. Five Italian submarines participated in Operation *Neuland*, primarily operating off Venezuela, with the Italian Marconi class submarine, *Da Vinci*, sinking the 3,500-ton Brazilian freighter *Cabedelo* on February 28, and the 3,600-ton Latvian freighter *Everasma* on the 28th. A further 17 ships sank to the bottom of the Caribbean from German and Italian submarines before Operation *Nueland* ended at the end of March. Merchant shipping losses between February and March 1942 totaled 52 sunk or damaged with 41 sunk totaling 220,600 tons.

Admiral John H. Hoover, Commander in Chief of the Caribbean Sea Frontier, Tenth Naval District, responded by pleading with Washington for reinforcements. Naval air power in the region was practically non-existent throughout for the first half of 1942, leaving anti-submarine work to the Army Air Force based in Trinidad and Curacao. The entire Army air strength in the Caribbean as of April 1942 consisted of 28 heavy bombers, 30 medium bombers and 16 light bombers, while the Navy had on hand PBY-5As of VP-31 and 92 at San Juan. VP-31 arrived in San Juan in January after having detachments-based Guantanamo, Antigua, Great Exuma, St Lucia, British Guiana, and Trinidad since December 1941, while V-92 transferred from the west coast in early March 1942. April

Vice Admiral John H. Hoover Commander in Chief Caribbean Sea Frontier. He later commanded a Fleet Air Wing in the Pacific. (Naval History and Heritage Command)

A damaged VP-31 Consolidated PBY-5 Catalina 31-P-8 (Bureau Number 2404) is being hoisted aboard the tender *Thrush* (AVP-3) in September 1941 in the San Juan PR area. (Bill Swisher Collection via Mark Aldrich)

saw the British and Americans increasing surface forces with the British sending 24 anti-submarine trawlers and transferring motor torpedo boats to Trinidad, while the Americans provided a few World War I four-stacker destroyers, 16 Coast Guard cutters, and some 19 other patrol craft.[3]

Meanwhile, *U-154*, *U-66*, *U-130*, *U-108*, and the Italian submarine *Calvi* were in the Caribbean primarily focused on the Windward Passage, Curacao-Aruba, and Trinidad areas, referred to as choke points for ships sailing between those islands. *U-154* commanded by Oberleutnant Oskar-Heinz Kusch opened up April on the fourth and fifth by sinking the 5,000-ton American tankers *Comol Rico* and *Catahoula*, both ships carrying molasses instead of oil. Three more merchantmen would be sunk by *U-154* during this patrol, including the British tanker *Empire Amethyst*, laden with fuel, sunk off Aruba on the 2th, claiming the lives of its 47-man crew. Korvettenkapitän Richard Zapp's Type IXC *U-66* made its appearance in the Caribbean known by sinking the Greek cargo ship *Korthion* south of Barbados on the 14th. During this fifth and final patrol by Zapp five more ships would be sunk between April 16 and May 2. Afterward *U-66*'s skipper took command of the Third U-boat Flotilla. April ended with 14 vessels sunk, but May 1942 would eclipse the previous month with the loss of 44 ships accounting for over 181,000 tons, including the Brazilian cargo ship *Parnanhyba* on May 1, pushing Brazil closer towards declaring war on Germany as U-boats had previously sunk five of her flagged ships. U-boats continued operations relatively unmolested by Allied surface and air forces although coastal artillery and enemy patrol boats chased *U-130* away while the submarine's deck crew used its 105-millimeter deck gun on a refinery in Curacao during the third week of April. A destroyer depth charged *U-108* depth unsuccessfully in early May. Yet, by May 12, U-boats operated in the Caribbean Sea Frontier with another nine dispatched during the month, as the Caribbean became the favorite hunting ground. With Allied forces stretched thin, U-boats operated day and night on the surface and crews would take time off from their duty to fish and bathe on uninhabited islands and, in some cases, would buy provisions from natives.[4]

Post-war assessments of enemy submarines sunk or damaged were largely based on captured German documents and quite a few claims had to be reversed. Such was a case involving a pilot from a PBY Catalina squadron. On May 26 1942, operating from St Lucia, British West Indies at the time, a submarine was on the surface at 2357 hours and the pilot dropped three depth charges on it in two diving attacks. The submarine appeared to settle slowly in the water in a sinking condition. The pilot called an American destroyer to the scene to access the situation. The destroyer's captain also had the opinion that the patrol plane had destroyed the submarine. The monthly squadron diary at that time stated, "This attack deserved special notice because it was the first night attack carried out successfully in that area." The pilot subsequently received one of the Navy's highest decorations for this action, but post-war examination of German Navy records did not record the loss of a U-boat in that area on that date.[5]

During the height of the U-boat blitz in the Caribbean, Gulf of Mexico, and Panama Sea Frontiers in June 1942, 66 ships were lost with a tonnage of 314,000 tons. The Army and Navy began shifting additional surface and air assets to the area and it paid off on June 13. U.S. Coast Guard *Thetis*'s (WPC-115) radar picked up *U-157* on the surface in the Gulf of Mexico between Cuba and Key West, Florida and, as the patrol vessel came into view, the submarine submerged, but it was too late as depth charges found her, sending it and its 52-man crew to the bottom. The first U-boat lost to Allied air power in the Caribbean occurred on July 6, when an A-20 Havoc of the 59th Bombing Squadron sank the Type IXC *U-153* with the loss of all hands northwest of Aruba on July 6. However, naval patrol planes failed to sink a submarine until the following month.

July 1942 saw a decrease in shipping losses as U-boats on station depleted their supply of torpedoes and returned to their bases in France while replacements took an average of two weeks to arrive in the Caribbean. Admiral Dönitz needed twice the number to strangle the Caribbean supply line and, if that had occurred, the war may have continued beyond May 1945. It was during the bloody months of May and June when the Americans and British came to terms on the importance of the Caribbean in the overall war effort, thus reinforcements began to pour into the region. The U.S. Navy strengthened aerial reconnaissance in August 1942 by establishing PatWing 11 at San Juan, PatWing 12 at Key West, Florida, and PatWing 3 headquartered at NAS

The *William Boyce Thompson* at anchor in Guantanamo Bay after being shelled and torpedoed by German U-boat *U-185*, southeast of Jamaica, 7 1943. The ship's master, Fred Charles Vosloh, lost a ship 4 months earlier to the same U-boat when his ship *Virginia Sinclair* was sunk in March 1943. (National Archives)

Coco Solo, Panama Canal, Panama. The establishment of the wings greatly increased the presence of naval patrol aviation between August and September, with PatWing 11 having VP-31 (PBY-5A), VP-53 (PBY-5A), VP-74 (PBM-3), VP-83 (PBY-5A), and VP-92 (PBY-5A) primarily operating from Trinidad and Cuba.

Caribbean Sea Frontier Merchant Shipping Losses (May–December 1942)

Month	Ships	Gross Tons
May	44	181,473
Jun	37	189,431
Jul	19	97,900
Aug	44	238,768
Sep	30	125,728
Oct	16	65,927
Nov	25	149,077
Dec	10	49,950

Stetson Conn, *Guarding the United States and its Outposts: The Caribbean in Wartime*, Ch. XVI (2000).

A PBY-5 Catalina of VP-92 (92-P-10) on Caribbean Patrol during May 1942. A squadron aircraft with the Canadian corvette HMCS *Oakville* sank *U-135* in the Caribbean on 27 August 1943. (National Archives)

U-boats, meanwhile, continued to have remarkable success in the Caribbean during August and September, with the number of ships lost numbering 74, totaling nearly 365,000 tons. However, the expansion of Allied surface and air units marked the high-water mark for U-boat operations in the region, as the total number and tonnage of ships dropped significantly during the last quarter of 1942, with Kriegsmarine losing two U-boats in August and one in September, one of them to a naval patrol plane. Type VIIC *U-94* became the first U-boat detected and sunk in the Caribbean Sea Frontier by the combined effort of a VP-92 PBY-5A Catalina and the Canadian corvette *HMCS Oakville* on August 27, 1942. *U-94* was a combat veteran of ten patrols with 25 ships sunk and one damaged totaling 149,000 tons. Kapitänleutnant Otto Ites, in command of the boat since September 1941, was one of the top U-boat aces with 76,882 tons sunk, for which he was the recipient of the Iron and Knight's Cross. *U-94* departed for the Caribbean from St. Nazaire on August 2, arriving east of Jamaica on the 27th, and waited for Convoy TAW-15 to appear. *U-94* had been on the surface for an hour under a full moon. Wind force and sea were four knots from east. Ites had maneuvered into position within the convoy screen to fire a torpedo at one of the escort destroyers when one of his lookouts sighted a plane. Ites cursed and remarked to his first officer, "I've avoided that plane all day, and now that I'm ready to attack he sees me."[6]

Lieutenant Gordon R. Fiss, in PBY-5A 92-P-6 was providing night air coverage for TAW-15 convoy when the fully surfaced submarine came into view three miles astern of the main convoy body. The Catalina went into a glide from 500 feet and when the submarine was at an estimated 200 yards (9,183 meters), the co-pilot released four depth bombs from under the port wing.

Lieutenant Fiss reported,

> A quick glance astern a few seconds later revealed the conning tower becoming obliterated by the bomb upheaval. Members of the crew in the waist hatch stated the stern of the submarine was raised clear of the water. However, I did not see this, my attention being necessary on the airplane which was close to the water.[7]

Fiss continued in his report, "A Corvette was sighted about two miles away while commencing a return circle and the word 'Sub Sub' was flashed by Aldis lamp." The *Oakville* commenced firing and continued to do so until it rammed into the *U-94*, the submarine passing under the corvette. The ship backed up and rammed again while firing its four-inch gun, which hit the conning tower and destroyed the U-boat's deck gun. Meanwhile, *U-94* increased its speed and turned hard to port. *Oakville* rammed the submarine's starboard side then dropped depth charges that exploded directly under *U-94*. The corvette rammed a third time hitting aft of the conning tower.[8]

It was time to abandon the submarine and Ites ordered the vessel scuttled. The corvette's machine guns continued firing to keep the Germans from operating their guns and Captain Ites was wounded in the leg. The crew left through the conning tower's hatch while the *Oakville* sent a boarding party. Leaping aboard two of the boarding party, they shot two of Ite's crew coming out of the conning tower. Nineteen of *U-94*'s 45 members drowned while inside the sinking boat, or died while abandoning ship. The boarding party went back into their boat and watched as the U-boat sank, bow first.[9]

The uncertainties in conducting war aptly coined as "The Fog of War" by retired British Army engineer Colonel Lonsdale Hale, defined it as "the state of ignorance in which commanders frequently find themselves as regards the real strength and position, not only of their foes, but also of their friends."[10] Thus, was the position in which Lieutenant John C. Lafferty of VP-74 found himself in when he nearly created an international incident on November 8, when he attacked a French submarine off the French-administered Martinique. The French administration on the island and the U.S. Government were in negotiations to allow American planes to operate from the island. However, the island's governorship was in a quandary as to whether to remain faithful to the Vichy government in France or ally themselves with the United States. The Americans could not allow a Vichy-aligned Martinique with its own submarine force with the possibility of German U-boats having a safe haven in the Caribbean. Until there was a solution, the two parties negotiated restricted area five miles out from the island banning Allied forces from within the five-mile exclusion zone. Squadron doctrine of VP-74, however, was to attack submarines at any place or time. Lafferty sent a message to base requesting instructions. He received the order to attack. The Mariner dropped four depth bombs in the swirling water where the submarine had submerged. The French vessel escaped undamaged. This encounter pales in comparison to the reaction by Vichy military forces towards the British and American landings in French North Africa taking place at that exact moment.[11]

The Kriegsmarine lost four U-boats in the Caribbean Sea Frontier proper during 1942, two from air attacks by Army planes and the other by VP-92, while American surface vessels sank Type IXC *U-157* off Cuba in June and *U-166* in the Gulf of Mexico in July. The following year, with adequate Allied naval and air forces positioned throughout the Caribbean, there continued to be a dramatic decrease in shipping losses, which were reduced to 26 ships totaling 141,000 tons. The capabilities of Allied air and naval forces in the Caribbean Sea Frontier decreased the effectiveness of the U-boat, with a steady downturn in the number of ships sunk between January and July 1943. The region became the grave for another five U-boats during 1943, four to naval patrol aircraft.

VP-207 Martin PBM-3C Mariners on the seaplane ramp at San Juan, Puerto Rico on 12 March 1943. A detachment of aircraft and crews operated from Jamaica during March 1943 in which time three squadron aircraft engaged a U-boat with negative results. Ensign Douglas Kelsey was wounded by a submarine's anti-aircraft fire during the first incident. (Steve Ginter via Mark Aldrich)

Caribbean Sea Frontier Merchant Shipping Losses (January–July 1943)

Month	Ships	Gross Tons
Jan	6	33,100
Feb	3	16,042
Mar	7	36,733
May	2	4,232
June	0	-
July	6	34,806

Stetson Conn, *Guarding the United States and its Outposts*

The Caribbean Won

The first loss occurred on March 8, when a PBY-5A of VP-53 sank Type IXC *U-156* east of Barbados. The squadron, established at Norfolk in March 1942, was operating from NAS Trinidad at the time. Korvettenkapitän Werner Hartenstein took *U-156* from Lorient on January 16, and had failed to attack Allied shipping by the date of its sinking on March 8. The U-boat with Hartenstein in command sank 19 ships and damaged five more totaling 117,000 tons between February 16 and September 19, 1942, including the passenger liner *Loconia* on September 12, 1942,

This swirl indicates the spot where German U-boat *U-156* met destruction in the West Indian waters. The submarine was sunk by depth charges and strafing by a PBY-5 of VP-53 on 8 March 1943. (National Archives)

referenced as "Laconia Incident". The ship carried 1,800 Italian prisoners of war and British military personnel when *U-156* torpedoed it. Hartenstein discovered who was aboard and called for assistance, which arrived in the form of a trio of U-boats along with an Italian submarine with most of the survivors either taken aboard or in tow in lifeboats. The five submarines remained surfaced with each displaying a large Red Cross flag, hoping Allied forces would not attack. However, a USAAF B-24 Liberator spotted the small convoy and radioed base asking for instructions. The base on Ascension Island replied to attack. The submarines cut the towlines to the lifeboats and scattered, escaping undamaged. A Free French destroyer picked up the *Laconia* survivors a few hours later. Afterward, BdU ordered U-boats to stop aiding survivors from ships they sunk.

VP-53's Lieutenant J. E. Dryden in PBY-5A 53-P-1 delivered an accurate depth charge attack on *U-156* sinking the U-boat and entombing most of its 52-man crew. However, an estimated 11 men stationed topside either jumped or were blown into the sea. Six of the men quickly drowned while desperately trying to hang on debris, leaving five in the water. The co-pilot dropped two life rafts and Mae Wests with provisions tied on towards the men below. The Germans reached the rafts and climbed aboard, one of them in defiance, shook his fist at the American plane. What happened to those men from *U-156* remains a mystery.[12]

The PBY dropped a life raft and provisions, and the survivors from *U-156* climbed aboard, but a subsequent search by the American destroyer *Barney* (DD-149) was unsuccessful in locating the men and the search was called off. (National Archives)

Pilot, Lieutenant (jg) Dryden, Jr., describing the sinking of *U-156*. The pilot sighted the submarine eight miles (13km) away, and he went into a 45-degree dive. As the submarine sank smoke and debris cascaded 40 feet (12m) into the air. The oil slick spread until it was a quarter of a mile wide and three quarters of a mile long. (National Archives)

"She just broke in the middle and sank," said Aviation Machine's Mate Third Class J.F. Connelly, waist gunner, as he described the event to a Rear Admiral (probably Admiral Hoover) and a Brigadier General. Lieutenant (jg) Dryden is standing on the right next to the Rear Admiral. (National Archives)

Lieutenant (jg) John E. Dryden finishes painting the submarine kill mark on his PBY-5A Catalina. *U-156* was the only submarined sunk by the squadron. (National Archives)

Over four months of unsuccessful attacks by FAW-11 squadrons followed until July 1943, when enemy activity increased resulting in the largest number of merchant ships lost in the region that year, although extremely few in comparison to that of 1942. VP-32, VP-204, and VB-133 conducted five separate attacks between the 15th and 28th resulting in the destruction of three U-boats. VP-32's Lieutenant R. C. Mayo aboard Mariner 32-P-10 spotted Oberleutnant zur See Rudolf Friedrich's Type VIIC *U-759* on the 15th, 252 miles (406 kilometers) southeast of Guantanamo Bay and, through intensive but inaccurate anti-aircraft fire, sank the vessel with its 47-man crew by depth charges.

Unsuccessful attacks were conducted on the 19th and 24th by VB-133 and VP-204. Lieutenant R. B. Johnson of VB-133 encountered a surfaced submarine 248 miles (399 kilometers) southwest of San Juan and dropped six depth charges from his PV-1 Ventura, but no damage was observed. That evening, a radar contact on a U-boat by a VP-204 Mariner occurred 84 miles (135 kilometers) east of Port

The commanding officer of VP-201 was Lieutenant Commander Magruder H. Tuttle and this is his personal PBM-2S Mariner (201-P-1). The squadron operated from Norfolk, with detachments in Bermuda beginning on 25 May 1943. On 19 August 1943, orders sent the entire squadron to Bermuda. (National Archives)

Attack on *U-134* by a VP-201 PBM-3S Mariner on 8 July 1943. The U-boat survived this attack, along with two others on 18-19 July and another on 21 August. The U-boat finally met her match when she was attacked by British Wellington aircraft and sunk near Vigo, Spain on August 24th, 1943. All hands were lost. (National Archives)

Attack on an unidentified German U-boat on 24 July 1943 by a Puerto Rico-based PV-1 Ventura of VB-133 piloted by Lieutenant R.B. Johnson. This may have been *U-466* and the aircraft was identified as a B-24 Liberator. The U-boat survived the attack. (National Archives)

PBM-3S anti-submarine Mariners based in the Caribbean during July 1943. The "S" in PBM-3S stood for "stripped" to increase range. They were stripped of the armor plating, bow and a deck gun; the navigator's position was moved from the flight deck to the starboard waist gun position. Twin, flexible-mounted .50-caliber machines were located in the nose and the tail position had a single hand-held .50-caliber machine gun. (National Archives)

This image, according to the description attached to it, shows an attack on an unidentified submarine by a naval patrol plane possibly on 31 July 1943. Three days later a PBM-3C from VP-205 piloted by Lieutenant (jg) C.C. Cox sank *U-615*, but his plane was shot down during the engagement. (National Archives)

of Spain, Trinidad. His plane took several hits from the unknown submarine, which escaped. Type VIIC *U-359*, under the command of Oberleutnant zur See Heinz Förster, was on its third unsuccessful patrol when Lieutenant R. W. Rawson's VP-32 Mariner P-12, temporarily based at San Juan Puerto Rico, located it on radar and sank it east of Jamaica on the 26th. There were no survivors.

VP-32's third victory was on the 28th against the highly successful Type IXC *U-159*. Submarine's skipper Oberleutnant zur See Heinz Beckman took over from U-boat ace Helmut Witte, who scored 23 ships sunk or damaged weighing a total of 119,819 tons. After leaving Lorient on June 12, and stationing southeast of Haiti on July 28, Beckman was having no luck in encountering Allied shipping. He and his crew wouldn't get another chance. PBM Mariner P-1 of VP-32, flown by Lieutenant (jg) D. C. Pinholster, picked it up on radar at a distance of five miles and soon spotted the boat's

A depth bomb dropped by a PBM-3C of VP-32 explodes near *U-359* south of Santo Domingo, Dominican Republic on 28 July 1943. This was the third German submarine sunk by VP-32 that month. (National Archives)

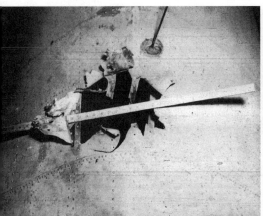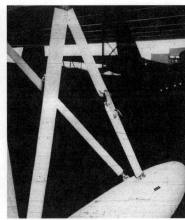

Two images showing the damage caused by *U-359*'s anti-aircraft fire to Lieutenant (jg) D.C. Pinholster's PBM-3C Mariner (32-P-1). Two crewmen were wounded by shell fragments. (National Archives)

wake. Machine guns mounted on the conning tower fired, inaccurate at first, as the Mariner crossed over the conning tower, the pilot released the depth charges. Men in the conning towered continued firing at the American plane as the Mariner into a steep left turn to circle the submarine and make a strafing attack. While circling in this strafing attack, the sub rose and fell back into the water from the exploding charges. After completion of the first full turn, while broadside to the sub, the plane received hits from anti-aircraft fire damaging the plane and wounding two crewmembers. With bow and tail turrets out, bombs expended, and two men wounded, the pilot felt it best to return to base without further observing effects of attack. However, two explosions enveloped the U-boat as the Mariner headed back to base.[13]

Two more U-boats would meet their fates between August 3 and 6; they would be the last submarines sunk by naval patrol planes in the Caribbean Sea Frontier during 1943. Between July 29 and August 7, 1943, Army and Naval aircraft engaged Kapitänleutnant Ralph Kapitsky's Type VIIC *U-615* after DF trackers located the vessel, following Kapitzky reporting the sinking of the Dutch tanker *Rosalia* off Curacao on July 28. An Army B-18 Bolo of the Tenth Bombardment Group attacked the following evening and, likewise, an Army B-24 on the first, causing some damage. A PBM piloted by Lieutenant (jg) J. M Erskine from VP-205, but failed to score additional damage. A second PBM piloted by Lieutenant A. R. Matuski, the following afternoon, damaged the U-boat further from depth bombs and radioed base, "Sub damaged with bow out of water making only two knots, no casualties to plane or personnel." Matuski, apparently conducted a second run in which *U-615* shot down the Mariner as the pilot radioed, "Damaged-damaged-fire." The plane went down with all hands.[14]

Depth-charge attack by PBMs (VP-204 and VP-205) and a PV-1 Ventura (VB-130) against *U-615* east of Curacao 6–7 August 1943. The submarine shot down two Mariners and mortally wounded the pilot of a third. (National Archives)

More aircraft appeared that afternoon with a PBM piloted by Lieutenant L. D. Crockett, spotting the submarine a few miles from where Matuski's plane crashed. The Mariner dropped a string of depth bombs through heavy antiaircraft fire in which one round punctured the starboard wing, bursting into flames. While the plane captain extinguished the flames, Crockett came around again and dropped another string of bombs exploding close to the U-boat's port quarter. By this time, Navy blimp *K-68* arrived on scene to provide any assistance if needed.

A Trinidad-based VB-130 Ventura piloted by Lieutenant (jg) Theodore M. Holmes sighted the German submarine southeast of Curacao, making several runs despite heavy antiaircraft fire, dropping several depth charges that further damaged the submarine. Soon after Holmes's attack, a pair of PBMs from VP-204 and 205 arrived between 1815 and 1834 hours, with the first piloted by Lieutenant J. W. Dresbach, joining Crockett and Holmes in a coordinated attack. The submarine's crew continued to fire heavy, accurate antiaircraft fire killed Dresbach and Lieutenant O. R. Christian took over the controls dropping a string of bombs. Below, the wounded and dead littered *U-615*'s deck from strafing attacks from the American patrol planes. Lieutenant Commander R. S. Null's Mariner arrived with bombing and strafing, killing more of the U-boat's crew. The destroyer *Walker* (DD-517) arrived the next morning at 0552 hours, and Kapitsky, seeing the ship bearing down, ordered abandon ship and 43 of the crew climbed into life rafts, not including the submarine's commander who went down with his boat. The *Walker* rescued the survivors shortly thereafter 35 miles north of Blanquilla Island off Venezuela.[15]

Lieutenant Junior Grade Holmes (VB-130-P5), in conjunction with a VP-204 Mariner piloted by Lieutenant (jg) John W. Dresbach, attacking *U-615* in which Dresback was mortally wounded. The U-boat finally sank after this massive and prolonged air action. (National Archives)

Type VIIC *U-572,* commanded by Oberleutnant zur See Heiz Kummetat, had previously sunk three merchantmen during the patrol including the 4200-ton Free French fleet oiler *Lot.* The ship as part of Convoy UGS-10 carried tons of fuel oil when Kummetat fired two torpedoes into it, in the middle of the Atlantic, 1100 miles from the Cape Verde Islands on July 5. Nearly a month later, a PBM-3C of VP-205 piloted by Lieutenant (jg) Clifford C. Cox, radioed Trinidad at 0025 hours on August 3, "Sighted submarine, making attack." caught the U-boat northeast of Trinidad and sank it with depth bombs, but in turn, was shot down by the submarine's gunners and the plane crashed into the water killing the crew.[16]

The Caribbean U-boat war effectively ended in August 1943 with a brief reprise in December. Shipping losses continued to decrease during the remainder of 1943 in the Caribbean Sea Frontier, due to the abilities of Allied forces to detect and destroy enemy submarines and with the Germans shifting operations further south into the South Atlantic. Only four ships were lost in the Caribbean Sea Frontier Shipping losses for the third and fourth quarters of 1943 in the Caribbean Sea Frontier totaled four ships. *U-516, U-518,* and *U-539* ventured into the Caribbean between December and July 1944, damaging or sinking five merchant ships combined. Farther south, in the short term, as in the Caribbean, U-boats operating in the South Atlantic enjoyed a target-rich environment relatively unmolested by the Allies.

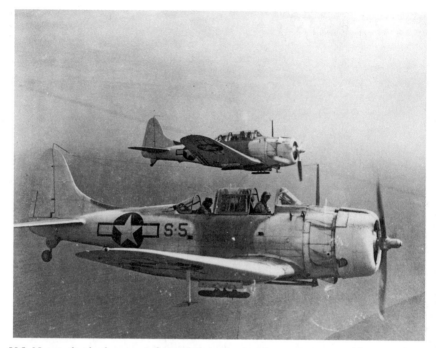

The U.S. Navy utilized other types of aircraft for anti-submarine operations in addition to the PBY, PBM, PB4Y-1, and PV-1. Two VS-37 (Scouting Squadron Thirty-Seven) Douglas SBD-5 Dauntless's in flight in February 1944 with Lieutenant William Matthews in Sugar Five (S-5). The aircraft have solid tail wheels and no tail hooks. The squadron operated from Hato Field, Curacao and Dakota Field in Aruba beginning December 1943. (Tailhook Association via CDR Harry Lewis (Ret))

CHAPTER 4

Battle of the South Atlantic
(January–June 1943)

"The Other World War II Battle of the Atlantic Everyone Forgets About"
TITLE OF AN ARTICLE BY SEBASTIEN ROBIN, *THE NATIONAL INTEREST*, MAY 14, 2017

The United States made the decision to deploy military forces to South America based primarily on a strategic necessity, in terms of Brazil's geographical location. Five months before Germany invaded Poland, the Joint Planning Committee of the U.S. Army-Navy Board concluded that French colonies in West Africa would be the most likely point for an invasion of South America by a European power. Specifically, the closest point on the northeastern tip of Brazil and West Africa named the Atlantic Narrows. South America, specifically the region in Brazil, extending from Belém in the northeast at the mouth of the Amazon River to Bahia in the southeast, was virtually undefended and beyond the range of American aircraft based in the Caribbean.

Efforts by the United States to establish a strong military presence began soon after the fall of France. With the possibility that German forces could use French colonies in West Africa to invade South America, Brazil quickly became the cornerstone for defending the Western Hemisphere. Therefore, the United States needed a foothold in South America to prevent either a possible invasion or, more likely, the military means to impede the introduction of regimes friendly to the Axis cause. Beginning in mid-1940, the Joint Chiefs of Staff and the Roosevelt Administration began sending military armaments and equipment through Lend-Lease to Brazil and other Latin American countries, as well as engaging in concerted negotiations to introduce thousands of American ground and air forces. Successful negotiations were not forthcoming with diplomatic efforts dragging on between 1939 and 1941, primarily due to the attitudes of a number of Brazilian officials who viewed an extensive American military presence as a threat to their nation's sovereignty. This was an understandable position since the United States had occasionally intervened in a number of Latin American countries.

The issue of basing American ground forces would not be successfully resolved to the satisfaction of the U.S. Army until late 1942. However, the Brazilians did grant two major concessions in 1940. First, the Brazilian Navy agreed, "to interpose no objections to advance discreet operations of U.S. naval forces in the Natal area and outlying Islands, both ashore and afloat."[1] This concession by the Brazilian government allowed U.S. Navy surface and air units to conduct patrols, in a "discretionary manner," in the South Atlantic. A second concession granted by Brazil involved building a series of airfields between Belém and Bahia, since airpower was crucial to Brazil's defense and the U.S. Army Air Force needed adequate facilities to base fighters and bombers. In November 1940, the United States Army and Pan-American Airways, with the approval of Brazilian President Getúlio Vargas, signed a secret agreement with the United States government to build airfields in Belém, São Luis, Fortaleza, Natal, Recife, Maceió, and Bahia. In return for this military cooperation, the Brazilian government received economic aid to build Brazil's industrial infrastructure in September 1940. The construction of Army airfields in Brazil soon caught the eye of the U.S. Navy, which viewed the airfields as highly desirable to base its own patrol aircraft and soon requested their use. In late April 1941, the Joint Chiefs of Staff approved the request by issuing a directive. This directive allowed the Navy to "use Army facilities as…necessary for the operation and maintenance of land-based, carrier-based, or amphibian type aircraft, subject to determination by the Army as to time and duration of such use, in order not to interfere with the primary purpose of these facilities."[2]

In mid-June 1941, Vice-Admiral Jonas Ingram's Task Force Three, later named South Atlantic Force, and then reorganized as U.S. Fourth Fleet, began surface operations in waters between Trinidad and the hump of Brazil. The Brazilians placed the two primary ports of Recife and Bahia at the disposal of the U.S. Navy for basing and support of surfaces while Natal would later become the major operating base for patrol squadrons. By January 1942, operations by the U.S. Fourth Fleet covered an extensive region known as the Brazilian Area. This area stretched from the border of French Guiana and Brazil down to Rio de Janeiro, to a point halfway across the ocean towards the West African Coast.[3]

However, the presence of American warships in Brazilian waters soon brought retribution with German and Italian submarine attacks commencing against Brazilian ships in the North Atlantic, Caribbean, and Mediterranean. Negotiations additionally led to the establishment of installations in British Guyana, Dutch Surinam, and French Guyana, while Venezuela, officially neutral, allowed U.S. warships and aircraft use of its ports and airfields.

German U-boat operations in the South Atlantic began materializing in autumn 1940, with activities centered in the Atlantic Narrows situated between Brazil and West Africa. During November and December 1940, *U-65* commanded by Korvettenkapitän Hans-Gerrit von Stockhausen sank six merchant ships in an

A merchant sinking in the South Atlantic after a German U-boat torpedoed her. The sinking of Brazilian-flagged vessels caused that nation to declare war on Germany. (Richard A. Wilson)

area off Sierra Leone and Liberia. U-boat activities tapered off and became almost nonexistent during the first three months of 1941, with only two merchant ships being lost between January and March. However, operations picked up during April and May 1941, as weak submarine countermeasures in the region became apparent to prowling U-boat commanders. In April 1941, seven ships went down in the Atlantic Narrows including one off South America. *U-124*, operating off Sierra Leone and Liberia, sank six vessels in April while Kapitänleutnant Georg Schewe, commanding *U-105*, scored Germany's first kill off South America by sinking the 5,200-ton British steamship *Ena de Larrinaga*.

U-boat successes rose sharply in the South Atlantic in May with 28 ships lost in areas below 10 degrees north, including three British and one American, off South America. *U-105* torpedoed the freighter *Oakdene* on the sixth while *U-103* dispatched the *City of Winchester* on the ninth and *City of Shanghai* two days later. The first American-registered ship lost off South America occurred when Korvettenkapitän Jost Metzler's *U-69* sank the Hog Islander SS *Robin Moor* on the 21st.

The number of losses in the narrows dropped considerably during June 1941, with only four ships being lost. The number steadily declined through the remainder of 1941 and 1942. The reason for the drop was that Dönitz scaled back South Atlantic operations due to the urgent need for submarines in the Mediterranean. Consequently, shipping losses fell, but they did not completely disappear. During September, U-boats sank three ships in the Atlantic Narrows near Pernambuco (Recife), Brazil. Two more went down in October, while *U-124* sank the British light cruiser HMS *Dunedin* on November 24. Of the cruiser's nearly 500-man crew, only 67 survived after spending three days in the water.

Although not nearly as significant to losses accrued in the North Atlantic and other areas, by mid-1941 German and Italian submarine operations off South America began to raise serious concern in Washington. This perceived threat warranted the introduction of U.S. military forces in Brazil, which would come into fruition after a series of diplomatic negotiations. The lack of surface and air assets, which prevented American naval forces from pursuing an aggressive ASW campaign, resulted in rising shipping losses along an area stretching from Trinidad down to French Guiana. German and Italian submarine interceptions of merchant shipping sailing between South America and Africa continued to go unchecked, with Jürgen Wattenberg in command of *U-162* sinking five vessels totaling over 10,000 tons between the first and ninth of May 1942. Wattenberg's first victim, the Brazilian freighter *Parnahyb*, went down near Trinidad. Three days later *U-162*, while operating off British Guiana, sank the American steamer *Eastern Sword* with torpedoes and the sailing vessel *Florence M. Douglass* with the boat's deck gun. The U-boat's success continued as the Norwegian *Frank Seamans* and the Canadian *Mont Louis* were sunk on the seventh and ninth respectively. In the interim, Italian submarines made a nuisance of themselves off Brazil with *Barbarigo* sinking the British freighter *Charlbury* on the 28th, while the Italian submarine *Cappellini* torpedoed the tanker *Dinsdale* on the 31st.

During the first week in March, *U-129* proceeded to sink the American freighters *Mary* on the third and *Steel Age* on the sixth. Shipping losses off Brazil did not materialize until the second week of April 1942, when the Italian submarine *Calvi*, operating farther south along the northeastern coast, claimed a pair of tankers and a freighter sailing between São Luís and Natal. Olivieri's first prize, the American tanker *Eugene V. R. Thayer*, went down off Parnaíba on the eighth. *Calvi* three days later sank the Norwegian freighter *Balkis* with torpedoes and cannon fire. Fortaleza, followed by the Panamanian tanker *Ben Brush*, sunk during the late evening hours of the 12th off Cape São Roque. The appearance of German and Italian submarines off South America caught the Americans just as unprepared as that of the Eastern and Caribbean Sea Frontiers during U-boat operations in those areas during 1942.

VP-83 Arrives in Brazil

PBY-5A squadron VP-83 relieved Lieutenant Commander VP-52 at Natal, Brazil in April 1942 and, in the months to come, VP-83 would become the most successful patrol squadron in the South Atlantic while under the command of three skippers Lieutenant Commanders Ralph Sperry Clarke, Ralph W. Mackert, and Bertram J. Prueher. The squadron performed convoy coverage, air-sea rescue, and anti-submarine operations for six months after forming at Norfolk on September 15, 1941 as part of Patrol Wings Atlantic Fleet. A considerable number of pilots assigned to patrol squadrons were enlisted men designated as Naval Aviation Pilots (NAP) who, although responsible for an aircraft and an entire aircrew, were denied most of the obligatory duties or benefits of commissioned officers. Frank Burgess was one such pilot, assigned to VP-83 and later VB-107.

> My being a full-fledged pilot and only being a Naval Aviation Pilot Second Class (NAP2c) had its shortcomings. First, I was not allowed in the conference room because I was not an officer and did not hold a secret clearance but when I became airborne, it was a different story. The officers tolerated me (rather us) because we did have quite a few enlisted pilots from Chief to Second Class In February 1942, VP-83 transferred to PatWing-5 and in mid-March, Commander Clarke informed his officers during a meeting to prepare to leave for Natal, Brazil for "temporary duty" with PatWing-11. He also instructed his men "take along your heavy clothes and winter flight gear. We'll be in the tropics about six months, and then move on into a colder climate."[4]

However, unknown to the men of VP-83, the squadron was destined to operate from Natal for the next 33 months. Eleven days later, Lieutenant Commander Clarke, leading 13 officers and 56 enlisted men in six planes, departed Norfolk for Natal. Meanwhile, the second division began temporary duty with the Fifth Naval District at Norfolk.

Maintenance of aircraft proved a problem due to a lack of spare parts and adequate repair facilities. Minor repairs to the aircraft did not present a problem but such major maintenance work as engine changes and major structural work required flying the planes back to Norfolk. This condition persisted until the spring of 1943, when Fleet Air Wing Sixteen (FAW-16) was established at Recife, Brazil, 140 miles (225 kilometers) south of Natal. However, a lack of spare parts

Two VP-83 PBY-5A Catalinas with 83-P-4 in the foreground circa 1942 at Natal, Brazil. The squadron began operations from Brazil in April 1942. (Richard A. Wilson)

continued throughout the squadron's tour having to cannibalize airworthy aircraft to remain operational.

The first division of VP-83, upon reaching Natal, set up an advance base of operations and began patrol and search operations four days later. In July, when the squadron was operating under full strength, it began systematic patrols of shipping lanes along the entire 3,800 miles of Brazilian coastline from Rio de Janeiro in the south to Cape Orange in the north. As the only aircraft squadron in Brazil, it became necessary to provide coverage for all convoys along a two thousand-mile route extending from Bahia to Cape Orange. This was in addition to normal anti-submarine searches under Commander Task Force 44 and Commander Fourth Fleet. Covering such a large area required planes to refuel at isolated airfields. Most of the bases along the Brazilian coast were completely inadequate, having no housing, mess, or repair facilities since they were initially built to provide only refueling points for Pan American Airlines operating along the Brazilian coast. On extended convoy coverage, when take-offs and landings occurred at all hours of the day and night, crews slept in the planes or on the wings, and they cooked most of their meals inside the aircraft.

VP-83's first experience with enemy action occurred on May 18, when three planes flew cover for the light cruisers USS *Milwaukee* (CL-5) and USS *Cincinnati* (CL-6), while they conducted a rescue effort for the burning Brazilian ship *Commandante Lyra*, a merchantman torpedoed and shelled by the Italian submarine *Barbarigo* off Cape San Roque, Brazil. During an effort to tow the ship into port, *Barbarigo* came up and launched an attack on the *Milwaukee*. The torpedoes missed. There was not any additional interference from enemy submarines and the seaplane tender *Thrush* towed *Commandante Lyra* into Fortaleza Harbor. Five days later Lieutenant Junior Grade (jg) Waggoner conducted an unsuccessful attack on a submarine, possibly the Italian *Niestlé* in cooperation with the USS *Milwaukee*. However, three months would elapse before the squadron would record a similar action against the enemy.

Merchant ships sailing off South America virtually unprotected were easy pickings and so Admiral Dönitz dispatched ten U-boats, along with several Italian submarines, to the area. Soon, Allied and neutral shipping losses began to rise. Four were lost off British Guiana and Surinam beginning with the Norwegian tanker *Hüegh Giant* sunk by *U-126* on the third, while the Italian submarine *Arcamede* dispatched the Panamanian *Cardina* on the 15th. In July, *U-160* torpedoed the Dutch freighter *Telamon* on the 25th and the Canadian freighter *Presrodoc* four days later. However, the height of submarine activity in the South Atlantic began in August 1942, and it did not drop off until January 1943. Losses in August started with Kapitänleutnant Heinrich Bleichrodt's *U-109* sinking the Norwegian tanker *Arthur S. Seawall*. By the end of the month, over two dozen merchant vessels would slip under the waves in the waters between Africa and South American—six were Brazilian-flagged.

The primary reason for Brazil's entry into the war on the side of the Allies was the sinking of six Brazilian ships by *U-507* commanded by Fregattenkapitän Harro Schacht. During the evening of August 15–16, the U-boat torpedoed the Brazilian passenger ships *Baependy* and *Araraquara* near the mouth of the Real River, between Sergipe and Bahia, resulting in over 400 casualties. Later in the morning, the *Annibal Benévolo* went down seven miles off the coast with the loss of 150 passengers and crew. Schacht followed up those successes on the afternoon and early evening hours of the 17th by sinking the *Itagiba* and *Arará*. The loss of the ships and over 800 casualties culminated with the country's formal declaration of war against Germany and Italy. Upon his country's entry into the war, President Vargas ordered Brazilian armed forces to operate under Admiral Ingram and to open all ports and air facilities to the Americans. Meanwhile, VP-83 continued searching for the enemy with the squadron recording several unsuccessful attacks on German and Italian submarines. Schacht's U-boat caught the attention of a VP-83 Catalina piloted by Lieutenant (jg) Lacey, who was patrolling the coastal shipping lanes on August 18. An attack was conducted on the surfaced *U-507* and the Catalina crew observed their depth charges straddle the submarine's bow, causing it to roll over 90 degrees before disappearing stern first. However, the U-boat escaped undamaged and went on to sink the 90-ton Brazilian sailing vessel *Jacira* by gunfire on the 19th and the 3,000-ton Swedish freighter *Hamaren* in the same fashion three days later. Two days after the attack on *U-507*, another VP-83 Catalina commanded by Lieutenant (jg) M. K. Smith conducted another unsuccessful attack against an unidentified submarine cruising at periscope depth. It was bombed, and debris and large bubbles rose to the surface, but the vessel apparently escaped.

Squadron personnel of VP-83 fueling 83-P-8 with a hand pump before setting out for convoy and ASW patrol over the South Atlantic. (Richard A. Wilson)

Admiral Ingram's air and surface forces had somewhat of a reprieve during the first two weeks of September 1942, without any shipping losses occurring within the fleet's operational area, that situation changed by mid-month. It began with Korvettenkapitän Werner Henke's *U-515* sinking the American freighter *Mae* off British Guiana on the 16th. Two days later, the Canadian steamer *Norfolk* went down in the same area after taking torpedo hits from *U-175* commanded by Kapitänleutnant Heinrich Bruns. Targets were plentiful and *U-175* and *515* claimed another five ships between the 20th and 24th. Farther down the coast, Kapitänleutnant Han Jürgen Auffermann's *U-514* sank the Brazilian vessels Ozório and Lages escorted on the 28th.

Another six ships went down during October in the Trinidad-British Guiana area beginning with the loss of the Dutch *Achilles* sunk by *U-202*. In approximately the same region, *U-175* torpedoed three merchantmen between the second and fourth of October. A week later the American *Steel Scientist*, a 5,688-ton steamer sank off Cayenne, French Guiana after from the torpedoes of *U-514*. The month closed with the loss of the British freighter *Marylyn*, torpedoed by *U-174* off the Brazilian hump. During November and December 1942, nearly three dozen merchant ships were lost in areas under the Fourth Fleet's operational control. During November, the Italian submarine *da Vinci*, operating off northeastern Brazil under the command of Lieutenant Gianfranco Gazzana Priaroggia, sank the *Empire Zeal* on the second, *Andreas* on fourth, *Marcus Whitman* on the tenth, and the Dutch freighter *Veerhaven* on the 11th. U-boats were also active from British Guiana to Brazil with *U-160, 154, 172, 174, 508*, and *UD-3* scoring kills.

An inadequate number of surface and air assets assigned to the Fourth Fleet, the lack of a coordinated convoy system, where ships often sailed alone, caused the rising losses of merchant shipping in the South Atlantic. As the lone naval patrol squadron in the Brazilian area of operations, VP-83 was beyond its capacity to patrol the entire Brazilian coast. In December, seven U-boats consisting of *U-128, 159, 161, 174, 176, 507, 508* and the Italian submarine *Tazzoli* continued to wreak havoc on shipping. *U-508* sank four British merchantmen during the first week starting on the second with the destruction of the *Trevalgen* and *City of Bath* off British Guiana. The next day, the *Solon II* felt the sting of *U-508*. Five days elapsed before another ship, this time the *Nigerian*, felt the sting of *U-508*'s torpedoes. Meanwhile, four ships fell to the *Tazzoli*, two on the 12th, one on the 21st, and another on Christmas Day.

Sightings and subsequent attacks on enemy submarines by VP-83 continued throughout the month but each time the enemy vessel escaped.

A day after the attack on *U-126* a pair of PBY Cats piloted by Lieutenant W. L. Wall and Lieutenant Commander Prueher damaged U-boats in two separate contacts. At 1320 hours, a Catalina piloted by Lieutenant W. L. Wall attacked the fully surfaced *U-174* commanded by Ulrich Thilo with depth charges, but the explosives overshot the target. However, the U-boat suffered minor damage from the near misses. Approximately four hours after Lieutenant Wall's contact with *U-174*, Lieutenant Commander Bertram Prueher conducted a depth charge attack on the fully surfaced *U-161* commanded by Korvettenkapitän Albrecht "Ajax" Achilles. Prueher's depth charges caused a considerable amount of damage to the U-boat, but the vessel slipped away only to be subjected to another attack from VP-83 the following morning. PBY Number P-9, piloted by Lieutenant Frederick C. Andretta, dropped one Mk-17 depth bomb 50 seconds after the submarine submerged, but again, Albrecht Achilles' U-boat slipped away. VP-74 subsequently sank *U-161* on September 27, 1943 in the South Atlantic near Bahia, Brazil.

Striking Back

Shipping losses in the South Atlantic began to decline beginning in January 1943, with the establishment of a convoy system for the Trinidad-Bahia route, under the control of Admiral Ingram, and the arrival of a sufficient number of escort vessels. Furthermore, the arrival of squadrons VP-74 in December 1942, followed by VP-94 the following January, greatly enhanced the Navy's ability to provide day aerial coverage of the convoys previously left entirely to VP-83 by allowing day coverage of convoys extending 2,000 miles from Belém to Bahia. The increased number of patrol aircraft conducting ASW operations over a broader area, marked the beginning of successful campaign to rid the South Atlantic enemy submarines.

A PBY-5A flown by Lieutenant (jg) William Render Ford of VP-83, scored first by sending Type IXC *U-164* and its crew of 54 to the bottom of the South Atlantic, 80 miles northeast of Fortaleza. Under the command of Korvettenkapitän Otto Fechner, *U-164* sailed from its base at Lorient, France, for its second voyage on November 29, 1942. On New Year's Day 1943, the crew celebrated its only success when it sank the *Brageland*, a Swedish freighter of 4,800 tons, which was sailing from Santos, Brazil to Philadelphia. Afterward, *U-164* continued towards its operational area, much of it on the surface. Northwest of Pernambuco, a white streak on the horizon attracted the attention of Aviation Machinist Mate Third Class (AMM3c) Billy Goodell, as Lieutenant Ford's plane flew back to base on January 6, after conducting a three-day convoy coverage. Lieutenant Ford, in his after-action report, described the attack:

> We were flying at 5,500 feet [1676 m] when Billy Goodell, who had made two sightings previously, advised me of his sighting. As soon as I sighted the sub, I turned ninety degrees to port and pulled the props and throttles all the way back. There was a small cloud between the sub and the plane. Air speed was 184 knots indicated with a rate of descent of about 2,000 feet [610 m] per minute. When about three to four miles away [5–6.4 km], I gave full power and approached the sub. The U-boat maintained her course and speed with several men on *U-164* lying on the deck, apparently in the process of bathing, seemingly unaware of the aircraft's presence. A moment before the bomb drop, two men caught on the submarine's deck realized they were under attack and ran to the bridge only to find it deserted and the hatch closed.[5]

Lieutenant Ford continued to push his Catalina into a nosedive until the aircraft was a mere 35 feet (11 meters) from the deck. The second pilot was in the bow and, on the order to drop, pulled the release and three Mk-47 epth bombs fell almost simultaneously, with a fourth falling a split second later. The exploding depth bombs blew the two hapless crewmen caught on *U-164*'s deck into the sea. With explosions occurring close to starboard and abeam of the conning

An unidentified U.S. sailor standing beside 83-P-2 while another rests under the wing. This particular Catalina may have been the aircraft that sank *U-164* on 6 January 1943. (Richard A. Wilson)

A depth bomb dropped from Lieutenant William Ford's PBY-5A 83-P-2 explodes near *U-164*. Only two men amongst the submarine's 54-man complement survived the sinking. (Richard A. Wilson)

tower, the submarine appeared to rise out of the water and break, at least partly, in two pieces.

Three of the U-boat's upper deck torpedo containers floated to the surface, along with several mangled bodies, and three men still alive, one of whom possibly killed almost instantly by the Catalina's gunfire. As the plane circled the first time just after dropping the bombs, one very large residue spot was seen with a smaller one about 50 feet (15 meters) away. The stern of the sub appeared at the forward edge of the large residue, rising almost vertically eight to ten feet out of the water and bobbing up. It remained so for some three minutes before it slipped under the surface. The aircrew dropped two life rafts but only two of the U-boat's entire compliment successfully climbed aboard one of the rafts and ultimately made their way to the northern coast of Brazil where they became prisoners of war.

While the men of VP-83 celebrated the sinking of *U-164*, other U-boats continued to ply their trade. Korvettenkapitän Johann Mohr's *U-124*, which had sunk the British light cruiser HMS *Dunedin* on November 24, 1941, stationed his boat off Surinam during the pre-dawn hours of January 9, 1943, when the 12 ships of Convoy BT-1 came into view. Two hours later, the U-boat's torpedoes sent to the bottom over 23,000 tons of shipping consisting of the tankers *Birmingham City* and *Broad Arrow* along with the freighters *Collingsworth* and *Minotaus*.

Badly shaken up by the experience, the remaining ships of the convoy made refuge in the Para River before proceeding again. Four months later, Korvettenkapitän Mohr and his entire crew were lost when the British corvette HMS *Stonecrop* and the sloop HMS *Black Swan* sank *U-124* on April 2, 1943.

VP-83 followed the sinking of *U-164* by hunting down Korvettenkapitän Haro Schacht's Type IXC *U-507* on January 12, 1943, when Lieutenant (jg) L. Ludwig and crew, while providing air coverage for a convoy, located and sank the U-boat northwest of Natal. Before being lost, *U-507* sank two British merchant ships within a period of five days in January, the *Baron Dechmont* on the third and the *Yorkwood* on the eighth. While Korvettenkapitän Schacht and his crew searched for vessels on the high seas off Brazil, Lieutenant Ludwig and his crew embarked on a ten-day tour of duty that stretched from Natal to Fortaleza. It began as the crew took off in Catalina Number P-10 at Natal on January 2, to cover a convoy. Richard A. Wilson wrote details the life of a patrol plane crew as they flew from one field to another with the primary mission of protecting Allied shipping from the vigilant U-boat force lurking off Brazil:

> Less than two hours after taking off, we sighted three lifeboats filled with survivors of a merchant ship sunk by a German U-boat. By Aldis lamp, we learned they had plenty of food and water. They just wanted confirmation of their position. This we did and advised Natal of their situation and we proceeded to our destination. Upon arrival at Belem, we were advised we were scheduled for a morning take off to locate the convoy.[6]

The following day, Ludwig found the convoy and stayed on station until relieved. For the next several days, three patrol planes alternated in tracking the ships with stopovers at San Luis, Belem, and Fortaleza where some of the crew spent each night at a local hotel.

> On January 12, we arrived at Fortaleza after nightfall. We bartered a local cab driver with a couple gallons of 100-octane fuel for a ride to a local hotel. After dinner and a bottle of cerveza, we retired for the night around 11PM [2300 hrs]. Before daylight, we were on our way back to the airport. Our plane had its interior lights on and the two radiomen, Aviation Mechanics [Machinist] Mate First Class (AMM1c) R. K Gernhofer, and Seaman Second Class (S2c) R. O Siemann were wide-awake. Gerbhofer handed me a message from Natal stating that a German submarine was shadowing the convoy and directed us to take appropriate action.
>   Before taking off the crew and I particularly co-pilot Lieutenant (jg) Mearl Taylor and Ensign Harry Holt, the navigator, the radiomen, and the two waist gunners named Merrick and Thurston reviewed our plan. We would not use the intervalometer [bomb release control unit] when we dropped the depth charges as there had been instances where they had hung up. We would fly around 6,000 [1829 m] feet using cloud cover where possible. If we made an attack, I would drop two depth charges by use of the handheld release button, namely the two outboard ones. Mearl, sitting in the co-pilots seat would manually drop the remaining right one and then Harry, kneeling between us, would drop the last one. Hopefully, they would drop within two or three seconds of each other. Gernhofer was to advise the base by sending a message in the clear that we were attacking. The two waist gunners would operate the .50 caliber machine guns and would fire upon advice from Mearl or me. We would not use the 30-caliber nose gun. We would fly to a point 50 miles [80.4 km] ahead of the projected convoy track, then back track. This way we would be looking down sun with a greater chance of surprise.
>   Lieutenant Ludwig's PBY became airborne shortly before sunrise and climbed to 6,000 feet [1829 m]. Northwest of Natal, the PBY Catalina crew found *U-507*: Nobody commented when right on course, we passed it on my side. Whatever it was, luck or lack of sleep for the past few days and clouds below, I did not see it. Shortly thereafter, Mearl leaned over and said, "Does that look like a pc boat?" One look is all it took, I answered, "That's a sub!" It seems like everything happened at once, power was cut, nose dropped, warning horn sounded, battle stations, and depth charges made ready. Harry Holt came forward and knelt between Mearl

and me. We were soon in a dive exceeding 200 knots. We were approaching the sub head on and so far no sign that the sub saw us. It seemed forever but in a matter of seconds, we were down to 1,200 feet [1931 m]. The sub had seen us and started to submerge. We shallowed the dive, but still nose down. Power was added to maintain our speed. Mearl was ready to pull the release on the right side; Harry was on the left. I had the pickeral, a hand held depth charge release, in my hand. We were about there and the sub had about submerged with only the conning tower awash. We were down less than 100 feet [161 m] altitude and still in a glide. I pressed the pickeral aiming just forward of the conning tower. Meal and Harry then released their depth charges as planned.

Fortunately, all four depth charges dropped because we were now down to 25 feet [7.6 m] and the loss of 2,000 pounds [907 kg] helped us level off. Soon we were in a climbing turn to the left. I looked back and what a sight. It looked like Niagara Falls turned upside down, a tremendous wall of water rose in the air, not as four columns but as one huge one. As we circled, we dropped a couple of smoke bombs but saw nothing of the sub except for the scum from depth charges. Harry Holt went back to the radio compartment, figured our position, and advised the base of an attack. I asked over the intercom "Did anyone see the convoy?" I believe it was the plane captain, Aviation Mechanics [Machinist] Mate Second Class (AMM2c) J. W. Dickinson in the tower, who replied, "We passed it about five minutes before we started the attack. I turned the controls over to Mearl to head for the convoy and went back to question the crew in the blisters. I asked them:

"Did you see the depth charges hit?"
"Yes."
"Did any of them skip?"
"No."
"Did they appear to hit the sub?"
"Right before the conning tower."
"What do you think about the attack?"
"I thought we were going to crash in to it."
"Well it was close but keep an eye on the smoke as long as you can, we are going back to advise the convoy."[7]

Lieutenant Ludwig contacted the cruiser *Omaha* that was escorting the convoy and the warship headed for the scene of the attack but failed to find any evidence of the U-boat's destruction. VP-83's intelligence officer received a report the following day while Ludwig's crew made a simulated run on a sub mock-up in the bush near the base at Natal. The squadron gave Ludwig and his men credit for causing minor damage to the submarine, but *U-507* didn't survive the attack.

The South Atlantic area stayed relatively calm during a period of six weeks after Convoy BT-1's experience with *U-124* on January 9, with only two ships being lost to German and Italian submarines between Brazil and the Guianas. Enemy operations picked up again during March, when U-boats set their sights on the northbound convoy BT-6 and six Italian submarines *Archimede, Bagnolini, Barbargio, Cappellini, Tazzoli*, and *Tortelli* began operations off Brazil. On March 1, while the Brazilian warships *Carioca, Caravelas*, and *Rio Branco* escorted the 29 ships of the northbound convoy BT-6, *U-518* sank the Liberty ship *Fitz-John Porter*. The *Barbargio* followed up by sinking the Brazilian *Afonso Pena* on the second and the American *Stag Hound* the next day. Meanwhile off Recife, a Navy surface group consisting of the destroyer

U-507 under attack by VP-83's PBY-5A 83-P-10 piloted by Lieutenant (jg) Ludwig on 13 January 1943. The submarine sank with her crew of 54. (Richard A. Wilson)

Borie, gunboats *Courage*, *Tenacity*, and patrol craft *PC-575* and *592* relieved BT-6's Brazilian escorts. The convoy proceeded north in a somewhat confused fashion with light and noise discipline being continuously broken. At 0210 hours on the ninth, as the convoy sailed 100 miles north of Cayenne, *U-510* commanded of Kapitän zur See Karl Neitzel commenced an attack. In a battle that lasted three hours, three merchant ships were lost consisting of *James K. Polk*, *Thomas Ruffin*, and *Kelvinbank* while another five were damaged. The U-boat escaped while the rest of the convoy made it safely to Georgetown, British Guiana and Port of Spain, Trinidad. U-boat successes in March ended with *U-518* sinking the freighter *Mariso* on the 20th and the Swedish *Industria* on the 25th off Bahia. A month later German and Italian submarines failed to sink any ships in the Brazilian area.

Since late 1941, the task of waging war against German U-boats, surface raiders, and blockade-runners in the South Atlantic fell to Vice Admiral Jonas Ingram's South Atlantic Force while air units fell under the operational control of PatWing-11. In March 1943, South Atlantic Force was redesignated as the Fourth U.S. Fleet while its naval air arm operated under Fleet Air Wing Sixteen (FAW-16) with Captain Rossmore D. Lyon as commanding officer. Vice Admiral Ingram expected Admiral Dönitz to move additional U-boats into the South Atlantic once the Allies won the Battle of the North Atlantic. He wasn't disappointed when two U-boats appeared off Brazil in May. At the same time, enemy submarines were operating 1,200 miles (1931 kilometers) off Brazil near Ascension Island, which was well beyond the range of patrol planes based in South America. German torpedoes sank four merchant ships

Unidentified sailors of VP-83 with PBY-5A 83-P-2 in background. Note the radar aerial under the starboard wing above the individual wearing the pith helmet. (Richard A. Wilson)

during the month off Ascension three of them sank. *U-182* sank a Greek freighter off Ascension on May 1. Five days later, *U-192* sent a Liberty ship down while *U-195* damaged the *Cape Neddick* and *U-197* sank a Dutch tanker on the 20th. Meanwhile, the two PBY Catalina squadrons, VP-83 and sister squadron VP-94, sent out five-plane barrier sweeps in hopes of intercepting German blockade-runners that were attempting to transport war materials between Japan and Germany. It was during one of those sweeps on April 15, that VP-83's Ensign Thurmond Robertson encountered the *Archimede*, a 237-foot-long (72 meters), 1,016-ton, Brin Class submarine of the Italian Navy, some 350 miles east of Natal.[8]

At 1500 hours, after being in the air for some ten hours, Ensign Robertson and his crew were proceeding back to base on what had been a routine patrol. The navigator Ensign Eugene Morrison was making his way forward to the bow to take a drift sight when Seaman Second Class Earl J. Kloss sighted a vessel below. Morrison immediately identified the object as a submarine and scrambled back to inform Robertson. By this time, the plane had already passed directly over the target, so Robertson began a turn to port in order to see the object himself. As he made the turn, the enemy began sending up antiaircraft fire, so Robertson attempted to make a horizontal run at altitude, drop one bomb, while his gunners cleared the submarine's decks. However, in the course of the bombing run, the *Archimede* started to submerge, forcing Robertson to start a dive from 7,300 feet (2225 meters). When the plane dropped down to 2,000 feet (610 meters), the target submerged, forcing Robertson to release all four depth charges. Immediately after the explosions, the submarine surfaced and began making erratic circles to port for about 20 minutes at a speed of four to five knots, apparently out of control. From the vantage point of the attacking PBY, the submarine was unable to steer to starboard and it was trailing heavy brown oil with heavy, grayish black smoke pouring from the conning tower. As it continued making erratic circles, some of *Archimede*'s crew kept up a valiant fight by firing rounds from the deck gun, in an attempt to shoot down Robertson's Catalina.

Immediately after the attack, Robertson sent a contact report and messages to four other patrol planes in the area. Lieutenant Bradford's plane received the messages and immediately proceeded to the position arriving on the scene an hour later. Bradford dropped four depth bombs from 50 feet on his first run and then conducted four strafing runs through intense antiaircraft fire coming from the submarine. During one of the runs, Bradford turned and faced the copilot with a look of complete amazement and remarked, "Gee, Brad, they're shooting at us!"

The submarine sank six minutes later. Members of Robertson's crew dropped life rafts to some 30 survivors in the water, but only two men managed to survive after spending several weeks adrift. VP-83's tour of duty concluded soon after Robertson sank the *Archimede* and the squadron returned to the United States. Three months later, after reforming as VB-107 and equipped with the Consolidated PB4Y-1 Liberator, the squadron returned for a second tour of duty in Brazil.[9]

In May 1943, Admiral Ingram had at his disposal a motley fleet of five Omaha class light cruisers, eight destroyers, five gunboats, and a hodgepodge of gunboats, seaplane tenders, patrol boats, and minesweepers. Fleet operations was based at Rio Janeiro and commanded by Captain Harold Dodd, who had under his command four task groups based at Recife, each consisting of two warships. To assist in the effort of clearing enemy submarines from the South Atlantic, Brazil placed under Admiral Ingram's operational control two thirty-four-year-old light cruisers, six modern minesweepers, patrol boats, and subchasers commanded by the Brazilian Contra-almirante Alfredo Soares Dutra. Admiral Ingram needed additional long-range patrol aircraft as his air assets in Brazil at the time consisted of three Navy squadrons and a few FAB units, the latter just becoming operational. The Brazilians, equipped with less than desirable aircraft, were undergoing ASW training at the time. The three Navy squadrons (VP-74, 83, and 94), consisting of some 36 long-range patrol aircraft, were the only units at his disposal capable of covering the coastal waters that stretched from French Guiana to Rio de Janeiro. At the end of April 1943, VP-74 moved to NAF Aratu, near Bahia, and by the end of May, two PV-1 Ventura squadrons had reported for duty at Natal. VB-127 arrived on the tenth and VB-129 joined them by month's end. By July 1943, FAW-16 air strength had grown to five squadrons with another five were deploying to Brazil by the end of the year.

Type IXC *U-128* departed Lorient, France on April 6, 1943, under the command of Oberleutnant zur See Hermann Steinert, his first patrol as a U-boat commander. The order for Steinert's boat was to escort the *Silvaplana*; a 4,000-ton blockade-runner coming from Japan loaded with strategic cargo. For about ten days, it cruised in the Bay

of Biscay and off the Spanish coast, pursued repeatedly and depth charged at least onc
by British corvettes and destroyers, but *U-128* suffered no damage from the attacks
However, around 16 April, Steinhert's initial mission of escorting the *Silvaplana* endec
upon receiving a message that the British intercepted and sank the blockade-runner

U-128 now set sail for its operational area off the northern coast of Brazil
traveling at its most economical surface speed. Although the U-boat sighted a few
ships, the commander did not consider them worthwhile. About a week before it
sinking *U-128* sighted a steamer on the evening of May 8, estimated at betweer
4,000 and 5,000 tons, possibly the *M. V. Motocarline*. The U-boat went in pursui
of the merchantman and, early in the morning, the executive officer fired three
salvoes of two torpedoes each. None found their mark and the ship finally wa.
able to elude *U-128* with the help of a patrolling Brazilian B-18B Bolo bomber
At 1120 hours on 16 May, VP-74's Lieutenant Gibbs took off from Aratu in PBM
Mariner Number P-2 to sweep a 200-mile sector (322 kilometers) to the northeast
At 1351 hours, the starboard bow watch reported from the bomber's window ar
object 15 miles distant. A few seconds later, the pilots saw a white wake and at the
end of two minutes identified it through binoculars as a submarine with decks awash
Lieutenant Gibbs turned the PBM slightly towards cloud cover to get between the
submarine and the sun, increased power, and came straight in. Squadron doctrine
for conducting an attack on a submarine according to William J. Barnard who flew
with VP-74 consisted of flying 50 feet (15 meters) above the surface, as the flying
boat approached the submarine. As the flying boat closed in for the kill, the pilot
or co-pilot released a string of 500-pound (227 kilograms) Torpex depth charges:

> The routine was to go full power at the time of sighting and point the nose over to reach the
> altitude for dropping about one mile to the stern of the sub if practicable. Somewhere along
> the way in (It was up to the pilot's discretion) the bomb bay doors were opened and the depth
> charges armed. When we nosed over and the power was thrown to it, the speed increased by
> 30 or 40 knots and when the bomb bays were popped open.[10]

Approximately halfway to the target, the U-boat submerged. Six minutes after the
initial sighting, a distinct swirl was reached and six Mk-44 depth charges were
dropped, which straddled the swirl, the last two 120 feet (37 meters) beyond its
leading edge. However, *U-128* sustained no damage from the attack and it continued
on course. During the evening, Oberleutnant zur See Steinert kept the boat surfaced
to recharge the batteries. Shortly after submerging at dawn, listening gear on the
U-boat picked up the presence of convoy BT-13. Upon establishing the convoy's
direction, the U-boat set off in pursuit, traveling at full speed on the surface, hoping
to close rapidly the estimated distance of 12 miles (19 kilometers) that separated it
and the convoy. However, escorting aircraft for the convoy forced Steinert to dive
several times, but, after surfacing the last time, he found the convoy about 14 miles
distant and again set out after it at full speed. Visibility on the morning of May 17
was excellent and the U-boat's lookouts were relied upon to warn of approaching

Two PBM's commanded by Lieutenant Howland S. Davis, USNR, and Lieutenant (jg) Harold C. Carey, USN, cripple *U-128* in South Atlantic on 17 May 1943. One plane dropped depth bombs bringing her to surface while the second machine-gunned to clear the submarine's deck to prevent its crew from operating anti-aircraft guns. (National Archives)

planes, as the G.S.R. was not mounted, partly because the commander would only use radar on a clear day.

Through the afternoon and evening of the sixteenth and into the morning of the seventieth, VP-74 kept aircraft on station over the area where the U-boat submerged. Known as a hold-down mission, it was a tactic to keep a submarine down until oxygen deficiency forced it to the surface. At 0843 hours, Mariner Number P-6, piloted by Lieutenant Davis, having just passed plane Number P-9, sighted the wake of a surfaced submarine 18 miles (29 kilometers) distant. Approximately, at the same time, A PBM picked up *U-128* on the radar from a distance of 28 miles (45 kilometers). Lieutenant Harold "Hog" Carey's radar aboard plane Number P-5 named the *Nickle Boat* made contact from an estimated ten miles astern of Number 6 on the east leg of an assigned 50-mile square (129 kilometers²) search sector. According to Carey in the after-action report:

> Through binoculars, I saw a fully surfaced submarine, and ordered an attack. Ensign Smolsnik, the regular patrol plane commander of P-5 was in the seat and I prepared the bomb panel. Soon after the run started, the U-boat started to submerge. We then first noted 74-P-6 going in for an attack about two miles ahead of us.[11]

The bridge watch on *U-128* had also seen the approaching plane, but, when the order to crash dive came, the boat couldn't dive due to a failure of vents in the high-pressure manifold. After opening the vents by hand, the U-boat finally submerged. Meanwhile, Lieutenant Davis started his run on the submarine by turning the PBM Mariner slightly to port in an attempt to use the sun. The submarine, running at about

15 knots, started to crash dive when our plane was slightly less than two miles awa and disappeared when it was still three-quarters of a mile distant. Crossing the patl of the sub at a 50-degree angle about 150–200 feet ahead of the swirl, six Mk-4 depth charges were released from an altitude of 50 feet (15 meters).

The depth charges detonated fifteen seconds after *U-128*'s submergence with th detonation pattern following the extended course of the U-boat. Immediately afte dropping the bombs, Lieutenant Davis conducted a sharp climbing turn in orde to observe the results of the attack.

> Halfway around the next circle the tail gunner reported the U-boat resurfacing on our starboar quarter. It was on a course near the reciprocal of its original course, apparently having made sharp left turn, and moved a quarter of a mile from the point of attack. We got into positio for a strafing run, observed PBM Number 5 coming in to attack, and turned to keep clear. W paralleled his course and photographed the attack, then circled left and followed him in on th first of several runs by both planes.[12]

Lieutenant Davis' attack severely crippled *U-128*. The pressure hull was ruptured nea the forward starboard torpedo tubes, water poured in through a four-finger wide gap through the forward galley hatch, and the electric motors were put out of commission as was the gyrocompass. Diving quickly and somewhat out of control, men were rushec into the aft parts of the boat to maintain trim. Realizing that his boat could not remair submerged without danger to the crew, the commander gave the order to surface. Abou three minutes after the first attack, *U-128* surfaced with both diesels running at ful speed. Immediately upon surfacing, and a course laid in the approximate direction of the South American coast. Members of *U-128* manned the antiaircraft guns but the other plane in the attack, Carey's PBM, took them by surprise.

A depth bomb from a VP-74 Mariner explodes near *U-128* south of Pernambuco, Brazil on 17 May 1943. The conning tower can be seen in the left center. (National Archives)

Ensign Smolsnik at the controls of a second PBM Mariner climbed to 1,500 feet (457 meters) before diving at an angle of 45 degrees. He crossed the now fully surfaced submarine at 100 feet altitude and an angle of 45 degrees, passing over the vessel just ahead of the conning tower. Lieutenant Carey, in the second pilot's seat, released the depth charges and the bombs straddled *U-128* just forward of the control tower, obliterating all view of the submarine from either plane. When the column of water subsided, the victim lay still in the center of disturbance. The pair of PBMs then executed the first of 20 or more strafing runs. During the strafing runs, both aircraft poured 4,500 rounds of .50 caliber machine-gun fire at the submarine's structure, gun emplacements, and later, at personnel attempting to operate the guns. Carey related the damage inflicted upon the U-boat,

> About a minute later, the U-boat got under way, leaving in its wake a large amount of oil, and was down by the stern to the aft deck gun. The bow diving planes had apparently been jammed in the up position by the previous attack.[13]

After 20 minutes of erratic maneuvering, the bow planes were fixed, and about four times the U-boat tried to dive, once succeeding in submerging to all but one quarter of the conning tower. Both planes maintained continuous strafing and on the fifth run, the crew aboard PBM Number 5 observed a flashing explosion just aft of conning tower lasting about a minute, which was believed to be from exploding ammunition.

This attack increased the damage to *U-128* by the first depth charging, and the subsequent 20 strafing runs killed or wounded several of the U-boat's compliment and prevented an effective defense against the aggressive PBM patrol planes. Aircraft gunners seriously wounded *U-128*'s second watch officer and a rating while commanding officer himself crawled onto the bridge to administer morphine to the

The explosion from the depth bomb has begun to subside. Lieutenant (jg) Carey and his crew were killed on a later mission when their plane crashed into the ocean while conducting an attack on *U-199* during July 1943. (National Archives)

second watch officer. Orders for steering the submarine from the conning became impossible and could only be conducted through the aft periscope, the forward one having been damaged in the first strafing attack.

Although not yet prepared to give up the boat, it was evident to most of the crew assembled in the control room and conning tower that only a miracle could save U-128. Some crewmembers went up on deck and took cover behind the conning tower to protect themselves from the strafing planes. One of the U-boat's crew later admitted that he had tried to signal the airplane that they were ready to give up. This attempt to surrender went apparently unnoticed; similarly, another crewman said that they were looking for a white sheet to signal surrender but couldn't find one.

Lieutenant Carey and his crew maintained the strafing attacks and kept other planes, the base, and surface ships informed of the progress of events for the next half-hour while Lieutenant Davis left to lead friendly destroyers to the scene. The U-boat's speed, which had been eight knots or more, dropped to three or four knots by 0952 hours and eight minutes later it was no longer making headway. The *Nickel Boat*'s patrol plane commander reported, "At 0952, the engines stopped, the decks were coming awash, and the crew started to abandon ship. Thinking they might man the guns or that scuttling might be prevented until the destroyers came, we strafed with all guns. Those who came on deck quickly took to the water."[14]

Lieutenant Davis returned to the scene and saw survivors were in the water astern of the U-boat. "We dropped a seven-man life raft in their midst and circled, observing the remaining men leave."[15]

About ten men were in this process of abandoning ship, including the commanding officer, when the destroyers *Moffett* and *Jouett* arrived at 1001 hours and started shelling. After firing 204 rounds and scoring four direct hits the, U-128 nosed over and sank at a 20-degree angle. Above the fray, the two Mariners continued circling while *Moffett* took aboard survivors. Less than two months later, Lieutenant Carey and his crew were lost while making an attack on U-199.

The *Moffett* rescued 51 of her crew, four of whom died aboard the warship. The engineer officer's death was diagnosed as chlorine poisoning and it is believed that chlorine developed during the latter stages of the sinking. A few superficial wounds from machine-gun fire, as well as one inflicted by a shark, were treated on the destroyer. During interrogation, most prisoners believed that U-128 could have effected repairs to the damage done by the first depth charge attack and might even had gotten away after the second one, but not after the destroyers come upon the scene.[16]

While U-164's crew became prisoners of war, their comrades continued searching for targets closer to Brazil. U-154 attacked convoy BT-14 on May 27, 170 miles northeast of Cape San Roque, Brazil, damaging a tanker and two freighters. The situation grew considerably worse during June as U-513 arrived off Brazil under the command of Kapitänleutnant Fritz Guggenberger who sank the British aircraft carrier *Ark Royal* in 1941, while in command of U-81. His first victim on this deployment was the Swedish steamship *Venezia*, which was torpedoed 300 miles southeast of Rio

The destroyers *Jouett* (DD-396) and *Moffett* (DD-362), led to the scene by one of the planes, finished off *U-128* with gunfire. The PBMs dropped life rafts and the destroyers picked up survivors. (National Archives)

de Janeiro on June 21. Upon hearing of the *Venezia's* loss, Admiral Ingram issued a submarine alert from Rio de Janeiro to Bahia and sent a three-plane detachment of VP-94 Catalinas to operate from the tender USS *Barnegat* (AVP-10) in Rio's Harbor. Meanwhile *U-513* moved farther south and torpedoed the American tanker *Eagle* off

Line-up of VB-107 PB4Y-1 Liberators with a PV-1 Ventura in the foreground during summer 1943. The Liberators are "D" models with the Plexiglas nose. The squadron formed from VP-83 and included many members of the former squadron. (Richard A. Wilson)

Side view of Admiral Ingram's personal PB4Y-1 requisitioned from VB-107 stock was named *Southern Cross*. Under the wording is the astronomical star pattern of the Southern Cross. The aircraft's name is also shown about the admiral rank on both aft sections. (Richard A. Wilson)

U.S. Navy PV-1 aircraft from NAF Natal, Brazil flying in formation on 6 October 1943. The aircraft could belong to any of the four Ventura squadrons operating from Brazil at or near that time: VB-129, VB-130, VB-143, or VB-145 (National Archives)

Cape Frio on June 25. A Brazilian FW-58B from Galeão, sent out the same morning to search for *U-513*, instead found *U-199* but it escaped unharmed and continued on patrol. *U-513* followed up the sinking of *Venezia* by torpedoing the Brazilian freighter *Tutóya* off São Paulo on the 30th and the Liberty ship *Elihu B. Washington* on July 3.[17]

The Fourth Fleet and FAW-16 had an enormous task with protecting the Trinidad-Rio convoys as well as other shipping spread across the waters off Brazil. FAW-16 consisted of five patrol squadrons and the Brazilian Adaption Aircraft Group. Admiral Ingram knew that additional long-range aircraft were required and sent a message to Admiral Ingersoll requested for such who informed Ingram that reinforcements in the form of VB-107 operating the PB4Y-1 Liberator would be arriving in early July. In the interim Admiral Ingram rearranged his air assets to extend coverage farther north by ordering a detachment of 32 men and eight PV-1 Ventura bombers from VB-127 to NAF Fortaleza. Renewed enemy activity and the inability of the Ventura squadrons VB-127 and 129 to operate at great distances from the convoy lanes required the further splitting of VP-94 into separate detachments. Four planes of VP-94 went to Santos-Dumont airport for operations with the extension of the convoy system southward from Bahia to Rio de Janeiro.

CHAPTER 5

U-boat Blitz off Brazil
(July 1943)

"My husband so often said he would just as soon be buried at sea and he always said
when his time came, he hoped he'd go fast."

FLORENCE CAREY, WIFE OF LIEUTENANT HAROLD "HOG" CAREY

During July 1943, air and surface units of the Fourth Fleet battled against a heavy
concentration of U-boats off Brazil, in what Admiral Ingram named the *July Blitz,*
during which time FAW-16 aircraft sank six U-boats. The blitz began on June 28,
when *U-172* sank a British freighter approximately 550 miles (885 kilometers) off
Cape San Roque. A week later, Oberleutnant zur See der Reserve Werner Kruer's
U-590 sank the Brazilian freighter *Pelotaslóide* off Pará. On the night of July 7–8, the
southbound convoy TJ-1, consisting of 20 ships, was attacked by Kapitänleutnant
Alfred Eick's *U-510* off Cayenne in the Trinidad area, resulting in the loss of a
tanker and two freighters. Two days later, Kapitänleutnant August Maus's *U-185*
discovered the Trinidad-bound Convoy BT-18 consisting of 18 to 20 merchant ships
and escorted by four Brazilian patrol boats 90 miles from Cape San Roque. Maus
proceeded to torpedo four of the ships, which resulted in the sinking of the tanker
William Boyce Thompson and Liberty ships *James Robertson* and *Thomas Sinnichson,*
while the damaged tanker *S. B. Hunt* reached the safety of a Brazilian harbor.

On the morning of July 9, surface units of the Fourth Fleet and FAW-16 aircraft
spotted several submarines at a distance indicating that the enemy was tracking
convoys BT-18 and TJ-1. The track of BT-18 required five of VP-94's aircraft at
Belém to provide both day and night coverage. At approximately 1235 hours,
Lieutenant (jg) Frank F. Hare's PBY was sweeping the area immediately east of convoy
TJ-1, when the surfaced Type VIIC *U-590* was sighted at a distance of 12 miles
(19.3 kilometers). Lieutenant Hare immediately began closing in for an attack.
Approximately a mile from the submarine, orange flecks of antiaircraft fire from
the U-boat's deck guns began appearing in front of the plane. Almost immediately,
a shell entered the PBY's bow on the port side, exploding against the instrument
panel, Hare, wounding the radioman, and setting a fire, which filled the flight deck
with a billowing cloud of black smoke.

Admiral Ingram, right, conferring with Admiral Dodsworth Martins of the Brazilian Navy during Wor War II. (U.S. Naval History and Heritage Command)

Co-pilot Lieutenant (jg) J. P. Phelps took over the controls, the bombing run w. continued, and he released two starboard depth bombs, which landed close togethe approximately 25 to 35 feet (7.6–10.6 meters) from *U-590*'s stern, but the U-bo appeared to be unharmed. Meanwhile, the bow gunner, Aviation Mechanics Ma Third Class (AMM3c) Clifford Eisaman, fired his .30 caliber guns continuous during the approach while the port blister gunner, Aviation Radioman Third Cla (ARM3c) Thomas Brown trained and fired on the U-boat. After circling the U-bo; for approximately a half an hour, the PBY departed leaving *U-590* still surfaced. A 1300 hours, shortly after Phelps began the flight back to Belém in his battle-scarre Catalina, another VP-94 PBY along with a PB4Y-1 Liberator belonging to VB-10 arrived over the scene but found no trace of the U-boat.

VP-94 Catalina aircrews continued searching for the enemy submarine by extend ing the search area beyond *U-590*'s last reported position and one of the aircraf piloted by Lieutenant (jg) Stanley Ernest Auslander, spotted the surfacing *U-59* at 1424 hours off Maraca Island. The plane was flying at 3,700 feet (1128 meter over a broken overcast and had just passed through a heavy cloudbank, when member of the crew spotted the U-boat. The pilots couldn't see the target from their position, so Auslander brought the PBY's nose over to bring the U-boat int view. As the PBY approached, water ran from the boat's decks, and within a fe seconds, *U-590* appeared fully surfaced, cruising at about 15 knots. The pile ield the plane in a dive directly toward the submarine without changing course and threw on the bombing switch. Lieutenant (jg) McMackin blew the warning horn and rushed to the waist compartment to take pictures of the enemy craft through the port blister. At an altitude of about 150 feet (46 meters), the co-pilot Lieutenant (jg) Elliot released the depth bombs by intervalometer with a spacing of 75 feet (53 meters).

The fully surfaced submarine proceeded on course, the crew seemingly unaware of the approaching plane. As the depth bombs landed in the water and detonated, the PBY made an easy turn to port. Below the plane, no trace of the submarine was visible as the water from the detonations subsided. While the Catalina circled, a greenish-brown slick appeared, and in the center of it, two men swimming among several pieces of debris. A moment later a member of Auslander's crew reported seeing three additional men in the water, but they apparently drowned very quickly. The plane dropped a life raft, but it drifted away before the remaining swimmers could reach it. Members of the flight crew tossed four life jackets out of the PBY and survivors appeared to get into the inflated ones. Four minutes after the *U-590* disappeared, a large amount of oil appeared on the surface, two or three hundred yards from the slick, along the sub's track, with the slick continuing to grow in length and breadth. The men that struggled in the water after their U-boat sank apparently succumbed to the ordeal, as none of *U-590*'s 45-man crew survived.

Kapitänleutnant Fritz Guggenberger's Type IXC *U-513* became the next enemy submarine to fall victim to FAW-16 aircraft when it was caught on the surface by VP-74, about 90 miles northeast of Florianopólis. During the previous month, Guggenberger sent three merchant ships to the bottom of the South Atlantic followed by two more vessels in July. The last victim of *U-513* was the 6,500-ton American freighter *African Star* dispatched with two torpedoes on the 12th. Guggenberger, quite happy on the successes, became somewhat overconfident over the ease of attacks in South Atlantic and made the decision to send a lengthy message about his successes back to BdU, which helped home in American patrol planes to *U-513*. The sky was hazy with a visibility of nearly 20 miles (32 kilometers) on July 19, 1943, as the submarine traveled on the surface.

Meanwhile, VP-74's *Nickle Boat* this time piloted by Lieutenant (jg) Roy S. Whitcomb, made a radar contact on the U-boat and closed in for the attack. On *U-513* the bridge watch caught sight of the approaching PBM, and general-quarters was called. Guggenberger rushed to the bridge, and realizing that it was too late to dive, ordered the 37-millimeter and 20-millimeter antiaircraft guns manned. He could hardly believe that the plane would be foolish to attack a surfaced U-boat with defensive weapons manned and ready. When Lieutenant (jg) Whitcomb's PBM flew within range, the U-boat's antiaircraft guns opened up on the American flying boat but, within a few seconds, *U-513*'s defensive fire was cut in half when its 20-millimeter gun jammed after firing only a few rounds.

VP-74 Martin PBM-3S Mariner, 7-4P-5 Nickle Boat was flow by Lieutenant Howland Davis on 19 May 1943 when it shared credit for sinking *U-128*. The second kill mark was for Lieutenant (jg) Roy S. Whitcomb's kill of *U-513* on 19 July 1943. (Mark Aldrich via Steve Ginter collection)

Two days after VP-74's Lieutenant (jg) Whitcomb's successful sinking of *U-513*, VP-94 scored its second U-boat kill of the month when *U-66* fell to depth charges from a PBY-5A Catalina commanded by Lieutenant Roland on July 21, 1943. Typ VIIC *U-662*, under the command of Kapitanleutnant Heiaz-Eberhard Müller, began its fourth and last patrol in the company of *U-591* and *59*, after departing St Nazaire, France. None of those U-boats would return from their tour, as each fell victim to FAW-16 aircraft during the next few months. The four traveled together for a few days before proceeding to their respective operational areas of South America. Three weeks later on July 19, Müller's surfaced U-boat, in the midst of tracking Convoy TF-2, drew the attention of a USAAF B-18

bomber about 200 miles (322 kilometers) off Cayenne. The lumbering Army bomber dropped four depth charges but caused no damage, and Müller continued to track the convoy only to come under attack off Surinam by an Army Air Force B-24. A third unsuccessful attack occurred the following day by a VP-94 PBY piloted by Lieutenant (jg) S. E. Auslander, the patrol plane commander responsible for sinking *U-590* near the mouth of the Amazon River on July 20, 1943. Auslander's eventual attack on *U-66* began as a routine patrol when he and his crew departed in a Catalina from Amapa, Brazil, at 1030 hours to relieve another squadron plane covering convoy TF-2. After sweeping ahead of the convoy at 1341 hours, the Catalina's bow lookout reported a ship to port at a distance of five miles. It took Lieutenant Auslander only a moment to recognize it as an enemy submarine. From the Catalina's altitude of 4,000 feet (1219 meters), he nosed the PBY over and made a turn to port to intercept *U-662*. Meanwhile, the co-pilot turned the bombing switch on and grabbed the "pickle" used to release the depth bombs hanging underneath the Catalina's wings.

Thick puffs of exploding antiaircraft shells burst in front of Auslander's PBY mingled with orange-colored tracers from machine-gun fire as *U-662*'s gun crew attempted to bring down the approaching American patrol plane. The pilots pulled back the throttles to the Catalina's two engines and the plane lost altitude but picked up speed as the pilot executed several skidding turns in order to evade the U-boat gunfire. About a mile away from *U-662*, Lieutenant Auslanger briefly leveled the

BY before pushing back over in a gliding turn towards the U-boat. He pulled out of the dive and briefly held his course before making a sharp turn to port. Coming in towards the target, the Catalina's bow and blister gunners opened fire while the co-pilot, on signal from the first pilot, made the bomb drop as the plane flew at an altitude of 100 feet.

According to the navigator, who was in the starboard blister, the drop was over with the bombs landing 30–50 feet (9–15 meters) over the submarine on the starboard side. Lieutenant Auslanger contacted the escort vessels of the convoy, which were nearby and advised them of the attack and its position. Without any remaining depth bombs, the plane circled the U-boat from 5,000 feet (1524 meters) and waited for the escort vessels to arrive on the scene. Approximately 40 minutes later, the patrol plane's crew saw the wake of an approaching escort and course was changed to guide the approaching warship to the U-boat. When the plane was halfway between *U-662* and the escort vessel, a crewmember in the after-station reported the submarine attempting to submerge. The pilot immediately turned the plane and dove, while a member of the crew stood by to drop a fluorescent dye marker to mark the spot. The U-boat seemed to have difficulty in completely submerging and attempted to do so several times before finally succeeding at 1445 hours. The PBY circled, notified the escort vessel, and flew a 20-mile square (52 kilometers²) around the point of submergence before PBY 94-P-12 arrived as relief at 1610 hours. Lieutenant Auslander's attack caused no damage to *U-662*, but its luck finally ran out when another PBY from VP-94 found it on the surface

A PBY-5A of VP-94 approaching *U-662* for a depth charge attack on 21 July 1943. The commander Oberleutnant zur See Heinz-Eberhard Müller and two other crewmen were rescued. Müller was repatriated back to Germany in March 1944 due to severe injuries received during the attack. (National Archives)

the following day. Lieutenant (jg) R. H. Roland in PBY Number P-4 took o
from Belém at 0230 hours to relieve P-7 on coverage of convoy TJ-2. The plan
arrived in the area at 0530 hours and started a search for the convoy. The plane
bow gunner thirty minutes later spotted *U-662* at a distance between two to thre
miles with its deck slightly awash and making six to seven knots. The plane was a
1,200 feet (366 meters) with an indicated air speed of 95 knots as Roland rolle
the plane slightly to bring the submarine into view. As the plane approachec
U-662's antiaircraft guns began firing, but they were short of ammunition an
two 20-millimeter cannons soon jammed. Inside the PBY, the bow gunner wa
having trouble of his own as he went into action to prepare the single machin
gun. However, he couldn't free the barrel group, which allowed the breech loc
to disengage, rendering the weapon useless throughout the attack run. Rolan
immediately turned to attack but seeing that his bow gunner was having troubl
with his machine gun and encountering heavy antiaircraft fire, veered slightly t
port for about five seconds before starting a shallow diving run. Gunfire from th
submarine was persistent and accurate. The PBY's rudder took hits during the fin
turn and a piece of shrapnel wounded the radioman in the lower leg and ankle. A
the same time, machine guns from the plane delivered a lethal hail of fire, whic
killed the U-boat's entire bridge watch and members of the gun crews. Defensiv
fire ceased as the plane approached from an altitude of 75 feet (23 meters).

The patrol bomber's pilot pressed the pickle, but one of the bombs on th
starboard wing hung up; however, two others fell away and detonated almost unde
the U-boat's port side, just aft of the conning tower. While the PBY pulled out of it
shallow dive and turned to port, the U-boat appeared emerging from the geysers c
water caused by the detonating depth bombs. Inside *U-662*, an explosion occurre
in the control room, fuel oil caught fire, and water began to pour into the divin
tanks, the conning tower, and the control room. Topside, the explosions hurle
Kapitanleutant Müller into the water with serious injuries.

Rowland continued turning the Catalina for approximately one minute in orde
to remain in the immediate vicinity as *U-662* began breaking apart. The entire bo
rose into the air, broke in two, and sank almost immediately, stern first. Five c
the U-boat's compliment, including the commanding officer, survived the sinkin
but one soon died. Upon re-establishing sight contact with the U-boat's positior
Rowland saw no submarine, but in its place an oval oil patch, which increased i
size to 200 yards (183 meters) in length and 150 to 175 yards (137–160 meters) i
width. On the second pass over the area, the PBY's crew dropped rubber life rafts t
four men seen in the water. The men climbed into them, but for the next 16 days
the survivors drifted in the Atlantic until USS *Siren* (PC-494) finally picked ther
up on August 6. One of the men died aboard the ship, leaving only Kapitanleutant
Müller, Matrosenobergefreiters Herman Grauff and Ferdinand Marx as the onl
survivors.

J.S. Navy personnel help one of the three surviving crewmembers of *U-662* out of a VP-94 Catalina ~~f~~ter spending sixteen days adrift in the South Atlantic. Five men survived the sinking but one died ~~ʒ~~on afterward and another shortly after rescue. (National Archives)

A day after VP-94 sank *U-662*, VB-107's Lieutenant Commander Turner found Type ~~V~~IIC *U-598*, under the command of Kapitänleutnant Gottfried Holtorf. *U-598* on its ~~ʒ~~ourth patrol arrived off Brazil on July 22, but Liberators of VB-107 quickly found it ~~a~~nd, within 24 hours, most of the U-boat's crew became entombed in the boat at the ~~ʒ~~ottom of the South Atlantic. The submarine's final journey began at 0925 hours with ~~t~~he first of a series of attacks by PB4Y-1 Liberators of VB-107 beginning with Lieutenant ~~C~~ommander Turner. While on a training flight near Bocas Reef, Turner and his crew ~~ʒ~~potted *U-598* and proceeded to drop a string of six depth charges 11 seconds after ~~t~~he submarine submerged. The depth charges apparently caused no damage and Turner ~~ʒ~~egan a hold-down over the area with Liberator Number B-8, piloted by Lieutenant ~~j~~g) John T. Burton. Turner spotted the target again at 1052 hours and attacked with ~~h~~is three remaining bombs, which appeared to straddle the conning tower. Turner left ~~f~~or base as Liberators Numbers B-5 and B-8 continued a hold-down throughout the ~~n~~ight. Lieutenant (jg) Baldwin, flying bomber Number B-12, arrived at midnight and ~~w~~as still on the scene when *U-598* resurfaced at 0635 hours six miles (10 kilometers) ~~f~~rom the plane's position. Baldwin conducted a depth charge attack a minute later and ~~t~~he U-boat received extensive damage. Within *U-598*, concussions from the exploding ~~ʒ~~ombs destroyed the radio equipment, ruptured the oil and freshwater tanks, jammed ~~t~~he diving planes, and the engines failed. Upon receiving messages from Lieutenant (jg) ~~ʒ~~aldwin, Lieutenant (jg) Waugh in B-6, and Lieutenant W. Ford in B-8, proceeded ~~t~~o the scene and made an attack run on the target. Waugh had arrived from Norfolk, ~~V~~irginia only three days earlier. Lieutenant Ford and his crew were also fresh from the ~~S~~tates as Aviation Machinist Mate First Class (AMM1c) Paul Richter recalled,

About two weeks after our arrival back in Natal we were out on a training flight, about 150 mile (241 km) off the coast, when we heard one of our aircraft in the vicinity calling to say that h had attacked an enemy submarine and it was damaged and apparently couldn't submerge. W immediately went full bore towards his position to see if we could finish the job. I left my radi op station and manned the top turret, which we used to strafe during an attack. On the wa we overheard one of our other aircraft (B-6) calling to say he was on the way also, I remembe cussing to myself because I was afraid that they would get there before we could.[1]

When additional American patrol planes arrived, Holtorf, realizing the situation t be hopeless, gave orders to abandon ship. Upon the order to abandon ship, the crev launched a pair of rubber boats and began climbing into them. Approximately half dozen men boarded each of the boats, while a few more succeeded in jumpin into the water before the Americans began a second attack. Half of the U-boa compliment was still below deck when the two Navy Liberators piloted by Waug and Ford attacked. Waugh's bomber went in first, but at such a low attack angle, th detonations of its own bombs immediately sent the plane plunging into the ocean leaving no survivors. Lieutenant Ford, closely following Waugh's plane over th target, flew through the spray of the exploding bombs but managed to keep his shi airborne. Paul Richter had a bird's-eye view from the top turret of Ford's Liberato

We were flying at about 3,000 feet (914 m) when we sighted the sub. Our pilot swung aroun to come in at him out of the sun to give us some advantage in the antiaircraft fire that was sur to come. As we were ready to start our run, we saw B-6 in the middle of his run! He made good drop at an extremely low altitude (which is the way we made all our attacks) but incredibl he didn't pull out but went straight in to the ocean. I remember remarking later that he didn even make a good splash. When our pilot saw this he nosed our plane over like a dive-bombe a B-24 wasn't built for that, He apologized later but said, "I was going to get that sub even if had to ram him!" The bow guns and my top turret were strafing on the way in. After a shar pullout, I am not sure whether I blacked out momentarily, but the next I remember my gur were pointed skyward and at an angle from dead ahead. I also smelled something burning. thought, "Oh shit, we've been hit!" but then I found that I was sitting on two shell casings tha had failed to drop into the sleeve provided and they were scorching my flight suit.[2]

Lieutenant Ford continued the run and made a very accurate drop on the vessel witl his bombs detonating so close to the U-boat that it sank immediately. Crewmember of *U-598* managed to launch two rubber lifeboats, but the suction from the sinkin vessel caught one of them and pulled him under; only two of its occupants manage to break free and remain afloat. Above the carnage, Paul Richter saw the results of heavy bomber crashing into the water and the U-boat's destruction by depth bomb filled with 500 pounds (227 kilograms) of explosives,

As we circled the scene, we saw two life rafts from B-6, which had popped out during the cras and inflated automatically. Shortly thereafter, two large black looking rafts came up, followe by sub survivors. In fact, there were so many that they filled both of their rafts and the tw yellow rafts from B-6. We were running short of fuel by this time and when relieved by anothe aircraft we returned to base. The other planes covered the rafts while waiting for a destroye dispatched from Recife to pick up the survivors.[3]

More than half of *U-598*'s crew remained trapped below deck while approximately two dozen men succeeded in boarding life rafts or jumping into the sea as their vessel sank. One of the life rafts drifted out of sight during the night and its occupants disappeared while the others drowned when pulled under the suction of *U-598* sinking. Only two men: the boat's executive officer and an enlisted rating stayed afloat with the American tug *Seneca* (AT-91) rescuing them 13 hours after the *U-598*'s loss.

FAW-16 had become successful at tracking and hunting down enemy submarines and it continued a week after the destruction of *U-598* with Type VIIC *U-591* sunk by a Ventura of VB-127 on the thirtieth. Lieutenant (jg) Walter C. Young found *U-591* on its eighth patrol and under the command of Oberleutnant zur See Raimer Ziesmer off Recife, Brazil. Young, flying Ventura B-10 on aerial coverage of convoy TJ-2, spotted the wake of a U-boat from an altitude of 4,000 feet. A few minutes later, the aircrew visually sighted the boat at a distance of 12 miles (19 kilometers).

At 1228 hours, Young's Ventura came out of the sun and completely surprised *U-591*, releasing a string of six Mark-44 depth bombs from a height of 50 feet (15 meters) and a speed of 260 knots. Young's attack wasn't the first experienced by *U-591*'s crew. After crossing the Atlantic from its base at St. Nazaire, the U-boat's demise began with depth charges from VB-107 Liberators.

As the PV-1 Ventura dove for an attack, there was no time to operate *U-591*'s antiaircraft guns as the bombs fell on or near the submarine. One exploded on the starboard side tearing a hole in the pressure hull while another landed squarely on the

An unidentified crewmember of VB-107 (possibly Richard Wilson) standing next to VB-107's PB4Y-1 *Gallopin' Ghost of the Brazilian Coast*. The plane was damaged beyond repair while taking off from the base at Natal, Brazil on 15 October 1943. (Richard A. Wilson)

20-millimeter gun mount, demolishing the cannon and the upper deck. However, U-591's engines continued to run, and the boat continued to make headway, but water began pouring through a rupture in the starboard side hull and soon all electric power was lost. Zimmer, realizing his boat would not survive, gave the order to abandon ship. Inside the conning tower, as the water rose to about three to four feet deep, the last man climbed up the ladder, onto the bridge, and dove into the water. Young's Ventura came back a second time for a strafing attack, firing 280 rounds of .50 caliber machine-gun fire as U-591 sank. Circling, the Ventura's crew dropped a life raft to the survivors, wounded men placed onboard, while the rest took turns hanging onto the raft. Five hours later, the *Saucy* picked up twenty-eight out of the crew of 49, including the commanding officer. While the American ship picked up U-591's crew, some of *Saucy's* crew fired their rifles at sharks following the life raft.

VP-74 Loses a Crew

U-199 became the last U-boat kill in the South Atlantic by FAW-16 aircraft and Brazilian PBY Catalina during July 31, 1943. Before the fate of U-199 was finally sealed, the hunt for this U-boat claimed the lives of Lieutenant Harold "Hog" Carey and the men aboard his PBM-3C Mariner. In the proceeding days prior to the loss of Carey's flying boat, a detachment of VP-74's flying boats stationed at Rio conducted nightly patrols.

Under the command of Kapitänleutnant Hans Werner Kraus, Type IXD2 U-199 cast off from the pier at Bergen in the evening of May 17, 1943, and crossed the equator in early June. There was no celebration, as Kruas considered it unwise to relax his watch while the U-boat sailed in the narrows between Freetown and Natal. After receiving orders to intercept and destroy enemy shipping, Kraus gave his ship company permission to celebrate *Crossing the Line* (a celebration for crossing the equator the first time). As usual, the ceremony consisted of the traditional ceremonies and an address by the U-boat's skipper about the nature and approximate operational area of their mission. After the celebration, U-199 altered course in order to pass southwards along the Brazilian coast, remaining at a distance of approximately 200 miles (322 kilometers) from shore.[5]

On or about June 18, 1943, U-199 arrived in its operational area and from then on, Kraus adopted the policy of remaining submerged all day at a depth of 20 meters (66 feet), occasionally rising to periscope depth for reconnaissance. At dusk, he would generally surface and not dive again until dawn. Kraus and his ship's company were very disappointed with the small number of targets that offered themselves in this area. Apart from a few Spanish and Argentine vessels, the crew sighted almost nothing. However, on the night of June 26, the American merchant ship *Charles William Peale* sailing about 50 miles (80 kilometers) south of Rio caught the attention of Kraus who fired one torpedo that missed. Kraus decided that the area allotted to him was unlikely to provide any worthwhile targets so in early July, without receiving any orders to do so, he altered course and proceeded eastward. He subsequently patrolled on an east-west line of bearing to the south of Rio de Janeiro, the patrol line extending approximately 300 miles (483 kilometers).[6]

A few days later, on July 4, it was patrolling the surface at night in its new patrol area, when it sighted to starboard the phosphorescent wake of the Brazilian vessel *Bury*, sailing a southwesterly course. Kraus thereupon fired a spread of three torpedoes at it from its bow tubes. The torpedoes missed and *Bury*'s crew responded by firing a number of rounds from its deck gun at the U-boat. Following this engagement, *U-199* signaled headquarters that it had torpedoed and sank a vessel, which in fact, managed to reach Rio de Janeiro. Kraus feared that the torpedoed vessel would report his presence and decided to leave the area. The U-boat was patrolling on the surface at about 2100 hours when a PBM piloted by Lieutenant Carey spotted her. Kraus immediately went to the bridge and ordered an increase to full speed. He also ordered the guns manned.

The flying boat's searchlight was apparently turned on to pinpoint the submarine as it approached the U-boat for a bombing run, but the plane crashed into the water killing all hands-on board. The exact cause of the crash remains a mystery. The U.S. Navy officially attributed the loss to enemy action; however, captured members of *U-199* denied they shot down the plane. The Mariner's onboard searchlight mounted on the starboard wing may have played a role in the crash as it reduced the pilot's ability to see his instrument panel according to William J. Barnard of VP-74, "It [the searchlight] was large enough to affect the aerodynamics of the wing and change the characteristics of the controls to a certain degree. We hated them...When we practiced with it; the million-candle power could cause problems...when the searchlight was turned on, a previously dark cockpit suddenly being flooded with light."[7]

Presumably, Lieutenant Carey picked up a contact on the radar and assuming it was a U-boat started his attack at an altitude of 50 feet (15 meters) according to squadron doctrine. A PBM was difficult to handle even during a normal bombing run because the entire control characteristics of the plane shifted, and the pilot had to be prepared to handle the changes. With the spotlight hanging out on the wing, it may have magnified those changes. Barnard theorizes,

> Carey put his nose over and gained a considerable amount of speed to around 180 knots, which was 40 knots above cruising speed. He was in a dive to lose altitude from maybe 3,500 feet [1067 m], which was our normal search altitude for best radar coverage and he had to get down to 50 feet [15 m] in a hurry. Somewhere in his dive, when his speed was probably the greatest, he opened the bomb bay doors and armed the DC's [depth charges]. When Carey thought that he was in position, he had his co-pilot flip on the searchlight. When the light came on, he suddenly had the cockpit brightly lighted at a relatively low altitude. At that time, he lost sight of his instruments, especially his radio altimeter, and he could not see the water and never pulled out of his dive. They hit the water at a steep angle [indicated by the crushed wing tip float]. The plane disintegrated on impact instantly killing all aboard. The death charges, dropped to the

depth where the fuses were set for explosion, 35 feet [11 m] below the surface, detonated directl under the spot where the plane had crashed. If anyone had lived through the crash, they woul have certainly been killed by the two tons of high explosives going off right underneath them.

U-199 patrolled the scene of the crash for a short time looking for survivors or debri but found nothing. After the crash of the American patrol bomber, Kraus altered cours to southward back to the operational area originally allotted to him. William Barnar and his crew of Mariner 74-P 6 were alerted after Carey's plane failed to report an went out to look for the missing crew. Barnard's bow gunner spotted debris in the wate "We descended to a couple of hundred feet and got down to the spot found abou a half-square mile of aircraft wreckage. The wreckage consisted of a badly collapse wing-tip float, blankets, charts, life jackets, and dish-shaped pieces of aluminum."[9]

Families from both sides of the conflict mourned the loss of their son, brothe husband, or father. Unfortunately, few first-hand stories of a lost loved remains afte so many years since the war. Lieutenant Carey left a wife, Florence, and an infan behind. In a letter dated 4 December 1943, she wrote to the mother of Willam F Magie Jr., a member of the crew.

> I do not know if she told you anything about us. So[,] Harold and I were married Nov. 23 1940 and our baby was born May 31, 1943. Harold never saw him. I was a nurse before was married and knew Harold then. He came up the hard way and was given a Commissio after he was graduated from Pensacola, Florida Navy Flight School Was Ensign then and Lieut (j.g.) at the time of his crash. We were married when he as second class so you see I've see the Navy from 2 sides. I went to California, Hawaii, Florida and Virginia with him so sav some of our great country. I can honestly say no other young couple could of been more happ than we were. I so regret he never saw his son. I was alone all during pregnancy except th 2 times you mentioned your son returned to the States and called you. Harold was home the too, but for such short times. Harold left Sept 23rd, 1942 and we didn't know the baby wa coming then. I named him Michael Harold—he didn't want him named for him.
>
> My brother came to Virginia and helped me drive back here. I still have our car. I hardl know what to do. I have been staying with my folks but now plan to move and have my ow place. I think I'll feel better when I can do my way. After a girl has her own home it's hard t go back home and live.
>
> Yes, I think the boys were all ready to go. They realized their danger and yet I know the all loved their job. My husband so often said he would just as soon be buried at sea and h always said when his time came he hoped he'd go fast. I don't believe any of them suffered If they must go—I'd rather it be this way than think of them being tortured and starved i a prison camp or come back mental or physical cripples for life. I think our boys preferre to go this way.
>
> It's hard in your own family but there are so many more just like us or worse. Sometimes think I can't go on and yet I know I have to for Mike. He is so sweet and precious.
>
> Do you live near Mrs. Roberts or did you meet her since news of the crash came. I've trie to get in touch with other families but haven't so far. Except Roberts, Helms, Smith and no you. There were 13 men on the plane and I do wish we knew the rest.
>
> We always had a soft spot in our heart for the regular Navy men—they seemed to know th Navy and were better men than so many of these that came in lately with commissions becaus they had some college education. So your son was greatly admired by Harold and all the crew

Your son had to study and work hard just as Harold did and they were getting ahead fine. I know it's hard to realize why they should be taken right in the middle of a promising career but "The Lord's will be done." I can't seem to believe they are gone and can't give up hopes and yet I know it's time. Just time and many prayers will heal the wound of losing Harold. I think I know how you feel too.[10]

After vainly searching the area for survivors, PBM 74-P-6 radioed base and reported what they had found. The flying boat stayed on the scene for several hours and increased the search area but nothing more could be located. On returning to his original operational area, Kapitänleutnant Kraus formally asked permission to abandon this area and patrol closer inshore. He felt convinced that headquarters had been wrong in its estimate of enemy shipping in the area and his only hope of sinking anything was to operate closer inshore. C-in-C U-boats concurred, and Kraus accordingly returned to the patrol line where he had conducted his first attack.

For several days, Kraus spotted no worthwhile targets. At about 0900 hours on or about July 25, 1943, U-199 cruising at periscope depth located the unescorted westbound British vessel Henzada, proceeding at about 10 knots towards Santos. Kraus fired a spread of three torpedoes at it from his bow tubes, but all missed. After the failed attack, Krauss maneuvered U-199 until it was ahead of the Henzada and waited at periscope depth for an opportunity to attack the merchant ship again. About midday, Kraus considered the boat to be in a favorable firing position and fired both his stern tubes at the merchant ship. One of these torpedoes hit the vessel amidships causing and it to break in two and sink. The U-boat continued to search for shipping but the sinking of the Henzada proved to be the U-boat's last victory.

At 0718 hours on July 31, 1943, Lieutenant (jg) Walter F. Smith's radar operator, onboard VP-74's Mariner Number P-7, made the initial detection of U-199 at 19 miles (31 kilometers). The pilot held the flying boat's speed and altitude at 120 knots and 4,000 feet (1219 meters), from a distance of 15 miles (24 kilometers), he sighted a faint wake. Smith immediately pushed the plane over into a power glide, headed it towards the wake, and soon visually sighted the vessel 10 miles (16 kilometers) ahead. The plan of the day for ASW operations involved contacting a Brazilian PBY to cover convoy JT-3 from Rio Harbor then sweep ahead. Smith's plane would make a barrier sweep to the harbor approaches paralleling the convoy route. Upon receiving Smiths' report at 0720 hours, A Brazilian PBY and a Hudson went to the scene, along with two additional VP-74 Mariners. However, Mariner Number P-4, the first U.S. plane to depart, couldn't locate the U-boat's actual location due to an incorrect position given by P-7.

Meanwhile, U-199 proceeded on the surface with the intention of reaching the 100-fathom line before submerging to wait for passing ships. The U-boat's G.S.R. set was not manned at the time when Lieutenant Smith's PBM was visually sighted some miles away. Immediately upon seeing the patrol plane the U-boat's Quartermaster,

U-199 as seen from a PBM-3C Mariner of VP-74 piloted by Lieutenant (jg) Walter F. Smith. On of the attacking Mariner's was shot down by the submarine's anti-aircraft fire. The submarine wa sunk by a coordinated effort of American and Brazilian aircraft. Twelve of the 60-man crew survived (National Archives)

who was on watch at the time, gave the order to put the helm hard to starboard and increase power to full speed.

However, those below deck misunderstood the Quartermaster's order due to the alarm bells ringing and ordered the forward tanks flooded in preparation for a crash dive, before the correction was given. As soon as Smith's plane was within range, every anti-aircraft gun aboard the vessel opened fire. The PBM's gunner returned fire, scoring several hits on the conning tower. Smith opened the bomb bay doors before entering the dive and, about a mile from the U-boat, leveled of at 150 feet (241 meters) with an indicated airspeed of 180 knots. Seeing a bean attack as probable, the pilot ordered bomb spacing changed to 65 feet (266 meters and then made a bombing run while avoiding antiaircraft fire, which was heavy though inaccurate. The plane crossed *U-199* from the port side, just forward of the conning tower, at an altitude of 75 feet (121 meters), as Smith dropped a string o six depth charges.

After bombs were away, Smith maintained the same altitude and made four turns to the left to deliver a second attack. The PBM headed down the U-boat' axis, from bow to stern, releasing last two depth charges from an altitude of 40 fee (64 meters) and a speed of 160 knots. The PBM then began series of strafing run on the U-boat, which continued until the vessel sank. Approximately 15 minute later, the U-boat straightened out on a northerly trek, altering course as the plane came in for strafing runs. At 0804 hours, the U-boat cleared the decks of personne and made an unsuccessful attempt to submerge. However, it lost control and sank, submerging completely without diving. A few minutes later, it resurfaced in the same spot with difficulty, with its stern completely awash. Aboard the PBM Mariner, Lieutenant Smith followed the U-boat from a safe distance and waited for reinforcements to arrive.

The damage caused by the Mariner's depth charges rendered *U-199* unable to submerge. It was, moreover, incapable of proceeding at more than very slow speed surfaced. Kraus thereupon determined to find shallow water to permit him to lie on the bottom and effect repairs. He felt convinced that if the boat remained surfaced it would come under further aircraft attacks. He accordingly instructed his quartermaster to take soundings constantly until the depth of the water below the boat's keel was no more than 135 meters (70 fathoms). Kraus accordingly altered course and proceeded slowly inshore with the echo sounder constantly checking the depth of the water. As *U-199* reached an area with a depth of 443 feet (135 meters), when another enemy aircraft appeared.

At 0840 hours, a Brazilian Hudson flying out of Rio and piloted by Sergio Candido Schnoor arrived and attacked, crossing over the submarine's starboard bow, while Lieutenant Smith's Mariner drew the sub's fire. The Brazilian plane released two Mk-17 charges, from an altitude of 300 feet (91 meters), at a speed of approximately 220 knots. The U-boat turned to starboard and the bombs exploded, some 150 feet (46 meters) from the boat's bow. The Hudson departed and immediately Alberto Martins Torres in a Brazilian PBY named *Arara* arrived and attacked. Again, Smith's crew provided suppressing fire, while the PBY closed in from *U-199*'s port quarter, firing its guns, and released three Mk-44 depth charges. The submarine attempted to alter course, but it was too late. The depth charges detonated alongside *U-199*, causing the boat to rock back and forth.

As soon as the bombs began to fall, Kraus realized that the position was hopeless and ordered his men to abandon ship. Most of the seamen personnel were already on deck while the remainder of the ship's company made a desperate effort to climb up the conning tower hatch. Only the Quartermaster managed to escape as the water reached the 20-millimeter gun mount. *U-199* sank a few minutes later leaving behind wreckage and men floating in the water. Two hours after the sinking, the tender USS *Barnegat* picked up Kraus and 11 of the U-boat's 62-man crew.

The July U-boat blitz resulted in the sinking of some 50,000 tons of shipping, but at the cost of six submarines sunk by FAW-16 aircraft. Those losses, compounded by the loss of several replenishment submarines, effectively ended the blitz.

For those German submarines still operating in the area between Natal to Rio, air units of the U.S. Fourth Fleet continued to hunt for them upon receiving radio transmissions between *U-172, 185, 604* and BdU. *U-604* began sending messages for assistance to nearby U-boats after suffering severe damage from Lieutenant Commander Thomas D. Davies' PV-1 Ventura from VB-129 on 30 July. The attack

Survivors of *U-199* photographed from a Brazilian PBY-5A Catalina included the boat's commande Kapitänleutnant Hans Werner Kraus. The tender Barnegat (AVP-10) picked up the survivors (National Archives)

jammed the vessel's starboard hydroplane, knocked out a motor, damaged severa tanks, and two of the boat's crew mortally wounded. The damage was severe enough that Kapitänleutnant Horst Höltring reported to Admiral Dönitz that he couldn' get his boat back to port, to which Commander-in-Chief of U-boats responded with the order to scuttle the vessel. Additionally, BdU ordered *U-591* to meet with *604* and provide assistance, but a PV-1 Ventura of VB-127 sank *U-591* on July 30 Kapitänleutnant August Maus's *U-185*, operating further south, was ordered to take over in assisting Höltring and his crew. Since the attack, the men aboard *U-604* marked time until help arrived while proceeding with difficulty to the predetermined rendezvous with *U-185*. While heading for the rendezvous, *U-185* met up with Convoy TJ-2 and sank the Brazilian freighter 8,235-ton *Bagé*.

Messages between *BdU*, *U-185*, and *604* caught the attention of the Allies who were able to pinpoint Höltring's boat and an extensive air-sea search ensued. On the morning of August 3, 1943, four days after *U-604*'s near fatal encounter with a PV-1 Ventura, Lieutenant Commander Prueher, piloting a PB4Y-1 named *The Spirit of 83*, took off from Recife to sweep the estimated position of a German submarine At 0722 hours, Lieutenant Commander Prueher spotted Höltring's U-boat and an attack commenced with Mk-47 depth charges 16 seconds after the vessel submerged Moments after the bombs detonated, observers aboard *The Spirit of 83* saw a large oi slick. However, the U-boat received no damage from Commander Prueher's attack and it remained submerged from the time of the attack until the evening when it came up for air. Almost immediately upon surfacing, it was subjected to fire from the destroyer *Moffett*'s guns and Höltring pulled the plug and *U-604* submerged only to have the U-boat subjected to depth charge attacks from the American destroyer Höltring kept his boat submerged until the next morning and surfaced only after

Under attack by a VB-129 PV-1 off Bahia, Brazil on 30 July 1943 *U-604* was badly damaged in this attack but survived until scuttled on 11 August 1943. Note her double level AA gun position. (National Archives)

the sounds of the American destroyer faded away. Afterward the U-boat continued towards a rendezvous with *U-185*.

While Höltring and his men were evading the *Moffett's* depth charges, *The Spirit of 83* flew back to Recife where it was re-armed and re-fueled. Commander Prueher and his crew went out again in search of the enemy and at 1735 hours, just as darkness settled, the Liberator's radar locked onto *U-185*. Prueher headed towards the target in the semi-darkness and ascertained the U-boat's exact position by tracer fire emanating from the submarine while the plane was still four miles away. As the PB4Y-1 Liberator closed into effective machine gun range, its crown turret and bow guns opened fire, which was very accurate as rounds ricocheted off the U-boat's superstructure. Prueher dropped four depth bombs and, after the plumes from the explosions subsided, observed the submarine making a sharp starboard turn. Prueher immediately swung the big four-engine bomber around and conducted a second attack on *U-185* with two remaining bombs. The drop was from an altitude of 175 feet (53 meters), but both bombs fell short by some 250 feet (76 meters). During this run, *The Spirit of 83* experienced heavy and accurate antiaircraft fire and the bomber received hits to the starboard wing and number three engine forcing a return to base. The crew inspected the plane and counted 23 perforations in the starboard wing.

Although VB-107's commanding officer conducted a gutsy attack, the U-boat escaped unscathed, although one crewmember received serious wounds from machine-gun fire. With a wounded man onboard, *U-185* required medical supplies and *U-172* received orders to provide assistance along with instructions to meet with *U-604*, take off its fuel, provisions, crew, and scuttle the boat. While on its way to the rendezvous, *U-185* sank the British *Fort Halkert* a 7,133-ton freighter off Recife on the sixth with torpedoes and gunfire. Planes of FAW-16 continued to search for several days without any luck until August 11, when the Fourth Fleet located the position of two U-boats. At 0900 hours, Commander Prueher, at the controls of *The Spirit of 83*, departed Natal with an unprecedented gas load of 3,400 gallon (12870L) with the goal of finding the Uboats. It was destined to be the last flight for this courageous officer and crew. Meanwhile, *U-185* and *604* rendezvoused and *U-604*'s crew immediately began the transfer of provisions, oil, and equipment to the other U-boat, which required several hours. When the transfer was almost completed, *U-172* commanded by Kapitänleutnant Karl Emmermann surfaced and took over one-half of *U-604*'s crew.[11]

Shortly after *U-172* arrived, Commander Prueher's Liberator dove out of the clouds in a surprise attack on the unsuspecting German submarines. *U-604* was in a near helpless condition, damaged, without fuel, and most of its crew was on the top deck waiting to transfer to *U-172* and *185*. Prueher put his plane through two attack runs over the U-boats, strafing and dropping four bombs, which further shook *U-604* but caused no damage. However, strafing from the PB4Y-1's

.50 caliber machine guns killed or wounded several of *U-172*'s crew and knocked out it antiaircraft guns. Kapitänleutnant Emmermann decided to pull the plug and submerge because his antiaircraft guns were out of action, leaving the other two U-boats to battle it out with the American patrol bomber. Meanwhile *U-185* began circling *U-604* in an effort to protect it. In so doing, it passed over the spot where *U-172* had dived. As the Liberator turned from an altitude of approximately 1,200 feet (366 meters) for another bombing run, the U-boat crews suddenly saw it wobble and then plunge into the sea.

Preparations to scuttle *U-604* continued however, *U-172* didn't return immediately and *U-185* had to accommodate the rest of *U-604*'s crew as *U-172*'s rudder had been jammed to port by the Liberator's exploding depth bombs causing the boat to run in a circle until it was freed by use of the hand steering gear. Höltring ordered his men overboard, who proceeded to swim approximately 100 yards (91.4 meters) to

Lieutenant Commander Bertram J. Prueher, the 30-year-old skipper of VB-107, was killed with his crew when their PB4Y-1 *The Spirit of 83* was shot down by *U-185* escorting damaged *U-604* which had been attacked by VB-129 five days before. (Jean Prueher)

U-185 while the captain, still recuperating from the wounds sustained in VB-129's attack, boarded a raft that rowed him over. *U-604*'s engineer officer was the last man to leave *U-604*, after opening the boat's vents and setting four explosive charges with eight-minute fuses. He then climbed quickly through the conning tower, dived overboard and swam to *U-185*. Before he reached it, the scuttling charges exploded, and *U-604* sank by the stern.

Throughout the remainder of August and into the last week of September, U-boats operating off South America successfully evaded Allied air and sea searches; that ended with the sinking of Type IXC *U-161* by VP-74 east of São Salvador da Bahia, Brazil on September 27. Twenty-nine-year-old U-boat ace Korvettenkapitän Albrecht Achilles headed his boat out of Lorient on August 8 for the vessel's sixth patrol; the previous five had netted 18 ships sunk or damaged totaling over 95,000 tons. His crew barely escaped death from attacks by VP-83 during the previous patrol. The submarine arrived off Brazil approximately on September 10, and continued southward for the next nine days without conducting an attack. The following day at 1050 hours, the British merchant ship *St. Usk* took a torpedo from *U-161*. The

A combat aircrew posing next to the PB4Y-1 Liberator *Subduer* during late 1943. This crew would be responsible for the sinking of *U-849*. The first names of many of these men remain unknown. Back row unknown order: (?) Preston, Jack McCabe, Lee Bergstrom, (?) Peterson, (?) Grocki, Richard A. Wilson, (?) Russell, (?) Fyffe. Front row unknown order: Richard Riggs, Marion Vance Dawkins, (?) Debler, Jean Cook, (?) Blauvelt. (Richard A. Wilson)

The seaplane base at Naval Air Facility (NAF) Aratu, Brazil on 13 September 1943 showing three PBM-5D Mariners of VP-74 parked on the ramp. The squadron at the time had detachments at Aratu, Bahia, and Galeao, Brazil. Squadron crews sank four U-boats between May and July 1943. (Sean Hearn via Mark Aldrich)

A PBM-3S Mariner of VP-211 (211-P-1) flying off Brazil during 1944. The squadron flew ASW missions beginning in September 1943 from Aratu, Bahia, and Galeao and conducted one unsuccessful attack possibly against *U-863* on 28 September 1943. VB-107 sank her the following day near the vicinity of VP-211's attack. (Mark Aldrich)

48-man crew climbed into lifeboats and abandoned ship. The submarine surfaced and Achilles took three of the ship's crew aboard for questioning including its master George H. Moss. Two of the men were let go but Achilles kept Moss aboard, who would perish along with the U-boat's crew a week later.

The Brazilian merchant ship *Itapagé* became Achilles's last victim on the evening of the 26th at 1850 hours, when two torpedoes slammed into the ship's starboard side. It sank in four minutes killing 20 passengers and crew of the 106 aboard. The radar operator aboard Lieutenant (jg) Harry Patterson's Mariner 74-P-2 picked up the submarine from a range of 38 miles at 1050 hours the following morning. Patterson reported,

Closing range, the wake of a submarine was first sighted visually by the second pilot [co-pilot] about 10 miles dead ahead, his [the U-boat] course at right angles to ours headed to our right. Battle Stations were manned, as we immediately increased speed and commenced a shallow turn to [the] left to take advantage of the sun, as well as to get in position for a stern attack. No clouds were in the area. I believe we were sighted at this time. About 7 to 8 miles [11–13 km] distant, the sub opened fire in a left turn, apparently attempting to bring his after guns [guns located on the boats aft section] to bear on us. This was puzzling as in the past the subs usually turned to present a beam target.

The shells were exploding short, leaving white puffs in a line across our course. As we came within range approximately 3 to 4 miles [5–6 km] distant, some large brown puffs could be seen. The gunners were very accurate and the explosions made the air vey turbulent. The bow gunner opened fire at 3,000 yards [2743 m], the fire falling short [of the U-boat], getting on the target as the range closed. Lieutenant (jg) Fergerson, co-pilot, dropped a string of 6 MK-44 Torpex-filled D/Cs [depth charges] as I passed over, or just forward of the conning tower from the sub's port quarter at an angle of about 20 [degrees] from stern, between 75 and 100' [feet] altitude, airspeed 185 knots.

I made a sharp left turn. [The] sub appeared to be just emerging from slick [the area of water where the depth charge exploded] most of which seemed to be on [the] starboard side of the sub's track. The sub started turning right. When the plane was broadside, the sub again opened fire, the shells exploding off out port side. After reaching 800' [feet] [244 m] altitude, I gave orders to standby and commenced [a] 2nd attack. During this run, the fire was heavier and more accurate. We were hit just forward of the galley door by a shell that exploded just as it struck. Ensign Brett was emerging from [the] bombing compartment after reset[ing] the intervalometer. He was severely wounded by shrapnel and aluminum from this shell, as was radioman Bealer. At this time I did not know that Bealer was hit nor where or how badly the plane was damaged.

Lieutenant (jg) Fergerson dropped the remaining two bombs and the plane passed directly over the target from stern to bow at about 165 knots [and] at 160' [feet] [49 m] altitude. I immediately gained altitude believing there was a possibility that my engines or fuel tanks were damaged. Ensign Larson, [the] navigator, carried Ensign Brett back aft to a bunk where Karsen [crewman] administered first-aid…The flight engineer reported that we were hit in many places and that our inverter line [provides electrical power] was shot away putting our electronic instruments out of commission. Just before reaching 2500' [feet] [672 m] altitude at which I leveled off, I glanced back and noticed Bealer was wounded in his right leg. He was still at his station helping Ensign Larson with the amplifying report [radio or Morse Code transmission] and had never reported being hit. After checking Ensign Brett's injuries and the damage to [the] plane I realized that he needed medical attention quickly. Although we were out of range at this time, the sub kept up

A PV-1 Ventura taking off from a Brazilian airbase in late 1944 or January 1945 as the PB4Y-1 Liberators in the background are those of VPB-107, which deployed to England in January 1945. Three PV-1 squadrons were in operation between October 1944 and January 1945: VPB-126, VPB-134, and VPB-145. (National Archives)

Patrol squadrons continued deployment to Brazil and conducted ASW sweeps off Brazil through May 1945 but no further enemy submarines were sunk by such units. Seen here is a PBY-5A of VP-45 at Belém, Brazil during 1944. The squadron deployed to Brazil at the end of April 1944 until 22 May 1945. Detachments operated from Belém, NAF Amapa, Sao Luiz, Fernando de Neronha Island, Galeao, Ascension Island, and Bahia. (Mark Aldrich)

a continuous fire. It maneuvered erratically after the 2nd attack and the speed was noticeably reduced. It squared away on a straight course of 140° T [true] [southeast] and submerged at 1122. I flew over the swirl and dropped D/C Marker, and then departed for base.[12]

Achilles and the 52 men aboard presumably perished when *U-161* probably imploded when it went beyond the maximum depth of 755 feet (230 meters). It was a quick, painless death, once it reached that point, but slow and painful as the boat descended with the crew fighting to bring *U-161* back to the surface.

Fleet Air Wing 16 (Recife, Brazil) December 1943

Squadrons	Seaplane Tenders
VB-107	*Barnegat* (AVP-10)
VB-129	*Sandpiper* (AVP-9)
VB-130	
VB-143	
VB-145	
VP-94	
VP-203	
VP-211	

Alan C. Carey, *Galloping Ghosts of the Brazilian Coast* (2005)

CHAPTER 6

Ascension Island Operations
(November 1943–April 1944)

"The fishing was good."

RICHARD WILSON, VB-107

U-boat activities moved away from the Brazilian coast to waters around Ascension Island during the last quarter of 1943. Therefore, to facilitate anti-submarine barriers in the narrows of the South Atlantic between Africa and the "hump" of Brazil, Admiral Ingram ordered a detachment from VB-107 to Wideawake Field Ascension. A pair of the squadrons' PB4Y-1 Liberators arrived on Ascension at the end of September. However, the crews chosen for the assignment found living conditions not to their tastes. According to Richard Wilson a member of Lieutenant Hill's crew,

> There was not much to do on Ascension Island, no women, no bars, no grass, and very little fresh water. There were movies, mostly ones we had already seen elsewhere, and some passing USO shows. Fishing was very good at southwest bay about 300 feet [91 m] lower than the airstrip. Flying was welcomed since the sooner you got over 100 hours on your plane, the quicker you returned to Brazil. In one 30-day period, my plane flew 103 hours in 13 flights. I was a radioman and was kept busy in flight operating either the radio or radar. My battle station was the crown turret.
> One night we came upon a Spanish freighter, which we suspected of refueling German submarines. The pilot called everyone to battle stations and started a bombing run. In placing the .50 caliber ammo belts in the twins in the crown turret, I shut one of the covers on my denim jacket sleeve. I could not get my other hand up to pry off the cover. I called down to Chief Bergstrom to loan me his knife and not to ask any dumb questions. I cut a U-shaped piece out of the sleeve and pried the cover off in time to be ready to fire if necessary. I kept the jacket long after the war. It was a good conversation piece. There I was, 6,000 feet [1829 m] altitude, in the dark, my left arm hung up on a 50 cal machine gun etc.[1]

Between November 1943 and April 1944, the Ascension detachment conducted successful attacks that resulted in the destruction of three U-boats and the severe crippling of a fourth. The first enemy contact occurred on October 27, 1943 when Liberator Number B-6 piloted by Lieutenant P. J. Haverty attacked a submerging submarine. However, there was no evidence of any damage inflicted on the vessel. It was a different story nine days later at 1125 hours on November 5, 1943 when, bomber Number B-12, piloted by Lieutenant Charles A. Baldwin, came upon Korvettenkapitän Wilhelm Rollmann's *U-848* while on an ASW sweep southwest of Ascension,

Ascension Island in the South Atlantic became home for several patrol squadrons beginning in the latter part of 1943. Detachments from VB-107 began ASW sweeps beginning in September 1943. (National Archives)

This first of seven images were taken by crewmembers aboard PB4Y-1 Liberators on 5 November 1943 showing the attack on *U-848* southwest of Wideawake Field, Ascension Island—an isolated volcanic island lying south of the equator, 1,400 miles (2,250 km) off Brazil and 1,000 miles (1,600 km) from the African coast. Four PB4Y-1s of VB-107 and two B-25 Mitchells of the Army Air Force First Composite Squadron participated in the submarine's sinking. The first image shows the submarine's gunners crouching down during a low-level pass by one of the Liberators. (National Archives)

> After being out about five hours and ready to start the return to base, I decided to transfer fuel from the outboard wing tanks. This requires turning off the radios and radar. While transferring fuel and passing through a small front with a base of 1,000 feet [305 m] and flying at 3,500 [1067 m] feet my bow watch reported the sighting of a ship through a break in the clouds. At the same time, the co-pilot and I sighted the same object at about five miles, two points off the port bow; I recognized it as a German submarine and sent everyone to battle stations.[2]

Type IXD2 *U-848* was heading for the Indian Ocean to join the Monsoon wolf pack that operated from the Japanese bases at Penang, Jakarta, and Sabang in Indonesia between 1943 and 1945. Three days earlier Rollmann's boat sank the British steamer *Baron Semple*, which was the only U-boat victory in the South Atlantic between November 1943 and February 1944.

Lieutenant Baldwin turned the radios back on as his PB4Y-1 cleared the storm at an altitude of 3,500 feet (1067 meters), and the U-boat was picked up visually one and a half miles (2.41 kilometers) from the rapidly approaching patrol bomber. The Liberator's pilot conducted a diving turn to port at a speed of 250 miles per hour (402 kilometers per hour) and within seconds the bomber had dropped down to an altitude of only 75 feet (23 meters),

> I dropped six bombs, one just forward of the conning tower. I pulled up into a steep port bank and began a second run. This time the sub was turning about on his starboard side and I was unable to straighten the plane out in time and passed over the sub about 60 feet [18 m] inside of his turn. I turned again to port for a third run. At a target angle of 60 degrees and an altitude 25 feet [7.6 m], I dropped the three remaining bombs, which were seen to explode short. Then pulling out to port and away, saw the sub still in his turn and losing a great amount of oil. I was also able to see three puffs of smoke, which I believe were the only shots fired at me during the three runs. There was enough personnel topside to man all guns but the reason for the light fire was the excellent shooting of my gunners and the element of surprise.
>
> After pulling out, I was able to contact 107-B-4, Lieutenant W. R. Ford's plane, by voice and tell him of the attack and started sending messages to home him in on the target. In the meantime the sub was still losing oil and appeared to be down by the stern steering an erratic course in a southerly direction making about four or five knots.[3]

Before *U-848* finally sank at 1900 hours, four PB4Y-1 Navy Liberators and two Army B-25 Mitchell bombers conducted ten separate attacks, expending a total of

A second attack on *U-848* conducted by Lieutenant Charles A. Baldwin flying 107-B-12 dropped three Mk-47 depth bombs from an altitude of only 25 feet. The bombs fell wide missing the submarine by some 200 feet. The bomber encountered heavy anti-aircraft fire causing damage to a vertical stabilizer. (National Archives)

33 depth charges and 12 demolition bombs. Lieutenant W. R. Ford in command of 107-B-4 arrived at 1245 hours and started his first bombing run while Lieutenant Baldwin made a strafing run. The submarine's gunners directed their fire at B-4 since it had the bombs. Ford reported,

> When about one and one half miles away the sub opened up with heavy antiaircraft fire. This was mostly to our port and below. Believing they would correct and make hits on us we turned to port and lost altitude until we were within the smoke puffs of the AA (antiaircraft) fire. Their subsequent fire was then on our starboard bow and beam in our former position. As we straightened out our diving run, our crown turret and both bow guns opened up with very accurate fire on the conning tower, scoring either very good hits on personnel or scaring the hell out of the sub crews, which resulted in stopping all AA fire [antiaircraft].[4]

With bomb bays open, Ford's Liberator's, at an indicated airspeed of 220 miles per hour (354 kilometers per hour), approached *U-848* from an altitude of 25 feet (7.6 meters), and dropped a string of depth charges. On pulling up from the bombing run, the Liberator's tail turret opened fire and scored accurate hits on the U-boat, "When we gained 500 feet [152 meters] and started our turn as B-12 advised we had dropped short. We completed our sharp left turn and made a second run with our guns firing very accurately encountering no opposing fire. We dropped our last three bombs at 100 feet crossing the sub at 25 feet [7.6 meters]."[5]

The bombs from Ford's plane fell approximately 30 feet (9 meters) short of *U-848*, which continued moving and putting up strong defensive fire against the two circling Liberators. Without any depth charges and low on fuel, Lieutenant Ford called in additional help from Ascension before heading back to the island, while Baldwin's

Lieutenant William T. Ford in 107-B-4 conducting a third attack on *U-848* dropping six Mk-47 depth bombs from an altitude of 125 feet. The bombs fell far off the mark by some 250 feet. (National Archives)

B-12 stayed to monitor the U-boat's position. Meanwhile, Lieutenant William E. Hill and his crew in Number B-8 took off at 1209 hours and homed in on B-12's messages. Hill reported,

> At 1230 hrs, B-4 was contacted on voice frequency and he gave me information concerning the tactics of the sub and the amount of AA fire I might encounter. At 1235, I arrived at the sub's position and saw the oil slick it was trailing. I contacted B-12 and suggested a combined attack, providing he had sufficient ammunition to do so. At the western end of the oil slick, I spotted the conning tower and deck of the sub from a distance of 10 miles at a speed of 4 to 5 knots, with its stern low in the water.[6]

Five miles from the target Lieutenant Hill sounded general quarters, placed his Liberator into a power glide from 1,800 to 1,400 feet (549–427 meters), applied full throttle, and started his run at an indicated airspeed of 200 miles per hour (354 kilometers per hour).

> At about two miles [3.2 km] from the sub, I noticed three puffs of white smoke from explosive shells that were above and to the left. I heard something hit the plane and believed it to be in the fuselage. The bow gunner was strafing the sub's deck where the enemy gunner was located. The crown turret gunner failed to fire because of an error in assembling the gun switches in the gun bolts. On the bombing approach, the co-pilot could see flashes of gunfire from several places on the platform aft of the conning tower, also some tracers going by the plane. For every one you see there are four you don't see. We crossed over the sub just aft of the conning tower, altitude about 100 feet [30.4 m]. I released five depth charges, all landed short, and the closest about 100 feet from the sub.
>
> On the pull out, I started a climbing turn to the left. The port waist gunner, Ensign Williby Scholar, called on the interphone and informed me that number two engine was on fire. Our flight engineer, Aviation Machinist Mate First Class [AMM1c] William J. Dickinson, and I feathered the prop, cut the engine, and the fire went out in a very few seconds. I then started a climbing turn to the right and was able to get to 4,000 feet [1219 m] where I leveled off. We remained in the area until 1410 and then set a course for the base, landing at 1612. I considered dropping the remaining four depth charges on three engines but since Army B-25 planes were approaching with bombs, B-4 was being reloaded, the sub was damaged and could not submerge, and base was only two hours away, return to base would be the intelligent thing to do. Lieutenant
>
> Baldwin informed me after the attack that my plane was surrounded by puffs from explosive shells, but most were behind. The plane suffered no other damage and there were no injuries to the crew.[7]

U-848 had survived three attacks by VB-107 Liberators. A crew led by Lieutenant S. K. Taylor in 107-B-4 was the next to take a crack at the U-boat, taking off at 1513 hours from Ascension. For him and the third pilot, Ensign Whyte, it was their first run of the day while the remainder of the crew had just returned from a previous engagement with the same sub,

> At 1625, we picked up the MOs (radio messages) from B-12 who made the first attack and was still circling the area. Over the earphones came reports from two B-25s that had made horizontal drops with 500-pound demolition bombs [227 kg]. They reported coming close but not close enough. One B-25 had its hydraulic system shot out.

At 1650, we sighted the oil slick made by previous attacks. B-12 then departed for base because of fuel shortage. At 1655, we sighted the sub approximately eight miles ahead and 12 miles west of the oil slick. We estimated the speed of the sub to be between eight and ten knots.

We turned to the right of the sub and began a wide counter-clockwise circle hoping to attack from the bow. Our altitude was 2,200 feet [671 m]. The sub continued on course until we got even with his bow, about five miles away. Then he began turning to starboard, bringing his bow toward us. We then began turning left maintaining 2,000 feet altitude. He continued his starboard turn as if attempting to present a beam target. We applied high rpm and 44 inches [112 cm] manifold pressure and began our dive turning sharply to the left again.[8]

As the Liberator turned, *U-848* sent up a heavy barrage of antiaircraft fire that barely missed the bomber's number-three engine. Lieutenant Taylor straightened out his turn and pressed on with an attack across the U-boat's bow dropping five depth charges from 70 feet (21.3 meters) at 200 miles per hour (644 kilometers per hour). Throughout the bombing run, the Liberator's bow and top turret laid down continuous fire aimed at the boat's conning tower and as the patrol bomber passed over its tail guns went into action,

We immediately followed up the first drop by pulling up to 400 feet [122 m] and 160 miles per hour [258 kmh] and whipped around making a run over the sub's starboard bow, the four remaining depth charges falling along the starboard side. The speed this time was 190 miles per hour [306 kmh] and an altitude of 50 feet [15 m]. In this attack, the sub appeared to be turning to starboard and listing but making headway. After pulling out of the dive and coming around in position to see the submarine, it appeared to be settling straight down. Suddenly, from the conning tower forward, shot up in the air, and then there was a terrific cone shaped explosion, coming from, and surrounding the entire sub, which rose high in the air.[9]

Tenth attack by Lieutenant Taylor conducted at an altitude of 50–100 feet. Three bombs exploded very close to the submarine's starboard side. (National Archives)

Ninth attack against *U-848* by Lieutenant S.K. Taylor's PB4Y-1 107-B-4. One depth bomb has exploded and another (center, right) can be seen in the air. (National Archives)

The explosion ripped *U-848* apart leaving behind debris, oil, and men struggling in the water. Lieutenant Taylor and his crew, the men responsible for the U-boat's destruction, watched the carnage below,

> The next instant there appeared in the middle of the oil patch a group of men, 25 to 30 in number, three life rafts, and a dark object, which looked like part of the broken sub. The apparent part of the sub soon disappeared below the surface. We then estimated there to be between fifteen and twenty men, part of them in life rafts, part hanging on and others swimming or floating. One of the rafts failed to open and sank. We dropped one raft and men were seen to get in it.[10]

An Army PBY dropped three life rafts to the men while other aircraft attempted to divert the HMS *Fort Cumberland*, located some 35 miles away, to pick up the survivors of *U-848*. According to Lieutenant Taylor, "We told the ship by blinker about survivors, giving position, bearing, and distance from ship and requested they pick them up. They receipted for the message but did not say they would pick them up. We then returned to the PBY and survivors. It was getting dark and nothing more could be done out there."[11]

The Liberator departed for Ascension leaving some 20 men in the water. A lone survivor of *U-848*, picked up in a life raft by the light cruiser USS *Marblehead* (CL-12) nearly a month later on December 3, 1943, confirmed the U-boat's demise. The man died three days later in a hospital at Recife.

The First Lady of the United States Eleanor Roosevelt pins the Distinguished Flying Cross on Lieutenant Taylor for his role in the sinking of *U-848* (Richard A. Wilson)

VB-107 continued to be successful in protecting merchant shipping sailing in the South Atlantic at the expense of the U-boat service. On November 25, 1943, Liberator B-6, commanded by Lieutenant (jg) Marion V. Dawkins Jr., departed Ascension Island on an anti-submarine sweep along with bomber B-8. The two aircraft departed company after take-off and Dawkins was unable to communicate with B-8 when his co-pilot Ensign Marvell E. Eide spotted a submarine. It was *U-849*, another Type IXD2, on its first patrol, commanded by Kapitänleutnant Heinz-Otto Schultze, a recipient of the Knight's Cross. Kapitänleutnant Schultze's boat, like the *U-848* sunk a month before by a Liberator of VB-107, was heading for the Indian Ocean to join the Monsoon wolf pack. Dawkins called the crew to battle stations and gave instructions to the navigator, Ensign George H. Valentine to check the intervalometer and the U-boat's position. Dawkins reported,

At about five miles, I began rapid a descent through clouds and broke through at 2,000 feet [610 m], one mile astern of target. I attacked the U-boat, releasing bombs in a steep glide with spacing of 60 feet [18 m] at 200 mph [322 kmh]. My target angle was about 160 degrees and at an altitude 25 feet [7.6 m].[12]

The pilot shown here is Lieutenant (jg) Vance Dawkins, USNR who served with a detachment of VB-107 on Ascension Island. Operations from the island increased the squadron's ability to patrol larger areas off Central Africa. (National Archives)

It was a sudden attack that took most of the Liberator's crew by surprise. The attack also apparently took the crew of the U-boat off guard, as the American bomber didn't receive any antiaircraft fire until it had passed over the conning tower,

> Six bombs were released, which were observed to envelop the submarine in one large detonation; two bombs falling close to starboard quarter, three close to beam, while the sixth possibly struck the U-boat's deck. After the drop, my tail gunner, R. D. Gilpin, strafed the conning tower and deck areas on which a few personnel were seen. The crown turret and nose guns did not fire due to the suddenness of the attack.
>
> As the plane passed over the conning tower, I felt a loss of control in the rudders while the nose dropped badly. I lost further altitude and nearly struck the water, but pulled heavily back on the yoke and plane climbed slowly to 800 feet [244 m] where I observed AA [antiaircraft] fire short and below the plane.[13]

After completing the bombing run, Lieutenant Dawkins circled his bomber to see the damage inflicted on *U-849* by the depth charging attack,

> The U-boat, blown 45 degrees to port gave off a large oil slick. I ordered the navigator to prepare the three remaining bombs for a drop and the co-pilot to contact B-8 and advised them of the attack and our position. I climbed to 1,500 feet [457 m] and out of range of AA fire. B-8 could not be contacted but Ascension picked it up and relayed it. I observed that the U-boat was severely crippled and not knowing the extent of damage to my plane, I did not think it advisable to deliver a second attack until B-8 arrived. However, I kept the plane within striking distance and ordered all hands to observe closely any attempt by the U-boat to submerge. While circling, I was advised by the after station that the U-boat's crew was abandoning ship.[14]

While Dawkins circled, *U-849* exploded and sending debris some 200 feet (61 meters) in the air. The plane continued to circle at 500 feet (152 meters), taking photographs

The first two depth bombs from PB4Y-1 Liberator 107-B-6 piloted by Lieutenant (jg) Vance Dawkins miss *U-849* during an attack on 25 November 1943 off Africa. (National Archives)

A depth charge explodes and small splashes from the Liberator's gunners are seen in this image. The submarine was mortally crippled, and as the boat's crew began abandoning ship, *U-849* exploded. The bomber's crew saw survivors in the water but none survived long enough for rescue. (National Archives)

of the survivors in the sea before departing the area at 1130 hours. Dawkins finally contacted B-8 and advised them of the attack and the U-boat's sinking. B-8 made a short unsuccessful attempt to locate the survivors then followed B-6 to base. None of *U-849*'s crew survived the attack.

After landing, the bomber's crew realized they came very close to becoming victims of their own attack. Fragments of a depth charge, which apparently broke upon striking the water, caused a considerable amount of damage to the Liberator. One fragment lodged in the center leading edge of the starboard vertical stabilizer of the plane.

After completing barrier patrols searching for German blockade-runners, VB-107 at Ascension returned to its primary task of hunting U-boats. On February 6, 1944, squadron planes conducted two attacks. One resulted in the sinking of *U-177*. It proved to be the last U-boat sunk by an Ascension-based PB4Y-1. Bomber B-3, with Lieutenant (jg) C. I. Pinnell at the controls, was on patrol off Ascension Island when the bow gunner sighted an object off the starboard bow. Pinnell's plane was cruising at about 170 miles per hour (274 kilometers per hour) and had just emerged from a cloudbank when the pilot ordered, "All hands to battle stations," and then nosed to the starboard 70 degrees and went into a glide. The submarine was approximately 12 miles off (19 kilometers), running full surface at a right angle to the course flown by Pinnell.

U-177, another Type IXD2 submarine, previously credited with sinking 14 ships totaling 87,388 tons was commanded by Korvettenkapitän Heinz Buchholz on its third and final cruise. The U-boat was sailing on a southeasterly course when the bridge watch spotted the incoming bomber. A momentary lapse in sounding the alarm by Matrosenobergefreiter Helmut Roch combined with the somewhat lethargic attitude exhibited among many of the gun crews to operate the guns, which were tired of frequent false alarms, sealed the fate of *U-177*. Pinnell in the after-action report stated,

> I don't think they saw us until we were just a little way off. I maneuvered around until I was almost directly head-on. The submarine's 20-millimeter [cannon] opened fire on the plane and our bow gunners opened with our .50 caliber [machine guns]. As soon as our guns opened fire, the enemy stopped. We dropped depth charges as we passed over. At first, I thought we dropped short, and immediately climbed, flew back, and dropped the remaining depth charges on the submarine.[15]

Bucholz ordered flank speed and the U-boat turned to starboard just as the Liberator dropped a load of depth charges. The ordnance straddled the submarine with one landing directly on the deck, another near the galley, and a third just forward of the control room. All three detonations shook the boat so drastically that a number of men received injuries from objects torn loose from their mountings or by flying glass. Almost immediately, the U-boat settled and water started to pour into the control room through the hatch. The engineering officer, making no effort to regulate the boat's trim shouted, "She's going down, everybody out!" As one survivor clambered out, the conning tower was already under water, and the flow of water into the U-boat was so strong that he could hardly reach the bridge. About 20 officers and men, including Buchholz jumped into the ocean, all others remained trapped in the flooded, sinking boat. As they swam about, the bomber came over again and released three more depth charges on the swirl of the sinking U-boat.

On the second run, Ensign Robert R. Swanson and Aviation Machinist Mate First Class (AMM1c) Stanley S. Shedaker reported the submarine had completely submerged. However, Pinnell and the co-pilot, Ensign John M. Leonard Jr., thought they saw it in the disturbed and oil coated water. After the second drop, the conning tower appeared and started a slow turn to starboard. The detonation of the charges killed about six of the swimmers, including Buchholz, and wounding several others. A moment later, there was a strong detonation from the area of the U-boat, which survivors believed were the batteries exploding. The bomber circled and flew low at 50 feet (15 meters) above the survivors, who expected to be machine-gunned, as the plane had strafed the U-boat while dropping the first string of depth charges. Instead, Shedaker photographed them while Pinnell radioed the exact location of the attack back to base. Shortly thereafter, a second plane, which dropped an inflatable rubber boat and another with provisions amongst the survivors, relieved Pinnell.

Fourteen officers and men reached the rubber boat. As the boat was far too small to accommodate all of the survivors, the men sat with their legs in the water.

Leutnant Hans Brodt, as the senior survivor, took command, and ordered sail set for the Brazilian coast. During the first night, a freighter passed within 800 meters (2,625 ft) of the survivors, but all efforts to attract the ship's attention failed. The rations dropped by the relief plane were more than adequate and there was no particular discomfort except that occasioned by overcrowding of the boat.

However, as the time went on, Brodt's attitude became insufferable, as he was unable to control his fury at Helmut Roch, blaming him for the U-boat's loss since Roch was the lookout from whose sector the bomber had attacked. According to the accounts, had the group remained intact much longer, Brodt would have provoked a mutiny by his conduct and been killed. 56 hours after the sinking, the USS *Omaha* hove into sight brought aboard the men of *U-177*.[16]

A pair of VB-107 Liberators conducted the last successful U-boat kill by a Brazilian-based Navy patrol squadron on September 29, 1944, which resulted in the loss of Type IXD2 *U-863* under the command of Kapitänleutnant Dietrich von der Esch. The day before PBM Number P-4 of VP-211 identified a surfaced submarine by radar and closed in to investigate but driven off by intense antiaircraft fire before conducting a bomb drop. However, an accurate fix on the U-boat's position allowed a pair of PB4Y-1s from VB-107 to find it the next day.

Lieutenant John Burton piloting Liberator Number B-9 sighted the boat east-southeast of Recife and dropped five depth charges on the first run damaging the submarine to such an extent that it could not submerge. Burton remained on scene, making strafing runs in coordination with Lieutenant Edward A. Krug Jr., in Number B-7 after the latter had homed in upon seeing antiaircraft fire near Lieutenant Burton's position. Lieutenant Krug in Liberator Number B-7 conducted three runs dropping depth charges that ripped *U-863* apart, and it quickly sank leaving some 20 men in the water. The Liberators dropped life rafts, but subsequent searches failed to locate any survivors.

By fall 1943, the number of shipping losses in the South Atlantic coincided with the reduction of U-boats operating in the region with only 15 merchant ships reported lost between August and December. Between September 28, 1943 and September 28, 1944, planes from several different squadrons located U-boats, but were unable to complete a successful attack. From January 1944 to May 1945, U-boats sank six ships in the areas patrolled by the United States. Fourth Fleet and FAW-16. Besides the loss of the *Nebraska* by *U-843* in April, U-boats sank four other merchant vessels during 1944, three in May and one in July. *U-181* sank the British *Janeta* on May 1, while *U-129* sank the British steamships *Anadyr* on the sixth and the *Empire Heath* on the 11th. Two months later Convoy JT-39 lost the American steamer *William Gaston* to *U-861*. The last Allied merchant ship lost in the South Atlantic was the *Baron Jedburgh* sunk by *U-532* on March 10, 1945.

CHAPTER 7

Mediterranean Operations
(November 1942–May 1944)

"Our losses…have reached an intolerable level. The enemy air force played a decisive role in inflicting these high losses."

ADMIRAL KARL DÖNITZ, *MEMOIRS: TEN YEARS AND TWENTY DAYS*

U-boat operations in the Mediterranean Theater began in September 1941 and ended in May 1944, with the Kriegsmarine sending 62 into the sea during that period and a peak of 19 boats operating at once during November 1942. Allied shipping loses totaled 194 ships for nearly 650,000 tons. The British-controlled Straits of Gibraltar became the grave of nine German submarines attempting to enter the Atlantic with total losses in the Mediterranean, equaling the number sent. The region proved quite hazardous as the British and Americans operated a string of airbases after the conclusion of Operation *Torch*, the invasion of North Africa, in November 1942. However, the first submarines sunk by American planes during *Torch* were those of the Vichy French. The invasion of North Africa placed French Navy personnel in an awkward position of either joining the Allies or keeping the pledge to remain loyal to the French government of Marshal Philippe Pétain. Admirals André Marquis and Jean de Laborde pledged to defend the naval base at Toulon from the Allies, but they also prepared to scuttle the fleet to keep it out of the hands of the Allies and Germany. The French submarines *Le Conquérant* and *Sidi-Ferruch* attempted to evade capture by the Allies and attempted to sail into the Atlantic. U.S. Navy planes sank both vessels with the loss of their entire crews. Four TBF-1 Avengers of Escort Scouting Squadron 27 (VGS-27) from the *Suwannee* (CVE-27) spotted *Sidi-Ferruch* on the surface off Fedhala Roads, Morocco some 12 miles from Casablanca at 910 hours on November 11. Three of the aircraft used cloud cover and conducted a stern attack with at least six depth charges falling in the lethal range. One of the DCs blew the conning tower off as the submarine submerged and shortly thereafter, a large oil slick formed followed by air bubbles. VP-92 under the leadership of Lieutenant Commander J. A. Moreno arrived at Casablanca the day after the *Sidi-Ferruch*'s destruction. Three months earlier while operating out of

Guantanamo Bay, Cuba Lieutenant Fiss' crew shared with HMCS *Oakville* in the sinking of *U-94* three months earlier. Less than 24 hours after arriving in Morocco two planes from the squadron would sink the French submarine *Le Conquérant* Two squadron aircraft 92-P-4 and 92-P-5 spotted the submarine and began circling it as a crewmember aboard each plane used an Aldis Lamp to signal and identify the vessel. *Le Conquérant* didn't respond and Lieutenant H. S. Blake flying 92-P-4 made a depth charge run; the explosives straddling the conning tower. The second PBY followed dropped more depth charges that blew the conning tower off and the submarine immediately sank. Moreno's squadron along with VP-73 settled into months of routine daily patrols over the Mediterranean.

Fleet Air Wing 15 (Port Lyautey, French Morocco) May 1943

Squadrons
VP-72
VP-73
VP-92

On July 15, 1943 when VP-92's Lieutenant R. J. Finnie and his crew participated in the sinking of Type VIIC *U-135* with British destroyers HMS *Rochester*, *Mignonette*, and *Balsam* between the Canary Islands and Western Sahara. The submarine was on its seventh patrol after leaving Lorient on June 7, with Oberleutnant zur See Otto Luther as new its new commanding officer. At 1015 hours on July15, the submarine fired a spread of three torpedoes at the 4,700-ton British merchant ship *Twickenham* scoring one hit on the ship's stern. However, the vessel made it to Dakar, Senegal for repairs. Unfortunately, for *U-135*, the British warships made contact on the submerged boat and a heavy depth charge attack followed forcing *U-135* to the surface after some two hours where upon the ships circled and began firing their deck guns. Lieutenant Finnie's PBY arrived, and his bow gunner began firing towards the Germans operating the deck gun forcing them to jump overboard as four depth charges fell from the aircraft from an altitude of 60 feet. The explosives detonated off *U-135*'s port side between the conning tower and bow. Geysers of water cascaded over the boat washing away three crewmembers attempting to operate the stern deck gun. Finnie circled and came back around at 150 feet, his port waist gunner strafing the deck, with .50 caliber rounds hitting one of the U-boat's crew and forcing another three men to jump ship. The PBY's guns swept the deck clear of any further attempt to operate the submarine's deck guns allowing for one of the warships to approach and ram it. *U-135* sank at 1305 hours, leaving 41 survivors in the water, including Oberleutnant zur See Luther, for pickup by the warships. Seven months of routine operations in the Mediterranean followed few hours of intense conflict between a U-boat, British warships, and a PBY Catalina.

M.A.D.-equipped PBY-5A Bureau Number 08245 of VP-63 at Pembroke Doc, England between August and December 1943. VP-63 armed the aircraft with retro bombs as shown, unique to this patrol squadron, on successful U-boat attacks conducted between February 1944 and April 1945. (National Archives)

The *Madcats* of VP-63 first served with FAW-7 at RAFB Pembroke Dock with RAF 19 Group Coastal Command and operated the PBY-5A Catalina equipped with M.A.D (Magnetic Anomaly Detection) and was viewed as a highly desirable tool to combat the U-boat. However, Coastal Command and the U.S. Navy soon realized the PBY, with a top speed of 90 knots, was no match for German fighters nor did the M.A.D gear live up to British Coastal Command's expectations. The squadron conducted patrols over the English Channel and Bay of Biscay from June 23 to December 23, 1943, in which time no U-boats were sunk while a Catalina piloted by Lieutenant William P. Tanner was shot down by JU-88 fighters of 13/KG40 on August 1. This engagement was the first aerial engagement by naval aviation and the Luftwaffe and the PBY's gunners shot down one of the eight enemy aircraft. Tanner and two crewmembers survived the crash. The squadron transferred to Port Lyautey, French Morocco where M.A.D proved its effectiveness in locating submerged enemy submarines.[1]

Squadron tactics, unlike other patrol squadrons, utilized detection gear, using propulsion smoke lights to mark a submarine's location and "Retro-bombs" to attack the target once located. The squadron based its anti-submarine doctrine on the inherent limitation of the M.A.D. gear, the extreme shortness of its range, but on the accuracy of its detection within that range. The squadron recognized immediately the impracticability of trying to sweep the entire ocean for submarines and that M.A.D. only could work in relatively small areas where the initial contact with a submarine visually, by radar, or by sonic detection. The submarine would likely have dived before the arrival of the aircraft, but if the swirl would still visible and then the aircraft would usually establish M.A.D. contact and proceed to "track" th submarine. Tracking procedure consisted of flying a "cloverleaf" patter, consisting of a number of 270-degree turns to the left at an altitude of 100 feet (30 meters) and firing a float light on each successive M.A.D. contact. When accurately flown, i would result in a line of float lights along the track of the submarine, which enabled the pilot to fly directly over the submarine for a bombing run.

There would probably be no trace of the submarine within a minute of sub merging in rough seas when a plane arrived over the area. Under those conditions the doctrine called for the plane to conduct a "spiral search" to secure contac by M.AD. The crew would throw a float light out towards the submarine's las known position as the plane flew a three-degree width turn to the left to a bearing of 180 degrees where upon another float light was thrown out while the pilot decreased the plane's rate of turn by one and one-half degrees. Flight personnel threw float lights out every ninety degrees as the spiral expanded. After eigh complete turns of the aircraft, the pilot would cease expanding the spiral and star a circle of constant radius. Placement of acoustic sonobuoys followed during the fourth circle with a buoy dropped every 90 degrees with the pilot reestablishing the spiral around any of the sonobuoys picking up submarine sounds. If at any point in the spiral search M.A.D. contact was established, the plane went into a bombing and tracking procedures.

In order to mark accurately the different positions on the water where M.A.D gear had signaled the presence of a submerged submarine, it was necessary to desigr a float light with the same retrofiring effect as the bombs. The Mark V Propulsive Float Light, which is a Mark V Float Light coupled with a propulsive motor, was developed and projectors were mounted in the tunnel hatches of the planes. The float lights could be fired either manually or coupled with the M.A.D. gear for automatic firing on M.A.D. signal.[2]

One of the first problems in using M.A.D. gear was that of deploying an effective aerial bomb when the gear made contact. Such a weapon, released at the instant M.A.D. signaled a submerged submarine directly underneath the plane, would have to strike the water far ahead of the submarine. Furthermore, multiple bombs would have to be pre-set to detonate at a given depth since the submarine might be at any depth up to about three hundred feet. The squadron chose a contact bomb containing 65.4 pound, (30 kilograms) of Torpex with a rocket motor that fired it in the opposite direction of the plane's course at a speed equal to the plane's speed. The bomb would hit the water at the exact position which was under the plane at the instant the bomb was fired. The pilot or M.A.D. operator could fire these "retro-bombs," (12 to 15) mounted on rails under each wing, automatically or manually in salvo or in spreads of eight or ten; only one was needed cause lethal damage.[3]

NAF Port Lyautey, French Morocco home to Fleet Air Wing 15 and patrol squadrons, such as VP-63, began U.S. ASW operations beginning in January 1943. (National Archives)

VP-63's successful use of its own tactics, gear, and weaponry occurred on February 24, 1944 against Type VIIC *U-761*, commanded by Oberleutnant zur See Horst Gelder at it attempted to pass through the Straits of Gibraltar from the Atlantic and into the Mediterranean. Ventura No. 15, Lieutenant (jg) T. R. Woolley, patrol plane commander, and plane No. 14, Lieutenant (jg) H. J. Baker, patrol plane commander, were flying the regular barrier patrol in the Straits when at 1559 hours when Woolley's operator picked up a M.A.D. signal Float light were fired, and the pilot immediately began a cloverleaf tracking procedure.

After plane No. 15 had tracked the submerged submarine and dropped three lights, plane No. 14 joined in the tracking, and the two planes flew the cloverleaf simultaneously, firing float light on each contact. At this point, a British destroyer, H.M.S. *Anthony* began to approach the area from a position two miles west of the point of contact. Six more float lights followed as the destroyer positioned itself within the cloverleaf pattern offering a serious hazard to the two aircraft flying at 100 feet (30 meters). On several turns, the *Anthony* was in the way, and the planes had to break off their tracking passes to avoid collision. The wingspan of a PBY is 104 feet (32 meters) and in a tight turn at 100 feet (30 meters), the wing tip isn't far above the water. Therefore, both aircraft requested the destroyer by voice communication to remain in the area but to stay clear of the tracking.

The destroyer then reported that it had a contact and was going to attack. However, it headed in the wrong end of the line of float lights, and Lieutenant (jg) Baker informed it that the target was at the other end. The ship promptly turned down the line of float lights and scattered them with its wake. Although it passed over the position of the submarine and was clear of the planes and other ships, it did not make an attack. Baker then told the *Anthony* directly that it should stay clear of the area if it was not going to make an attack. Up to this time, the aircraft had succeeded, under difficult conditions of interference, in placing the ten float lights on the track of the submerged submarine. After passing over its target, the destroyer announced that it had lost contact, and left the area, steaming off to the west, apparently having lost interest in the contact established by aircraft.

One of two Royal Navy destroyers depth charging the area in which M.A.D.-equipped PBY-5A of VP-63 located *U-761* in the Strait of Gibraltar on 24 February 1944. (National Archives)

The planes continued to make several fast cloverleaf passes over the suspected position of the submarine without success, and it appeared that contact had been lost. Baker directed Woolley to commence a spiral search, but not to expand it beyond the fourth turn. The spiral search is essentially a trapping circle, which increase in diameter and flown around the last known position of the submarine. The objective is to gain magnetic detection as the submarine passes through the circular barrier. Woolley commenced the spiral search, while Baker made several more cloverleaf passes before joining with him and taking up a right echelon position.

At 1645 hours, during the sixth turn of the spiral, Woolley regained magnetic contact about one mile south-southeast of the previous position. Both aircraft then re-established the tracking procedure. The British destroyer again headed into the area after several float lights had been laid, continued in it approach toward the line of float lights despite warnings from the aircraft to remain clear. The planes dropped ten float lights but both pilots wanted to lay two or three more lights before making their bombing runs. However, with the imminent possibility that the destroyer would again cause loss of contacts, both pilots decided to attack immediately. Woolley announced that he was making a bombing run, whereupon the destroyer "Rogered" for the message and turned slightly to port as Plane No. 15 passed abeam about 300 yards (274 meters) on the bombing run. 11 minutes after regaining contact, Woolley fired 23 retro-bombs, one bomb failing to fire.

Lieutenant Baker then fired a float light ten seconds after Plane No. 15 had bombs, made a 360-degree turn, and approached on his own bombing run. As he approached, he destroyer was within 100 yards (91 meters) of the end of the line of float lights and appeared to be backing down. Baker fired 24 retro-bombs on good M.A.D. indication about the two minutes after Woolley's attack. Twenty seconds later, the destroyer dropped ten depth charges at the position of the slashes of Baker's bombs.

At 1702 hours, the conning tower and bow of a U-boat broke the surface at the point of attack and directly in line with the string of float lights. It lost all forward speed, the stern sank until the bow was the only portion visible, about 40 degrees from normal trim, and then it disappeared stern first under the surface. Another British destroyer, HMS *Wishart* had arrived on the scene and it now attacked with depth charges over the point of submergence. Then the Anthony followed with another attack of ten depth charges. The submarine surfaced again eight minutes later, and personnel immediately began to abandon ship without attempting to defend the vessel. Both destroyers opened fire in the submarine, scoring a direct hit on the conning tower. At 1717 hours, a Venture, No. 46 of VB-127, Lieutenant P. L. Holmes as pilot, attacked the submarine with six depth bombs followed two minutes later with another depth bomb attack by RAF Catalina, Plane G of 202 squadron piloted by Flight Lieutenant John Finch. The bow of the submarine then rose to an angle of about 40 degrees, and at 1720 hours, it sank, leaving many survivors in the water. The destroyers remained in the area and picked up 48 survivors, one of whom died aboard the *Anthony*, with the balance sent ashore at Gibraltar.[4]

Oberleutnant zur See Henning Schümann and his crew aboard Type VIIC *U-392* made an ill-fated attempt to make a run passed the Straits of Gibraltar on March 16, 1944. At 0920 hours on the 14th, a PB4Y-1 Liberator of VB-112 spotted a periscope near Gibraltar. However, the periscope disappeared before the aircraft could attack. The following morning at 0457 hours, a Leigh light RAF Wellington operating from Gibraltar obtained a good radar contact not far from the initial

These two images show the attack on *U-761* in the Strait of Gibraltar on 24 February 1944 by two M.A.G-equipped PBY-5A Catalinas from VP-63 piloted by Lieutenant (jg) T.R. Wooley and Lieutenant R. J. Baker aided by two Royal Navy destroyers HMS *Anthony* (R-40) and HMS *Wishant* (I-67). (National Archives)

sighting. This contact disappeared at four miles, but the crew observed a definite swirl as the aircraft passed over the contact position. These two sightings gave every indication that another U-boat was going to try to run the Straits, and fleet operations estimated that the submarine would probably charge batteries the night of 15–16 March and would pass under the M.A.D. barrier sometime during the morning of the sixteenth. VP-63 assigned three PBYs to fly an additional barrier patrol near Europa Point at the eastern edge of Gibraltar to catch the submarine as it passed that position.

The three planes took-off at daybreak, Plane No. 8 flown by Lieutenant R. C. Spears and Lieutenant (jg) V. A. Y. Lingle in plane No. 1 would fly the regular M "fence," and Plane No. 7, Lieutenant (jg) M. J. Vopatek, flying the one plane "fence" at the eastern outlet of the Straits. As anticipated, the U-boat arrived at the barrier at 0853 hours, and Plane No. 8 obtained the first M.A.D. contact. Plane No. 8 notified plane No. 1 by voice communications, and two planes proceeded to track, firing float lights on each contact. They soon obtained nine successive contacts, and the line of float lights showed the submarine to be proceeding eastward at a speed of 3 to 4 knots.

At 0905 hours, Spears made a bombing run, but did not release due to failure to obtain M.A.D. contact. The planes then lost contact and were unable to regain it with standard tracking. A Free French submarine on the surface, escorted by a Free French sloop, was approaching from the west a distance on one-half mile, and

A line of float lights fired by VP-63 Catalinas during M.A.G. tracking of *U-392* on 16 March 1944. The British frigate HMS *Affleck* and destroyer HMS *Vanoc* contributed in the submarine's destruction. (National Archives)

's believed that the presence of those vessels caused the submarine to take evasive ction. A spiral search was then commenced by plane No. 8 and No. 1 around he point of last contact, and the 0935 hours, plane No. 8 regained contact three uarters miles east of the position where contact had been lost, and approximately hree miles east of the position of original contact.

Lieutenant (jg) Vopatek's plane No. 7 arrived at 0938 hours and joined in the racking. The float lights fired in the tracking shoed the submarine was continuing n an easterly course. At 0942 hours, Spears made a bombing run and fired 24 etro-bombs on a strong M.A.D. signal. Lieutenant Lingle followed with an attack f 23 bombs, also on good signal, one bomb failing to fire from the rack. The 3ritish destroyer HMS *Vanoc*, which was standing off while the planes tracked, eard explosions of three bombs from each plane's attack in its listening equipment, few seconds after each plane's attack.

The planes continued tracking and obtained signals indicating that the submerged ubmarine was still under way on the easterly course. Vopatek prepared to make bombing run but withheld his attack because of interference by the tracking of ther planes. At 1000 hours, Spears, the senior patrol plane commander, informed he *Vanoc* that the planes had a very good contact at the easterly end of the line f float lights and requested it to attack. The ship complied and moved in toward he position, while the planes continued to track in order to inform the ship of he latest position of the target. At 1028 hours, the destroyer fired a patter of 24 edgehog contact bombs. Following the attack, the destroyer that the results of its ttack were negative and that it had lost contact.

Vopatek making a second attempt at a bombing run, obtained an M.A.D signal mmediately after the attack by the destroyer, but since both the submarine and the lestroyer caused this signal, he didn't release his bombs. At 1030 hours, Plane No. 3 again obtained a good M.A.D. signal, but the float light intended to mark the position failed to fire; the planes then lost contact. It is probably that the submarine, f not too severely damaged by the retro-bombs, again took evasive action after earing the explosions from the destroyer's depth charges exploding bombs.

The British frigates *Affleck*, *Balfour* and *Core* now arrived on the scene from the vest. Plane No. 8 dropped a one-hour marine marker at the estimated position of he submarine and Spears informed the ships of the last contact of the planes and he estimated course and speed of the submarine. The frigates formed in a line and proceeded eastward at slow speed. At 1145 hours, the *Affleck* reported a possible contact, which was lost and then regained at 1200 hours and then warned the aircraft to stay clear while it attacked. The planes climbed to 500 feet (152 meters), while the *Affleck* continued east at slow speed and at 1212 hours, fired a pattern of 24 hedgehog bombs forward of its bow. It informed the planes that it had completed its attack, and the planes reduced altitude to resume M.A.D. search. Meanwhile the *Affleck* launched a boat, and crew rowed out and picked up debris on the surface at the point of its attack.

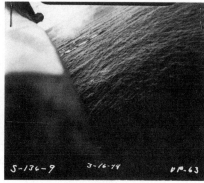

Attack on *U-392* on 16 March 1944 shows splashes from retro-bombs launched from 63-P-8. Th
submarine's crew of 52 perished with the submarine near the Strait of Gibraltar. (National Archives)

Oil and bubbles appeared on the surface followed by personnel aboard the Britisl
warships gathering pieces of wood, later identified as locker tops from the enemy
U-boat, and substantial pieces of human flesh. The *Affleck* later reported that it hearc
three distinct explosions five seconds after its hedgehog contact bombs struck the watei
One minute after the attack, a loud underwater explosion took place, possibly from
the U-boat's torpedoes exploding or from the vessel imploding. Twenty-four-year-olc
Oberleutnant zur See Schümann and his crew remain on the Mediterranean's floor.[5]

On May 15, the effectiveness of M.A.D.-equipped aircraft was again demon-
strated when Oberleutnant zur See Graf Alexander von Keller's Type VIIC *U-73*
attempted to make a daylight-submerged passage through the straits and into the
Mediterranean. Plane No. 12, Lieutenant (jg) M. J. Vopatek and Plane No. 1
Lieutenant H. L. Worrell, patrol plane commander, were flying the "fence" in the
Straits north of Point Malabata that afternoon, when two Spanish fishing vessels
were sighted approaching the area from the west. The planes left the "fence" to
investigate but nothing seemed unusual. They were proceeding at a speed of eight
to ten knots and passed by the south end of the patrol on an easterly course.
About twelve minutes later, while on a northerly heading, plane No. 12 obtained
an M.A.D. signal near Gibraltar; meanwhile, plane No. 1 on a southerly heading
immediately crossed over and obtained contact. The planes then proceeded with
cloverleaf tracking which resulted in a line of float lights showing the submarine
to be on an east-northeasterly course.

Vopatek called the British surface vessels in the area by voice and requested them
to close the position. Plane No. 12 then launched a sonobuoy, but did not have
reception from it, although Plane No. 1 tuned in on it and heard definite propeller
noises. The planes continued to track, and the line of floats showed the submarine
to be continuing on the same course at a speed of four to fine knots. At 1530 hours,
Plane No. 12 made a bombing run and Vopatek fired 30 retro-bombs in three
ripples of ten each on a good M.A.D. signal. The position of this attack was one

A pilot and ground crewman prior to the departure of PBY-5A 63-P-14 Bureau Number 08437 from NAF Port Lyautey during 1944. Note the radar antenna next to number 1 and the U-boat kill marking forward of the cockpit. (Mark Aldrich)

and one-fourth miles east of the initial contact. Following the attack by Plane No. 2, crews of both planes observed a number of pieces of splintered wood floating in the water at the position of the attack.

The planes continued cloverleaf tracking, and the signals obtained showed that the submarine was still under way on about the same course. Vopatek then launched three additional sonobuoys but couldn't pick up submarine sounds. The first radioman of Plane No. 1 however, again reported picking up screw noises from the buoy. This was before the arrival of any surface craft.

At 1550 hours, the first surface vessel was approaching from the east and Lieutenant Worrell in Plane No. 1 proceeded to attack while the area remained clear. At 1552 hours, he fired 24 retro-bombs on three ripples of eight on good M.A.D. contact off Tangier, French Morocco. One sizeable piece of wood, having the appearance of new lumber, was spotted on the surface following the attack. The escort craft, HMS *Kilmarnock*, and *Blackfly*, an armed trawler, and *Aubriettia*, arrived in the area shortly after the attack by Plane No. 1. The planes continued with cloverleaf tracking and instructed the ships by voice communication to make attacks ahead of the easterly end of the line of float lights.

At 1630 hours, the *Blackfly* made an attack with depth charges, followed a few minutes later by an attack by the *Kilmarnock*. The *Blackfly* then attacked again, but these attacks were all off target and indicated the ships were fooled by *U-731* deploying a BOLD sonar decoy called "submarine bubble target" by the Allies, a canister filled with calcium hydride that, when mixed with salt water, emitted a large quantity of

A VP-63 Catalina lifting off from Gibraltar circa 1944. Detachments of U.S. patrol aircraft would ba...
from Gibraltar during poor weather conditions at NAF Port Lyautey. (Mark Aldrich)

gas bubbles. The aircraft continued to track and to mark accurately the successiv...
positions of the submerged submarine so that the surface vessels could attack at th...
correct position. The pilots requested the ships to conduct attacks at the positio...
marked by the float light rather than at ASDIC contacts (the ship's sonar).

M.A.D. tracking was continuous until the *Kilmarnock* hoisted a pennant warnin...
of an imminent hedgehog attack, when the aircraft withdrew to avoid from being h...
by hedgehogs due to their considerably high trajectory. The final M.A.D. contact wit...
the submarine, obtained by Plane No. 1 at 1648 hours, appeared to be stronger tha...
any previous, indicating that the submarine was probably coming to the surface. Th...
Kilmarnock fired its hedgehog bombs three minutes later at a position immediatel...
ahead of the line of float lights, the exact point where the submarine should hav...
been at that time. The crews of both planes two minutes later observed underwate...
explosions and saw two great bubbles of air rise to the surface. A large stationary o...
slick appeared and continued to increase in size during the evening until it was mor...
than a mile (1.6 kilometers) in length and about 200 yards wide (183 meters). B...
the next day, it had spread over a distance of 12 miles (19 kilometers) in the Straits...
The attack left no survivors amongst the complement of 54 men.

Naval patrol squadrons continued operating in the Mediterranean but scored n...
further victories against German submarines. Squadrons VP-63, VP-92, and VB-12...
sank four of the 63 U-boats lost in the Mediterranean between July 1943 and Ma...
1944 while VGS-27 and VP-92 sank two unfortunate Vichy French submarine...
between November 11 and 12, 1942.

CHAPTER 8

Fleet Air Wing Seven Operations (August 1943–May 1945)

"The Bay (Biscay) is the trunk of the Atlantic U-boat menace, and the branches spreading far and wide, to the North Atlantic convoys, to the Caribbean, to the eastern seaboard of North America."

AIR MARSHAL SIR JOHN SLESSOR, C-IN-C COASTAL COMMAND,
MEMO TO COMBINED CHIEFS OF STAFF APRIL 1943

On July 8, 1943, the *Madcats* of VP-63 became the first Fleet Air Wing Seven squadron to operate from the United Kingdom after Admiral King sent secret dispatch 082220 to Royal E. Ingersoll, Commander in Chief, Atlantic Fleet. The dispatch directed the squadron to report to Commander, U.S. Naval Forces in Europe, for temporary assignment with British Coastal Command for Bay of Biscay anti-submarine operations (the temporary assignment of FAW-7 squadrons originally had a termination date November 1, 1943 but was rescinded for the duration.

The Americans and British developed a new strategy of increasing the number and presence of patrol aircraft in England with the mission of hunting German submarines as the boats left their bases in France, thus stopping them before they could enter the shipping lanes. AIRCINCLANT selected FAW-7's VP-63 and VB-103 as the first transfers to the UK. There were two primary reasons for sending FAW-7 units to England. First, because the Germans had adopted countermeasures against Allied patrol aircraft, the number of losses among aircraft and men were rising and this required additional reinforcements. Secondly, increasing the number of patrol aircraft would result in additional U-boat kills by broadening the area of operations. Consequently, a wider search area would force U-boats to travel greater distances submerged and they would have to surface to recharge batteries thus exposing themselves to patrol aircraft.

VP-63 under the command of Lieutenant Commander E. O. Wagner reported for duty with 15 PBY-5 aircraft at Pembroke Dock, Wales operations over the Bay of Biscay. The transfer of additional FAW-7 units to England intensified during the second week of August 1943 when Captain William H. Hamilton (later promoted to Commodore), Commander FAW-7, issued Operational Order 2-43 on July 13, 1943.

Hamilton's order ended the Wing's ASW efforts from Argentia and directed several wing squadrons to deploy to the British Isles. In short, the entire Argentia Air Group, except for Coast Guard Squadron VP-6, would begin deploying to the United Kingdom. Meanwhile in England, Air Marshal, Sir John Slessor, Commander-in-Chief of Coastal Command, issued secret dispatch 122120 that directed the movement of Army and Navy anti-submarine squadrons to bases in Britain. The RAF directed the USAAF's Fourth and Nineteenth Squadrons of the 479th Anti-submarine Group to base at Dunkeswell in Devon, England while VB-103, as the U.S. Navy's first heavy bombing squadron to operate from the UK, would initially operate from St. Eval in Cornwall. The Air Force's 479th would remain with Coastal Command until Navy Liberator squadrons were up to operational strength.

U-boats operating in the Atlantic were nearly all based in French ports on the Bay of Biscay. The Royal Air Force and Army Air Force B-24 Squadrons, with assistance from naval surface units, had been attacking U-boats on passage through the Bay of Biscay to and from their bases. It was an aggressive operation with a considerable number of U-boats sunk while impairing the effectiveness of those who did manage to evade the gauntlet by forcing them to make a large part of their passage through the Bay of Biscay submerged. Consequently, U-boat crews began experiencing lower morale and general aggressiveness knowing that a growing number of their brethren were falling victims to Allied aircraft. Coastal Command wanted to keep it that way.

U-boat crews called the Bay of Biscay the "valley of death" with some 69 German submarines being lost in the body of water that lies between Western France and Northern Spain. Frequent, violent storms in the bay made surface and air operations difficult to conduct, and a number of whale species inhabiting the area were often confused with submarines. Moreover, military personnel unfortunate to find themselves swimming in the Bay after surviving the loss of their ship or aircraft had a reduced chance of surviving the frigid water long enough for a rescue.

Unlike U-boat operations in the Atlantic and Caribbean in which the crews could only count on themselves to defend or elude prowling warships and aircraft, the Germans adopted three major countermeasures to address Allied ASW operations in the English Channel and Bay of Biscay. First, the Luftwaffe sent the long-range, twin-engine, Junkers JU-88 fighter out to intercept Allied patrol aircraft. Secondly, some U-boats were equipped with additional anti-aircraft weapons. The boats called Flak ships (submarines fitted with additional antiaircraft guns), sometimes operating in groups of three, posed a formidable opponent for a single patrol planes. Third, the Germans would target warships working together as hunter-killer groups with aircraft, some equipped with radio-guided bombs. Consequently, between mid-1943 and early 1944, the threat from German patrol and fighter aircraft forced Allied ships to reduce their operations in the English Channel and Bay of Biscay.

While American and British military officials ironed out the problems of supporting U.S. Naval Air Forces, Captain Hamilton on August 23, 1943 sent Secret Dispatch 211756 to Vice Admiral Patrick N. Bellinger, Commander Air

Delivery of the Glenn L. Martin PBM-1, the first production series of the Mariner, began in October 940 with VP-55. Shown here is P-55-1 circa 1940. (Mark Aldrich)

A PBM-1 Mariner of VP-56 in 1941. Delivery of the Martin PBM-1 Mariner to the squadron, only 20 were built, began in December 1940. (Mark Aldrich)

Martin PBM 1 of VP-55, which later became VP-74, during late 1940 somewhere along the Eastern Seaboard. Armament of the PBM-1 consisted of five .50-caliber machine guns. (Mark Aldrich)

A Martin PBM-1 of VP-74 on take-off in March 1942 has an overall blue-gray coloration with light gray lower surfaces that replaced the pre-war metal and yellow paint scheme. (Mark Aldrich)

Martin PBM-3 NAS at NAS Banana River, Florida during May 1943. PBMs based at Banana River were part of Fleet Air Wing Twelve headquartered in Miami. (Mark Aldrich)

A PBM-3 on the plane ramp NAS Pensacola, Florida c.1944. The PBM-3 replaced the PBM-1, 2-series didn't enter production, and the Martin company produced 679 of the -3 series. (Bill Derby via Mark Aldrich)

AS Norfolk circa 1944 showing a ramp area of PBM-3C, PBM-3D, and PBM-3S Mariners. The PBM-S was used exclusively in the Atlantic and Caribbean for anti-submarine operations. (Mark Aldrich)

ngine start-up on a PBM-3S in the Caribbean with one sailor standing by with a fire extinguisher in ase the engine catches fire. The Glenn Martin Company produced 94 of the -3s model and converted 2 PBM-3C Mariners. (Mark Aldrich)

Two mechanics working on a Martin PBM-3S Mariner radar housing, containing the AN-APS-15 search radar, on the ramp at NAS Norfolk in 1945. (Steve Ginter via Mark Aldrich)

PBM Mariner taxiing on the water at a Brazilian air station circa 1945 with three other Mariners in the background. U.S., Brazilian naval and air forces by late 1944 had no enemy submarines to hunt in the South Atlantic. (Naval Historical Center via Mark Aldrich)

An Aviation Machinist Mate refueling a Consolidated PBY-5 at NAS Corpus Christi, Texas, circa 194? while another PBY taxis out for a training flight. (National Archives)

A PBY-5A of VP-63 at NAS Port Lyautey, French Morocco, during 1944. Known as the *MAD CATS*, onducted ASW operations over the Bay of Biscay, Mediterranean, and the English Channel. (Mark Aldrich)

A PBY-5A of VP-92 at Port Lyautey in the squadron operated from 6 April to 4 December 1943. Afterwards, Navy Auxiliary Airfield, Agadir in Morocco was base of operations from 5 December 1943 :o 28 February 1944. (National Museum of the U.S. Air Force via Mark Aldrich)

A U.S. Coast Guard PBY-5A of VP-6 at Greenland during the war. The squadron carried out the sam missions as naval patrol squadrons. (Mark Aldrich)

Engine start-up of a Lockheed PV-1 Ventura NAF Natal, Brazil circa 1944-45. This is a later version with the .50-caliber "chin" machine gun package located under the aircraft's nose. (National Archives via Mark Aldrich)

Another view of a Brazilian-based PV-1 Ventura showing the three .50-caliber machine gun ports under the nose and one of two .50-caliber machines fixed on top of the forward fuselage in front of the cockpit (National Archives via Mark Aldrich)

A Navy Aviation Ordnanceman feeding a belt of .50-caliber machine-gun bullets into the Erco bow turret on a VB-107 PB4Y-1 Liberator base in Brazil circa 1944-45. VB-107 was the only Navy PB4Y-1 squadron based in Brazil during the war. (National Archives)

An early D-model PB4Y-1 of VB-103 outward bound for an anti-submarine patrol from Dunkeswell, England, during the late summer and fall of 1943. VB/VPB-103, VB/VPB-105, VPB-107, VB/VPB-110, VB-111, VPB-112, and VPB-114 operated from England. (National Archives)

An F4F/FM-2 Wildcat fighter preparing to launch from an escort carrier. The national insignia on this aircraft appeared only from June to August 1943. (National Archives)

A largely forgotten part of anti-submarine operations in World War II was that of squadrons that operated the Douglas SBD-5 Dauntless used as a scout plane and dive bomber. Squadrons equipped with this aircraft scored no victories against enemy submarines in the Atlantic but did locate some, thus helping to keep enemy submarines on the defensive. (Tailhook Association)

Operating from Southwestern England, U.S. Navy PB4Y-1 Liberator "C" B-3 of VB-103 heading towards the Bay of Biscay. Note, the PB4Y-1 was the U.S. Navy's designation of the B-24. Most patrols lasted 10–12 hours before returning to England. (National Archives)

Vice Admiral Patrick N.L. Bellinger, became the Commander-in-Chief Naval Air Forces Atlantic Fleet in March 1943. (Photo by Maurice Constant in 1943, U.S. Naval History and Heritage Command via Leahy Collection).

Force, Atlantic Fleet, with FAW-7 European Theater Detachment Operation Plan No. 1-43. This established the Dunkeswell Air Group consisting of PB4Y-l Liberator Bombing Squadrons 103 and later VB-105, and the St. David's Group, consisting of Bombing Squadrons VB-110 and VB-111. The group's mission-prosecute offensive ASW operations by conducting and supporting Bay of Biscay operations under the operational control of British authorities. Cooperate with British Isle forces in the protection of British Isles against enemy action or infiltration.[2]

American and British command made to establish FAW-7 Headquarters at the Area Combined Headquarters in Plymouth, England where the headquarters of the Royal Navy Commander-in-Chief and the Commanding Officer of No.19 Group of Coastal Command were located. The Royal Navy Commander in Chief had command of the Royal Navy Forces operating in the Bay of Biscay, western part of the English Channel, and Southwest approaches to the British Isles. The Commander of No. 19 Group had command of the Coastal Command planes operating from bases in Southwest Britain with patrol areas in the Bay of Biscay, English Channel, and adjacent waters. Since Plymouth made tactical decisions concerning the disposition of aircraft in the offensive against U-boats, the Wing Commander and his British counterparts could maintain close communication.

There were two primary reasons for British operational control over FAW-7 squadrons. First, the initial commitment of U.S. Navy Air Forces was but a small fraction of the total number of planes used in the offensive and, because the British had a complicated command organization, which had achieved considerable amount of success, an independent U.S. Navy command would only complicate matters. Secondly, the general rule at the time was that the nation supplying the largest forces in an area would usually supply the commanding officer in the area and all units would come under his command.

On August 15, 1943, Lieutenant Commander Easton and his squadron VB-103 began the movement across the Atlantic with 13 PB4Y-1 Liberators departing Argentia for St. Eval, England. Nearly three months would pass before the opportunity to engage the enemy transpired. The Dunkeswell Air Group's first successful attack on a U-boat occurred on November 10, 1943 when VB-l05's Lieutenant Leonard E. Harmon in Liberator "R", while on anti-submarine patrol sighted and attacked the surfaced *U-966*, commanded by Oberleutnant zur See Eckehard Wolf in the Bay of Biscay. Earlier that morning a British Wellington bomber of No. 612 Squadron attacked the boat with depth bombs causing damage to the periscope, motors, clutches, and drive shafts. Wolf's men repaired the damage and the submarine resumed a course towards the Atlantic only two have a Wellington of No. 407 Squadron arrive, which was shot down killing the bomber's six-man crew. At 0857 hours, Lieutenant Harmon closed in for an attack with depth bombs.

Checking the depth charges aboard a Navy PB4Y-1 Liberator of Fleet Air Wing Seven circa 1944. Navy Liberators could carry both depth charges and the Mk-24 acoustic torpedo for ASW work. (National Archives)

Intense anti-aircraft from the U-boat greeted the Liberator causing damage to the bomb bay doors and the bomb-release circuit and Lieutenant Harmon was unable to drop his explosives. However, he pressed on the attack and continued a running battle against the enemy submarine with the PB4Y-1's gunners firing 1,500 to 2,000 rounds of .50 caliber machine gun fire until a shortage of fuel forced a return to base. Three hours later, at 1145 hours, Liberator "E" of VB-103 piloted by Lieutenant (jg) Kenneth L. Wright appeared on the scene. Despite some anti-aircraft fire, Lieutenant Wright took the PB4Y-1 down and dropped five 325-pound depth charges with one landing close to the U-boat's port side. Circling around the Liberator's gunner strafed as *U-966* began settling by the stern and trailing oil. At 1305 hours a Liberator from VB-110 flown by Lieutenant W. W. Parish dropped six depth charges with one hitting the water 30 feet from the submarine's starboard side. A Czech Liberator of No. 311 Squadron, specially fitted with rocket launchers, sealed *U-966*'s fate at 1345 hours as the combination of depth charges and rockets damaged the submarine making it impossible to dive

Subsequently, Wolf ordered it scuttled two miles off the Spanish coast and 42 of the 50-man crew swam to shore or were picked up by Spanish fishing boats.

Two days later, during the night of November 12, VB-103 chalked up another U-boat kill, at the cost of an entire aircrew. While flying north of Cape Penas, Spain, Lieutenant (jg) Ralph B. Brownell in Liberator B-3 "C" named *Calvert & Coke* (Bureau Number 32032) spotted the Type IXC *U-508* running on the surface and apparently attacked the vessel. This submarine wasn't on her first patrol, but on its sixth, and her crew were combat veterans. Commanded by Kapitänleutnant Georg Staats, during the CT-boat's previous patrols, it netted 14 ships totaling 78,000 tons and earned the skipper the Knight's Cross.

Type VIIC *U-966* under attack by a VB-103 Liberator piloted by Lieutenant Kenneth Wright on 10 November 1943. The sinking of *U-966* off Porto de Bares, Spain was a combined effort of American, British, and Czechoslovakian aircrews. (National Archives)

Kenneth Wright number 8 flight crew who participated in the attack on *U-966*. Back row left to right: Carlton Lillie, Robert Zabic, and Kenneth Wright. Lawrence "Pete" Peterson. Robert Lacey. Front row: Richard McDaniel, William (Bill) Middleton. Bernie Faubian, Thomas Ryan, and Robert Erdman. Dunkeswell Memorial Museum)

VB-105 and VB-110 Liberators attacked a U-boat on 18 June 1944 when a Schnorchel was spotted. The unknown submarine apparently survived the attack. The Schnorchel allowed U-boats equipped with such a device to stay submerged for a longer period. (Dunkeswell Memorial Museum)

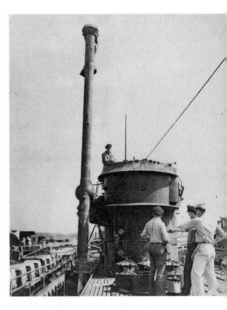

The Schnorchel in the extended position of a U-boat that surrendered to the Americans after Germany lost the war. The air intake was a relatively small target but not enough for the sharp eyes of aircrew aboard patrolling Allied aircraft. (National Archives)

Approaching the target, Lieutenant Brownell made his only call to base "Am over enemy submarine in position…" then the transmission ended. Perhaps at that point the bomber was under anti-aircraft fire and Brownell was committed to an attack with depth charges. For whatever reason, *Calvert & Coke* and its crew didn't make it back to base. The squadron sent aircraft piloted by Lieutenants Willis and Muckenthaler to search for the missing crew following day but they only revealed two-oil slicks, one large and one small, five miles apart, near Brownell's last transmission. The slicks strongly suggesting the final resting-place of the hunter and hunted. After reviewing intercepted radio transmissions from the Germans regarding *U-508*, the British Admiralty credited the Liberator's crew and the U.S. Navy awarded Brownell the Navy Cross.

It wasn't until the end of January 1944 that the Dunkeswell Group successfully attacked and sank an enemy submarine with VB-103 sinking a U-boat, while they flew cover for convoys SC-151 and ON-221 on the twenty-eighth. Lieutenant George A. Enloe, pilot of the PB4Y-1 "B-5" named The *Bloody Miracle*, caught Kapitänleutnant Kun Barleben's fully surfaced *U-271* west of Limerick, Ireland. The engagement would include the earliest sighting of a U-boat fitted with a Schnorchel. Aboard the plane sat Francis "Red" Dean, inside the small confines of the tail turret recounted the mission.

The tail turret was a particularly cold place. When the plane is in the air and the waist hatches are open so the waist guns can be moved into firing position, the air comes in through the hatches and out through the tail turret. To make matters worse, we removed the doors from the tail turret so it is easier to get out if an emergency arose. This left the full force of the air from the waist hatches to come directly against the tail gunner's back.[4]

Meanwhile, at his desk in the navigator's compartment, Ensign Emrick Pohling stood up, stretched, and walked over to the starboard waist hatch and, as he did so, he yelled over the intercom, "I see something in the water at two o'clock, it looks like a submarine".

Looking out his window, Enloe confirmed Pohling's observation and began turning and putting the bomber into a steep dive Barleben's gunners began firing as the bomber came within range, puncturing the plane's fuselage. As the PB4Y-1 approached the target, some 500 yards (152 meters) away, the bombardier Dallas Jones, ACOM (AB) [Air Bombardier], opened the bomb bay doors and released the six depth charges as Enloe flew the plane across the U-boat at an altitude of 50 feet (15 meters). "Red" Dean returned fire with his turret's twin .50 caliber guns but couldn't get on target as the plane was moving too fast.

Being in the tail turret[,] I had a full view of the submarine as we passed over it. The six depth charges straddled the sub, three landed just short of the port side; the fourth almost landed on the deck and the other two went in just over the starboard side. As the plane pulled up out of the dive, the charges started going off. The number-three depth charge had gone under the sub before it exploded. They had been set for a depth of 30 feet [9 m] and as they exploded, they lifted most of the sub right out of the water.[5]

As the U-boat began sinking by the stern, Enloe turned the Liberator around and prepared to drop a Mk-24 torpedo; however, the vessel was still above the water, and the torpedo couldn't be dropped. As the U-boat slipped beneath the waves, Enloe wanted to make sure of the submarine's destruction and ordered the sonobuoys dropped. The radioman, Clifton M. LeMarr (Aviation Radioman First Class), reported a positive contact and the pilot released a Mk-24 torpedo, called Zombie in the European Theater. A few minutes later, LeMarr heard a tremendous explosion inside his headset. The Liberator circled for 30 minutes but the crew spotted debris and Enloe pointed the plane towards the convoy. Later in the day, Enloe and his crew headed back to Dunkeswell where, after landing, the crew began their debriefing and told their story on the attack to an assembly of U.S. Navy and R.A.F. officers. As the debriefing officers concluded the questioning, one of them asked if the crew had seen anything unusual about the U-boat. Dean, then 19 years old, decided to tell them something he saw that was different about the vessel.

I stated that there were two periscopes on the submarine's conning tower. An R.A.F. officer asked me to explain what I meant two periscopes. I repeated there were two very distinct poles extending upward from the conning tower, which looked like periscopes. With this statement, a U.S. Navy Admiral in an annoyed voice stated that German submarines only have one periscope, and since the submarine was on the surface, the periscope would not be in the raised position. I answered that this submarine did have two periscopes and they were

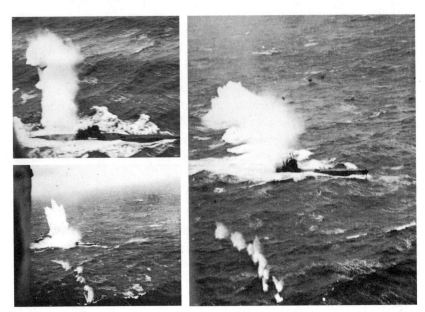

Three images showing Type VIIC *U-271* under attack by Lieutenant George E. Enloe and crew of VB-103 on 28 January 1944 off Limerick, Ireland. The submarine and her complement of 52 men commanded by Kapitänleutnant Curt Barlebern were lost when the Liberator sank her with six depth charges. (Dunkeswell Memorial Museum)

both in the raised position. The Admiral in loud voice said, "I repeat. German submarines do not have two periscopes you are mistaken, again."

I thought to myself, with all that gold braid on the Admiral's arm, I must have been mistaken and said no more.[6]

After the debriefing, the crew waited for the development of photographs that Roy "Slim" Carter (Aviation Machinist Mate Third Class) had taken during the attack while precariously hanging out the port waist hatch. The lab delivered photographs, which besides showing the depth charges lifting the submarine out of the water, showed what appeared to be two periscopes extending from the conning tower proving Dean's observation. However, he never did get an apology from the Admiral.

Five months of patrols followed for the men of FAW-7 without a successful interception of an enemy submarine. D-Day arrived on June 6 and wing aircraft provided aerial reconnaissance of the landing beaches while watching for German surface ships, submarines, and aircraft.[7] U-boat increased substantially as D-Day unfolded with FAW-7 Liberators conducting 11 attacks between June 8 and 23, with most of the action occurring on June 13, 22, and 23. Lieutenant Spalding's crew from VB-110 sank Type VIIB *U-988* in the English Channel off Cherbourg. The crew received no credit at the time but the submarine and its complement of 50 did not return.[8]

On July 8, the attack on *U-243* began when a Sunderland of No.10 Squadron spotted the fully surfaced submarine, commanded by Kapitänleutnant Hans Marten, at 1435 hours, off La Rochelle. A depth charge attack left the sub dead in the water

A pair of PB4Y-1 Liberators from VB-103 over the Bay of Biscay fall 1943. In the background is B-3 "C" Navy Bureau Number 32032 named *Calvert & Coke*, shown previously on page 125. She and her crew were lost on 12 November 1943 while attacking *U-508*. (Dunkeswell Memorial Museum)

and by 1500 hours, the sub crew began abandoning ship. At 1441 hours, Cooledge's PB4Y-1 was flying at an altitude of 800 feet (244 meters) when the radar operator reported a contact dead ahead at a distance of 8 miles (13 kilometers). Three minutes later, the submarine came into view along with a British Sunderland flying boat trailing behind the boat. Cooledge decided to attack at once and ordered battle stations as the PB4Y-1 approached from the submarine's port quarter at a speed of 200 miles per hour (322 kilometers per hour). Coming in at 200 feet (61 meters), the puffs of the U-boat's anti-aircraft fire began to appear in front and to the sides of the approaching Liberator and a number of explosions from bursting shells rocked the aircraft.

As the Liberator came within range, his top and bow turrets opened fire, scoring numerous hits on the U-boat's conning tower. Cooledge pressed the bomb release button, but nothing happened. The pilot pulled up and into a left turn while the equipment was checked, to determine why the depth charges didn't drop. It appeared to be in working order, and a second attack began at 150 feet (46 meters) altitude and the bomber directly passed over the U-boat's bow. The submarine's antiaircraft fire was noticeably weaker, but still accurate enough to bounce the approaching plane. Cooledge pressed the bomb release button and again the depth charges failed to release. The pilot pulled up and into a left turn while a crewman checked the equipment to determine why the bomb release malfunctioned. The circuits appeared to be in working order and the bomber went in for second run at 150 feet (46 meters), crossing directly over the U-boat's bow. The release mechanism failed again. Meanwhile, the Sunderland continued circling waiting to attack, as the Liberator began a third run. When the plane was in a favorable position for starting a bow attack, Lieutenant Cooledge turned and started his attack run. Just after he did so, he sighted a second Sunderland below and ahead of him also in an attack run. The interval between the planes was sufficient for both planes to make attacks without interference so the run was continued. The explosions from the Sunderland's depth charges raised a plume of water nearly 200 feet (61 meters) high and obscured any view of the submarine as the blast tossed the Liberator violently upward. As the plume subsided, the submarine again became visible on the far side of the explosion area. The Liberator now descended to about 80 feet (24 meters) altitude and at a speed of 200 miles per hour (322 kilometers per hour). As the plane reached the release point, Cooledge pressed both his own release button along with the co-pilot's and, this time the explosives fell away from the plane. The charges detonated at a predetermined depth with the twin plumes of water created by the explosions obscuring the target. The bombs fell along the starboard side of the submarine approximately 25 feet (7.6 meters) from the stern and somewhat more near the bow. The co-pilot, sitting in the bomb bay, was able to watch the bombs fall and enter the water close alongside the U-boat. The submarines rose vertically into the air as *U-243* began its death plunge stern first. Ships of the Fourteenth Escort Group homed in by the British flying boat, rescued 38 of the submarine's crew, including the mortally wounded Kapitänleutnant Martens. After the destruction of the *U-243* the Dunkeswell Air Group settled in for nearly six months of routine patrols as the Allies consolidated their positions in France and U-boat contacts diminished as the submarines began evacuating from their French bases starting in August.

By March 1945, with Germany's situation deteriorating rapidly, Coastal Command called on the squadron s for extra alertness and diligence in their patrol work. Lieutenant R. N. Field on 12 March, of VPB-103, spotted fully surfaced *U-681* a Type VIIC boat, under the command of Oberleutnant zur See Werner Gebauer Southwest of the Scilly Islands, a set of five small islands 28 miles (45 kilometers) off Land's End at the tip of Cornwall, England, the submarine had run aground while attempting to enter St Mary's damaging its hull and screws. Gebauer managed to bring the *U-681* to the surface but it wouldn't dive, a very dangerous predicament. Therefore the Uboat's captain decided that the safest bet was to head for neutral Ireland and internment. Gebauer and his crew didn't get the chance as Field's bomber came in low and fast, dropping a string of eight depth charges. The concussion from the explosions began flooding the boat and Gebauer decided to abandon ship Of the *U-681*'s 49 crewmembers, 38 managed to pile into dinghies while

This is PB4Y-1 "M" B-12 Bureau Number 32282 flown by Crew 7 of VB-110 during 1944. Coloration is navy blue on upper surfaces and light gull gray on sides and lower surfaces. It has the Erco bow turret that became standard on Navy Liberators. (Dunkeswell Memorial Museum)

demolition charges were set, and vents opened. As the American aircrew and the German submariners watched, the submarine slipped beneath the waves.

The Nazi regime was in its final weeks of existence, yet German submariners continued to operate offensively only, in many cases, spotted visually or by airborne radar from Allied planes. On April 25, VPB-103's Crew 5 led by Lieutenant Dwight D. Nott, sighted and attacked a submarine while on patrol southwest of the Brest Peninsula. This submarine previously identified as *U-326* was actually Type VIIC/41 *U-1107*, commanded by Kapitänleutnant Fritz Parduhn, which, eight days earlier, sank the two merchant ships *Cyrus H. McCormick* (7,100 tons) and *Empire Gold* (8,000 tons) sailing as part of convoy HX-348. Six members of *McCormick's* compliment of 53 perished while only four of *Empire Gold's* crew of 47 survived. On board Liberator K-103 was "Dick" Alsop.

> Our crew got in 43 missions at Dunkeswell. There were those long 24 hour duty stretches from Ops Chow [dining before and after a mission] to the briefing, loading the equipment, getting air borne, completing the patrol, debriefing, Ops Chow again, unloading the plane, and then secure until noon the next day. That is, if everything went according to plan, which it didn't.[9]

At 1938 hours, the co-pilot Lieutenant (jg) Robinson and R. L. Page (Aviation Ordnanceman Third Class), the starboard waist gunner looked out, and sighted a Schnorchel at a distance of two miles. The aircraft was flying at 800 feet (244 meters) and Lieutenant Nott immediately chopped the throttles and started a turn to starboard in order to deliver an attack. Nott sharpened his turn to starboard, keeping the target in view, at the same time reducing speed and altitude in order to set up for an attack. The Schnorchel continued on the same course and speed, apparently not aware of

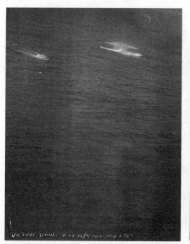

The attack and sinking of Type VIIC/41 *U-1107* on 25 April 1945 by Crew 5 of VPB-103 commanded by Lieutenant Dwight D. Nott. The three areas of water disturbance are indicative of the Mk-24 acoustic torpedo locating and detonating causing rapid loss of air pressure inside the submarine. The second image shows a large amount of oil rising to the surface. The sinking occurred off Brest, France and the crew of 37 perished. (Dunkeswell Memorial Museum)

the aircraft' a presence. The Liberator's approach and attack took place at 1940 hours with the pilot dropping two Mk-24 Zombies with maximum intervalometer setting of 150 feet (46 meters) at an altitude of 200 feet (61 meters). After the torpedoes were away, Nott continued a straight heading for 20 seconds before making a turn to starboard for a return heading to the point of impact. While the Liberator turned, the torpedoes homed in on the submarine's heading and a moment later, a large explosion occurred and the Schnorchel jumped five feet into the air and then disappear. Alsop remembers dropping the sonobuoys to track the submarine's path,

> Just a few seconds too late to pick up the sub's engine sounds but we did record a significant amount of underwater breaking up noises. At least that is what the Navy intelligence people in D.C. determined after they heard the tape. There was no chance for survivors.[10]

After circling explosion for several minutes, Lieutenant Nott and his crew continued sowing a standard 1,550-yard (1417 meters) sonobuoy pattern, completing it at 1954 hours. At 2015 hours, the crew observed an oil patch extending over an area of 150 yards (137 meters) in diameter approximately 250 yards (229 meters) south-southwest of the position of the explosion.

The last successful attack destruction of a U-boat by a UK-based American naval patrol plane by took place on April 30, when PBY-5A (Bureau No. 48318) with Lieut. F. F. Lake as patrol plane commander, attacked Type VIIIC *U-326* on

Lieutenant Dwight D. Nott Crew 5 VB-103 taken before leaving for England in 1944. They were responsible for sinking *U-1107*. Back row left to right: Robert Mayer (left crew before going to England), Renfro Pace, D.C. Pinholster, R.H. Roberts, Marco Vaccher, James R. Alsop, and Joseph Kirchdorfer. Front row left to right: left crew before leaving for England (replaced by Ensign K. Robinson), Lieutenant Dwight D. Nott, and Ensign John S. Walker. D.C. Pinholster served with VP-32 and sank *U-359* on 28 July 1943. (Dunkeswell Memorial Museum)

its first patrol under the command of Oberleutnant zur See Peter Matthes. While the submarine was sighted visually upon spotting a Schnorkel the attack was made due to a positive M.A.D. signal. There was one explosion resulting in considerable debris, and oil slick, which continued to expand, and it was impossible to secure M.A.D. signals after the attack. There were no survivors.

Two U-boats surrendering to a PB4Y-1 of Fleet Air Wing PB4Y-1 Liberators after Germany's surrender. Top: Type VIIC *U-249* surrendering on 10 May 1945 off Portland Isle located in the English Channel. Bottom: Type VIIC *U-825* surrendering at Loch Eriboll, Scotland on 13 May 1945. (Dunkeswell Memorial Museum)

Planes from VB-114, which normally operated out of the Portuguese-held Azores, were required to display dual national decals. Note the Leigh Light used to spot enemy submarines at night. Detachments of PB4Y-1 aircraft and crews from VB-111 and VPB-112 briefly operated as well from England between 1943 and 1945. (Dunkeswell Memorial Museum)

CHAPTER 9

Escort Carrier Operations
(April–December 1943)

"Escort carriers had many nicknames, only a few tinged with anything resembling affection: jeep carriers, baby flattops, Woolworth flattops, Kaiser coffins, one-torpedo ships. Wags in the fleet deadpanned that the acronym CVE stood the carrier's three most salient characteristics: combustible, vulnerable, expendable."

JAMES D. HORNFISCHER, *THE LAST STAND OF THE TIN CAN SAILORS: THE EXTRAORDINARY*
WORLD WAR II STORY OF THE U.S. NAVY'S FINEST HOUR

The dark characterization of escort carriers written by James Hornfischer does have its merits as the U.S. Navy lost five escort carriers through enemy action in the Pacific Theater and others suffered battle damage. American shipbuilding companies produced 124 of them during the war between 1942 and 1945. They lacked speed, armor-belts, and adequate anti-aircraft defenses compared to heavy carriers of the day. The typically length of 500 feet (150m) was approximately 400 feet (122m) shorter than heavy carriers and with a displacement over one-third smaller (8,000 compared to 30,000 tons). An escort's complement of aircraft was significantly smaller with an average number of approximately 24 fighters and torpedo bombers compared to some 100 on a heavy carrier. Operating in the Pacific escort carriers were largely vulnerable to Japanese aircraft and warships as shown during the Battle of Samar in the Philippine on October 25, 1944 when the *Gambier Bay* (CVE-73) and *St. Lo* (CVE-63) were sunk along with three damaged. Japanese aircraft would go on to *Ommaney Bay* (CVE-79) and *Bismarck Sea* (CVE-95) during January and February 1945. However, escort carriers operating in the Atlantic fared better then sister ships in the Pacific as threats from German aircraft was nonexistent.[1]

While land-based patrol aircraft hunted U-boats in the Atlantic and Caribbean the Navy established hunter-killer groups comprised of escort carriers with destroyers and destroyer escorts. Each carrier operated Navy Composite Squadrons (VC) equipped with the Grumman TBF/TBM Avenger torpedo bomber and FM/F4F Wildcat fighter.

The purpose of such groups was to protect convoys in the mid-Atlantic, which was out of reach of land-based aircraft. The concept began in December 1940, when Admiral William F. Halsey, C-in-C of the U.S. Fleet sent Admiral Harold S. Stark

Chief of Naval Operations, a confidential letter expressing the need for auxiliary aircraft carriers to supplement the six heavy carriers then in operation. President Roosevelt followed up with a memorandum requesting the conversion of merchant ships into small carriers to provide aerial protection of convoys.

The Newport News Shipbuilding Company received the 10,000-ton *Mormacmail* for conversion to the Navy's first escort carrier named *Long Island* (AVG-1). The *Charger* (CVE-30) followed as the second escort upon commissioning in June 1942. Conversion of additional ships quickly followed including four merchant ships at Newport News converting to escorts for the Royal Navy. Meanwhile, the U.S. Maritime Commission by December 1941 had agreed to release 20 class C-3 freighter hulls to the Navy for the construction of the Bogue Class escort carrier, a 442-foot-long (135 meters) platform with a top speed of 19 knots. The U.S. and British Navies received 21 Bogue class escort carriers, five of which, *Block Island* (CVE-21), *Bogue* (CVE-9), *Card* (CVE-11), *Core* (CVE-13), and *Croatan* (CVE-25), operated in the Atlantic Theater, while the converted oiler *Suwannee* (CVE-27) operated in the Mediterranean during Operation *Torch*. The Casablanca-class followed with 50 built with *Guadalcanal* (CVE-60), *Solomons* (CVE-67) and *Wake Island* (CVE-65) operated in the Atlantic.

The first mention of establishing a hunter-killer force appeared in a memorandum from Admiral Francis S. Low, Tenth U.S. Fleet, advocating the inclusion of an escort carrier to each surface support force to protect convoys and to establish anti-submarine hunter-killer groups.[2]

The escort carrier USS *Bogue* (CVE-9) operated in the Atlantic from March 1943 to April 1945. Her air arm and escorting destroyers sank twelve U-boats and one Japanese submarine. (National Archives)

The major breakthrough that allowed such groups to be successful was th decryption of German Enigma communications by Ultra, which provided th location of individual U-boats, allowed convoys to avoid wolfpacks and guide hunter-killer groups towards unsuspecting submarines. BdU never realized tha Enigma had been compromised and that communications between headquarter and submarines were being read by American and British intelligence. Allied cod breaking, the use of direction-finding equipment, and radar cost the BdU heavil with 244 submarines lost in 1943 and 249 in 1944. U.S. Navy composite squadron operating from escort carriers in the Atlantic sank 33 while contributing in th destruction of another eight, of those between May 1943 and September 1944.

Operations Summer 1943

VC-9 began operations from the *Bogue* in the Atlantic on February 20, 1943 a a time when the U-boat menace was at its peak. The first cruise ended on Marc 14, without the squadron scoring; although TBFs made two contacts, one onl 3,000 yards (2743 meters) from the carrier. The presence of aircraft in the ai prevented the unknown submarine from attacking. The second patrol started o April 20, under Task Group 21.12 and would be much different from the first wit sightings and attacks on U-boats beginning on April 28, when VC-9 attacked a full surfaced submarine with depth charges, possibly damaging it. Five separate attack in May followed with Type VIIC *U-569* becoming the *Bogue*'s first victim and th first by a CVE hunter-killer group operating in the Atlantic, on May 22, 1943 eas of Newfoundland while the task group provided protection for ON-184. Betwee the 21st and 22nd, the squadron conducted six attacks on U-boats attempting t launch attacks against the convoy. Two Avengers of VC-9 flown Lieutenant H. S Roberts and Lieutenant (jg) William F. Chamberlain caught the surfaced boat an badly damaged it with depth charges. The captain ordered *U-569* scuttled and 2 men of the 46-man crew survived.[3]

VC-9 struck again the following month as a flight element consisting of Avenger flown by Lieutenant Biros, Lieutenant (jg) Fowler and Fryatt sank Type VIID *U-21* operating 45 miles (72 kilometers) from the *Bogue* in the North Atlantic southwes of the Azores on June 5. There were no survivors. Type XB *U-118* minelayin submarine was lost a week later on the 12th when Avengers of VC-9 caught th surfaced boat west of the Canary Islands, 16 of 49-man crew survived and wer rescued by American vessels. *U-118* left Bordeaux on its fourth and final patrol o May 22, under the command of Korvettenkapitän Czygan Werner, at 38 years old who was old for an initial U-boat command, as was this sailing. The crew likec Czygan and viewed him as friendly, a stern disciplinarian but fair. The previous tou almost resulted in the loss of the boat and its crew when on December 7, 1942 as the vessel submerged; it went down by the stern at a 55-degree angle. The boa

Type VIIC *U-569* became the Bogue's first kill occurring on 22 May 1943 when two TBF(M) Avengers of VC-9 seriously damaged her with depth charges off Newfoundland forcing the scuttling of the vessel by the crew. Note depth bombs at the top right. (National Archives)

descended to approximately 210 meters (689 feet), the maximum depth for this type was 722 feet (220 meters), before Czygan ordered to blow the tanks sending *U-118* rapidly to the surface. There was minimal damage except for the crew's frayed nerves who believed death was imminent.

As *U-118* headed towards the Azores, the radio operator received an urgent message from *U-758*'s commanding officer from Kapitänleutnant Helmut Manseck, stating American planes had attacked his submarine severely damaging it and wounding four men. VC-9 had found Manseck's boat surfaced on the previous day, June 8, and crippled it with a series of depth charge and strafing attacks. *U-118* rendezvoused with *U-758*, which Kapitänleutnant Ebe Schooner's *U-460* arriving shortly thereafter. *U-118* sent over doctor to tend to the injured along with spare parts to the damaged submarine. Cyzgan transferred oil to *U-758* and continued towards his assigned area of operations. Shortly before 1400 hours, VC-9 spotted the U-boat, coming out of the sun to attack. Matrosenobergefreiter Wilhelm Doblies, one of four men on the conning tower for bridge watch saw the planes and shouted, "*Flieger! Flieger!*" (Planes! Planes!). The gunfire of Lieutenant (jg) R. J. Johnson's Wildcat answered Doblies' warning as the plane flew over at 15 feet (4.6 meters) from the submarine's stern to bow. Lieutenant (jg) Robert L. Stearns followed Johnson in his TBF-1 at 100 feet (30 meters), lowering his landing gear down, and then up, to cut air speed. A salvo of depth charges left the torpedo bomber's bay, straddling *U-118* amidships with the blasts causing water to pour into the diesel compartment, and for the U-boat to descend several degrees by the stern.

USS Bogue TBF-1 of VC-9 attacking Type VIID *U-217* in the mid-Atlantic on 5 June 1943. The submarine of her third war patrol sank from the attack with the loss of all hands. (National Archives)

TBF-1 flown Ensign Hodges of VC-9 approaching *U-217* to drop four Mk-17/2 depth charges. Moments before a Wildcat fighter had strafed the submarine's deck to keep the crew from operating anti-aircraft guns. (National Archives)

Type XB *U-118* under attack off the Canary Islands by VC aircraft from USS *Bogue* on 12 June 1943 Korvettenkapitän Werner Czygan was among the 42 killed while 16 survived. Only eight Type XB boats, the largest submarine built during the war by Germany, were built as transport submarines. Six XBs were lost and aircraft from escort carriers sank three of them: *U-117*, *U-118*, and *U-220*. (Bob Rocker via Tailhook Association)

Engineering Officer Herman Götze restored partial trim by ordering the men forward but, a few minutes later, more depth charges exploded. The clear water allowed the attacking planes to see the submerged vessel trailing oil and bubble. Lieutenant (jg) H. E. Fryatt arrived in an Avenger five minutes after Stearn's attack, dropping two depth charges, straddling the conning tower. The explosions caused the U-boat's two motors to stop, steering failed, wrenching the hydroplane and rudder loose. Engineer Götze yelled at Czygan, "*Das Boot ist nicht mehr Schwimmfähig!*" Czygan ordered the tanks blown upon realizing his boat couldn't be saved ordered the tanks blown. The commander then ordered his gun crew to fight it out with the American planes. Czygan and his gun crews climbed out of the hatch, the U-boat's captain climbing to the bridge. Nearly all of those who attempted to operate the guns were cut down by machine gun fire. Lieutenant Johnson's Wildcat ran out of ammunition and returned to base while Lieutenant (jg) Tennant, in another Wildcat circled and strafed only when men in the conning tower tried to man the guns. Each time he saw someone going to a gun he would strafe, and they would run below, or over to the other side of the conning tower. Lieutenant. (jg) Fowler, who participated in the sinking of *U-118*, arrived in his Avenger and he, along with Tennent took turns chasing the Germans on deck from one end to the other. The crisscross machine gun fire from both planes was accurate and deadly.

Czygan ordered abandon ship, he remained aboard, blood covering his white shirt. At least a third of the crew below did not hear the command. Lieutenant (jg) Chamberlain in an Avenger arrived eight minutes after the first attack, making three depth bomb attacks in succession; *U-118* blew up and broke into two. The attacking aircraft had hit the U-boat with sixteen depth charges and spent 4410 rounds of .50 and 800 rounds of .30 ammunition. The destroyer *Osmon Ingram* (DD-255) picked up seventeen survivors, one later died, and four bodies were left in the water.[4]

The destruction of German submarines continued during July with utility squadrons based on three carriers claiming eight U-boats sunk marking the start of a hunter-killer blitz against the U-boat with BdU losing six submarines between the thirteenth and thirtieth. Utility squadrons aboard the *Bogue*, *Core* and *Santee* sank three between 13–15 July while conducting operations in the Central Atlantic and off the Azores. Oberleutnant zur See Helmut Metz took the Type XIV Milch cow out from Bordeaux the month before for its first operational patrol and was on a continuing southeasterly course at 1921 hours on July 13, unaware the Americans had located the boat's location. A large group of the boat's complement sunbathing topside were taken by surprise when an Avenger and Wildcat from VC-9 appeared.

Lieutenant (jg) Earl H. Steiger strafed while the Avenger flown by Lieutenant R. P. Williams straddled the U-boat with four depth charges. Steiger came around for another strafing run but was shot down and killed. Two more Wildcats and an Avenger arrived on scene with the fighters providing suppressing fire while the

Engines running TBF/M Avenger torpedo bombers with F4F/FM-2 Wildcat fighters in the background on an escort carrier in the Atlantic preparing to depart for an ASW sweep during 1943. They are painted in Atlantic scheme one (also called ASW scheme I and II) of dark gull gray top surfaces, sides of nonspecular insignia white, and gloss white bottom surfaces. ASW scheme two consisted of nonspecular dark gull gray top surfaces, nonspecular insignia white sides, and gloss white bottom. (Tailhook Assocation)

A landing Signal Officer (LSO) directing an Avenger torpedo bomber for a landing aboard USS *Bogue*. The TBF-1D carried a radar pod housing the ASB system. The radio operator located in the aircraft's belly operated the radar. (National Archives)

Avenger, flown by Lieutenant (jg) Schoby dropped another four depth charges; the explosions lifted *U-487* out of the water and sank. 33 of the boat's complement who had been topside before and during the attack, survived and taken aboard the destroyer *Barker* (DD-213).

VC-29 aboard *Santee* conducted two successful attacks against Type IXCs *U-160* and *U-509* between the 14th and 15th. F4F-4 F-1 flown by Lieutenant Harry B. Bas, with TBF-1 T-7 flown by Lieutenant (jg) John H. Ballentine sighted the surfaced *U-160* south of the Azores. The submarine had sunk or damaged 31 ships during four previous patrols under the command of Kapitänleutnant Georg Lassen. On the fifth and final patrol of twenty-five-year-old Oberleutnant Gerd von Pommer-Esche was in command on its final voyage. Lieutenant Base made two strafing attacks to clear the boat's deck as the submarine submerged while Ballentine released a *Fido* striking the water 600 feet (183 meters) ahead and 100 feet (30 meters) to the U-boat's starboard side. 75 seconds after the torpedo's release an explosion appeared 1050 feet (320 meters) directly ahead of where the target submerged. The U-boat and its crew of 57 sank to the bottom of the Atlantic.[5]

The *Core*'s VC-13 followed VC-29's success the following day by sinking the homeward-bound Type IXC *U-67* southwest of Azores, in the Sargasso Sea. Günther Müller-Stöckheim commanded the U-boat on all seven patrols sinking three ships and damaging five between September 1941 and November 1942. No kills occurred

USS *Core* (CVE-13) underway in the Atlantic on 10 October 1943 began her first hunter-killer ASW cruise on 27 June 1943 and lasted until 31 July sinking two U-boats during that time. (Naval History and Heritage Command)

during the sixth and seventh patrols. Lieutenant Robert F. Williams dropped a string of depth bombs under the conning tower causing the boat to lift up 35 degrees, and then it sank stern first. Three men of the 51-man crew survived, Hans Bruck, Walter Otto, and Walter Younek stationed on the conning tower, were blown overboard and picked up by destroyer *McCormick* (DD-223).

The third U-boat lost to VC-9 occurred on July 23, when one of its Avengers piloted by Lieutenant Robert L. Stearns sunk, who sank *U-118* on June 12, caught Type IXC/40 *U-527* commanded by Kapitänleutnant Herbert Uhlig on the surface south of Azores, leaving 13 survivors from the boat's complement of 53. Those that survived, including Uhlig, were all topside on or near the conning tower when the depth charges exploded. The destroyer *Clemson* (DD-186) picked them up before transferring to the *Bogue*.[6] A week later VC-29 caught Oberleutnant zur See Hans—Joachim Schwantke's Type IX *U-43* southwest of the Azores on July 30. This was Schwantke's fourth patrol with *U-43* with two ships sunk to his credit but a Fido torpedo dropped by Avenger T-13 sank the U-boat taking the 55-man crew down with it. Six U-boat losses followed during August, four of them *U-117, 664, 525,* and *847,* by VC-1 aboard the *Card.* The *Card's* air group, as part of Task Group 21.14, sank three U-boats between 7 and 11 August with *U-117* becoming the first when five Avengers found the submarine on August 7, resupplying *U-65* in the North Atlantic, depth charges and a Fido sent the submarine and its 62-man crew to the bottom of the Atlantic.

Fregattenkapitän Hans-Werner Neumann took Type XB *U-117* out for its fifth patrol from Bordeaux on July 22. Only its previous patrol as a minelayer had been successful with two merchant ships damaged. West of Ponta Delgada in Azores, 82 miles from *Card,*

Type XIC/40 *U-527* as seen by TBF-1 of VC-9 USS *Bogue* by pilot, Lieutenant (jg) R.L. Sterns, at 1407 hours. Four Mk-47 depth charges were dropped and the submarine was sunk. USS *Clemson* (AVD 4) was sent to the scene and three hours later picked up thirteen survivors; the Captain, two officers, two non-commissioned officers and eight enlisted men. (National Archives)

A Mk-47 depth charged dropped by a TBF-1 flown by Lieutenant (jg) R.L. Sterns explodes near *U-527*. It may have been close enough to breech the haul as the kill radius of a standard depth charge was 10-13 feet (3-4m). (National Archives)

Crewmembers of *U-527* struggling to survive (top of image) among the bodies of shipmates killed by depth charges. The original caption stated the image shows only survivors of the sunken submarine; however, close examination shows several men floating head down in the water. (National Archives)

The Bogue-class USS *Card* (CVE-11) started its service life as a Type C-3 cargo ship before conversion as Auxiliary Aircraft Carrier 11 (ACV-11) and then CVE-11. (Naval History and Heritage Command)

First German submarine, *U-66*, sighted by TBFs from USS *Card* (CVE-11) on August 3, 1943. *U-66* was later sunk by USS Buckley (DE-51) on May 6, 1944. Piloted by Lieutenant Junior Grade R. L. Cormier. (National Archives)

a TBF-1 Avenger flown Lieutenant (jg) A. H. Sallenger, on an anti-submarine sweep, and spotted *U-66* refueling *U-117*. Neumann had also transferred a medical officer over to *U-66* to care for two injured men, wounded from an attack by VC-1 on the third.

According to Sallenger, "At first I thought it was a merchant ship, but I soon realized it was two submarines close together, fully surfaced, cruising very slowly with neither wake nor bow wave."

He made his run out of the sun; the men aboard the U-boats were unaware of an attacking plane until it was some 500 yards (457 meters) away, at 400 yards (366 meters), both boats began sending up heavy antiaircraft fire but none hit the plane. He dropped to Mk-47 depth charges set for 25 feet (7.6 meters), which straddled *U-117*.

> The bombs seemed to straddle the U-boat and about 3 seconds later there were two large explosions, one five to ten feet on the starboard quarter half way between the conning tower and the stern and the other just ahead of the conning tower 15–20 feet (4.6–6 m) out. I circled sharply to the left gaining altitude while the turret gunner strafed and the radioman took pictures. The attacked submarine immediately began to smoke badly throwing off a dark greyish black smoke. It began making erratic turns in a crazy quilt pattern trailing a heavy oil slick. I had made a preliminary contact report to the ship before the attack and now made another giving the bearing and distance.[7]

Through intense antiaircraft fire the Avenger circled around and made a run against the submerging *U-66*, dropping another depth charge; however, there was no damage to the boat and safely avoiding further attacks. Climbing up to a safer altitude to avoid antiaircraft fire from *U-117* he vectored a pair of TBF-1 Avengers and two F4F-4 Wildcats. Lieutenant C. R. Staple flying of the Avenger's called in one of the Wildcats piloted by Lieutenant Hodson to strafe while he went in for a bombing run. Heavy Anti-aircraft fire peppered the sky around the incoming Avenger.

As we came in, the submarine put up considerable AA fire which, judging from the explosions in front of us, were from 20 mm guns. I weaved somewhat on account of this fire, steadying down for the attack and then firing several bursts with my 30[-] caliber fixed gun.

At 1037 at a speed of 195 knots in a 200 [degrees] dive, I released the two depth bombs at an altitude of 185 feet [56 m]. My course was 2750 T [degrees west] and that of the U-boat was about 3000 [degrees northwest]. It had turned a little sharper than I estimated and its stern was transversing noticeably to port. The bombs landed very close aboard the port side just ahead of the conning tower, the explosion sending up a large geyser of water that almost completely covered the submarine.[8]

These three images by USS *Card* aircraft from VC-1 show the attack on Type XB *U-117* transport submarine (right) on 7 August 1943. U-117 was providing medical assistance for two wounded men aboard *U-66*. TBF-1s dropped depth charges and two Mk-24 acoustic torpedoes and one of the torpedoes apparently sank the submarine. Pilots of the TBF-1s were Lieutenant (jg) Asbury Sallenger, Lieutenant Charles R. Stapler and Lieutenant (jg) Ernest E. Forney. Two F4Fs flown by Lieutenant Norman Hudson and Lieutenant (jg) Ernest E. Jackson provided strafing fire. (Captain Lex Black, USN, via Emil Buehler Library-National Museum of Naval Aviation)

Lieutenant J. C. (jg) Forney, in the second Avenger, made his bombing run, while the fighters clear the U-boat's deck, thus stopping the AA fire. Forney signaled for Lieutenant (jg) Jackson, in the second Wildcat, to start his strafing attack. Forney recounted, "I made my run about 15° [degrees north-northeast] off the stern. After dropping, I pulled out to the left and observed both my charges go off slightly aft and on the starboard quarter 20–25 feet [6–7.6 m]. The explosion was close and also covered the sub from view."[9]

Two minutes after his first attack Staple went in to drop a Mk-24 Fido as *U-117* attempted to submerge, barely making headway.

> I dropped the Mk. 24 Mine about 200 feet ahead of the oil slick and 100 feet to starboard of the submarine's last track. The dropping course converged with that of the U-boat by about 10° [degrees]. At the instant of dropping, the plane was making 120 knots, altitude 205 feet [62 m].[10]
>
> Lieutenant Forney followed ten seconds later to drop his torpedo. *U-117*'s conning tower had just disappeared below the surface as the Avenger came in for the kill. "I then circled and half a minute after disappearance, at an altitude of 200 feet (61 meters), speed 120 knots, I dropped my mine about 400 feet (122 meters) ahead and to port of the spot the sub was last seen. There was no noticeable swirl."[11]

Ensign John Franklyn Sprague went missing in action on 7 August 1943 when his Grumman Wildcat fighter plane crashed into the water upon being hit by heavy anti-aircraft fire. He had strafed both submarines before gunners aboard *U-117* shot him down. (National Archives)

Lieutenant Forney circled the area and, according to his radioman, a shock wave appeared followed by air bubbles, this continued for five to eight minutes.

The *Card*'s hunter-killer group followed up two days later by sinking another submarine west of Azores. Oberleutnant zur See Adolf Graef left Brest on July 21, commanding Type VIIC *U-664* on its fifth patrol. Prior patrols resulted in the sinking of three merchant ships, one as part of convoy ON-153 and two sailing with ON-167. VP-84 had severely damaged it on November 1, 1942 during its patrol. Graef and his crew may have survived what became the final patrol as the submarine fired three torpedoes during the evening of 8 August but missed the intended target-the *Card*. Less than twenty-four hours later, a duo of VC-1 Avengers dropped depth charges while a Wildcat provided suppressing fire. Seven crewmen of *U-664* were killed but the destroyer *Borie* (DD-215) brought aboard

Graef with 43 other survivors. *Card* aircraft struck again two days after sinking *U-664* when Korvettenkapitän Hans-Joachim Drewitz's Type IX/40 *U-525* on its fourth patrol was located northwest of the Azores. Depth charges and a Mk-24 Fido sent the vessel and the 54 men aboard to the bottom.[12]

Two crewmembers wear life jackets (top right) on *U-664*'s conning tower looks towards a plane from VC-1 from USS *Card*. Another individual, bottom right) stands on the submarine's gun platform. Note, the laughing sawfish insignia on the conning tower of the 9th U-boat Flotilla. (Captain Lex Black, USN, via Emil Buehler Library-National Museum of Naval Aviation)

U-664 sinking by the stern after depth charges from TBF-1 Avengers of VC-1 ruptured her hau while located off the Azores in the North Atlantic on 9 August 1943. (Captain Lex Black, USN, via Emil Buehler Library-National Museum of Nava Aviation)

Another view of *U-664* showing the vessel slowly sinking by the stern while crewmembers are seen on the conning tower and gun deck. (National Archives)

Moments after depth charges mortally injured thei *U-664*, men on the conning tower prepare to go ove the boat's side during attack by two Avenger aircraf from USS *Card* (CVE -11), August 9, 1943. (Captair Lex Black, USN, via Emil Buehler Library-Nationa Museum of Naval Aviation) (National Archives)

Seven of *U-664*'s complement were killed but 44 survived the attack by VC-1. Crewmembers abandon the sinking vessel with the second and third image showing men in life rafts. (Captain Lex Black, USN, via Emil Buehler Library-National Museum of Naval Aviation)

U-185 carrying the survivors of *U-604* attacked by a PV-1 Ventura of VB-129 on July 30 was heading back for its base in France when aircraft from the *Core* on August 24 sank it with depth charges. During the attack, strafing killed or wounded *U-185*'s deck crew while a pair of depth charges cracked the batteries causing chlorine gas to form, which quickly incapacitated or killed several men. During the attack, Kapitänleutnant Höltring, the former commander of *U-604*, was in the officers' quarters as the U-boat's batteries began pouring out toxic chlorine gas. According to survivors, Höltring was lying on his bunk with his pistol nearby when the attack began. In the bow compartment, a member of *U-185*'s crew laid on the deck with a bullet wound to his leg sustained from the 3 August attack by VB-107's Lieutenant Commander Prueher's aircraft. As Höltring rushed into the bow compartment, the young man cried for *U-604*'s skipper to shoot him. According to survivors from *U-185*, Höltring shot and killed the boy before shooting himself through the head. Unable to escape the assault from the American warships, *U-185* surfaced and the remaining members of its crew, who had not succumbed to the chlorine gas, abandoned ship. The American destroyer *Barker* picked up Maus and 21 crewmembers, along with nine from *U-604*.[13]

Three days later after *U-604*'s loss, on the 27th, VC-1 scored its fourth kill in August by sinking Type IXD2 *U-847* with Fido torpedoes in the Sargasso Sea in the Mid Atlantic. The boat sank taking the compliment of 62 men with it. The boat had refueled several U-boats before Kapitänleutnant Herbert Kuppisch headed to the south Indian Ocean to join the Monson (Monsoon) wolfpack. *U-847* was one of eleven U-boats selected to participate in the operation but only five reached Japanese bases in the Far East.

VC-13 based on USS *Core* found Type IXC/40 *U-185* off the Canary Islands on 24 August 1943. Lieutenant Robert P. Williams flying a TBF-1 Avenger sank her with depth charges. Twenty-two of the boat's complement survived but 29 died. (National Archives)

Survivors of *U-185* and those of *U-604* rest on the flight deck of USS *Core*. *U-604* was scuttled after suffering serious damage from a U.S. Navy PV-1 Ventura. The men were aboard *U-185* when aircraft of VC-13 sank her. (National Archives)

Attack on Type IXD2 *U-847* on 27 August 1943 in the Sargasso Sea in the Atlantic Ocean by Lieutenant (jg) G.G. Hogan of VC-1 from USS *Card* leaving no survivors amongst the boat's 62 crewmembers. (National Archives)

Operations Fall 1943

Hunter-killer groups failed to sink a U-boat during all of September, although other Allied air and surface units sank six during the month. That trend ended in October when Allied forces sank 25 U-boats, six by CVE-led groups consisting of *Block Island, Card,* and *Core* with VC-9 sinking four, giving them seven U-boats destroyed while deployed on two carriers.

Card returned to Norfolk, disembarked VC-1, picked up VC-9 at the end of September, and returned to sea. October mirrored the successes of July and August with six U-boats destroyed, three of them by VC-9 when 13 squadron aircraft interrupted a resupply meeting of four submarines north of Azores on the third. Sunk were Type VIIC *U-422* under the command of twenty-three-year-old Oberleutnant Wolfgang Poeschel and Type XIV *U-460* commanded by Kapitänleutnant Ebe Schnoor at 48 one of the oldest in the submarine surface while *U-264* was damaged, north of the Azores. There were only two survivors from *U-460* out of the 64-man crew while all 49 aboard *U-422* perished. Then it was *U-402*'s turn. Korvettenkapitän Siegfried Freiherr von Forstner was one of the top German submarine commanders of the war and on his eighth patrol with Type VIIC *U-402*. He and his crew had escaped five attacks from British and American aircraft from April 1942 with the latest, prior to *U-402*'s loss, occurring on October 1, 1943 when a Ventura of VB-128 attacked with depth charges. VC-9 found it 12 days after surviving the latest attack and a Fido dropped from an Avenger claimed the boat and its 50-man compliment.

North of the Azores VC-9 pilot Lieutenant (jg) R.L. Sterns found four U-boats replenishing on 4 October 1943. VC-9 from USS *Card* sank Type XIV *U-460* and Type VIIC *U-422* while *U-264* and *U-455* escaped. F4F pilots Lieutenants (jg) Puckett and Heim and TBF pilot Lieutenant (jg) Weigle aided Sterns. (National Archives)

Type VIIC *U-402* and her 50 crewmembers, previously responsible for sinking 15 ships, became the next victim of VC-9 when a Mk-24 *Fido* torpedo sank her on 12 October 1943 north of the Azores. (National Archives)

VC-13 stationed on the *Core* as part of Task Group 21.15, sank *U-378* on October 20, north of Azores, when an Avenger and Wildcat caught it on the surface. A Fido sank the boat, killing the 48 men aboard. Closing out October 1943 saw *Block Island's* contingent of Avengers and Wildcats sink *U-220* with its 56-man crew on the twenty-eighth followed by the *Card's* VC-9 on the thirty-first sinking *U-584*, with all hands lost, north of the Azores. Sixteen U-boats were lost to Allied air and surface units during November 1943, yet only one was the result of an attack by a Navy composite squadron: *U-86* lost east of the Azores by *Bogue's* VC-19 on the 29th.

Attack on *U-378*, on 20 October 1943 by USS *Core*-based VC-13. The U-boat was sunk by a Mk-24 *Fido* torpedo and depth charges from Avenger and Wildcat aircraft north of the Azores leaving no survivors. (National Archives)

Oberleutnant zur See Herman Hoffman, at 22 years of age, was one of the youngest U-boat commanders as he took out *U-172* on his first and last voyage in November 1943. 27 days later, he and 12 of his crew lay on the Atlantic's bottom west of the Canary Islands, the result of a combined effort by *Bogue's* VC-19 and American destroyers. Four months after aiding *U-604* in the rescue of Captain Höltring and his men,

U-172's luck ran out when American aircraft and destroyers sank it on December 13, 1943, after a 27-hour fight west of the Canary Islands. After being submitted to some 200 depth charges from destroyers *George E Badger* (DD-126), *Clemson* (DD-186), *Osmond Ingram* (DD-255) and *DuPont* (DD-152), and MK-24 Fido homing torpedoes from aircraft belonging to the escort carrier USS *Bogue*, *U-172* sank, 46 of 58 aboard the boat survived were taken prisoner, Hoffman wasn't among them.[14]

The Sinking of *U-172*

A Lieutenant Porter with the Navy's public relations section interviewed Lieutenant (jg) Harold G. Bradshaw an Avenger pilot aboard the *Bogue* who discussed typical flight operations and the sinking of *U-172*. The following is a transcript of the interview that occurred on January 30, 1944.

We went aboard the *Bogue* the first part of November [1943] and our first contact was not made until, oh, it was towards the latter part of November and the first attack was sighted on a routine patrol and an attack group was sent out and a submarine submerged. We dropped sonic buoys and tracked him with sonic buoys. Eventually [we] heard an explosion and assumed that he [the U-boat] was killed. The destroyers came into the area sometime later and shortly after I left the area the destroyer picked up sound contact and continued to attack that sound contact all afternoon. The contact was decided later by the destroyer commander to have been a pinnacle in the middle of the Atlantic Ocean and no submarine at all. It is believed that in the original attack, the submarine was sunk and when the destroyers came in, due to the fact that the pinnacle was there, they attacked it all afternoon.

The ship went into Casablanca [and] had a couple of days there, rested up and then the Cominch report showed a concentration of refuellers [refueling U-boats] down south of the Azores. Captain Dunn [Commanding Officer of the *Bogue*] headed [the carrier] down there, and we had a report that there were two submarines, so we went down and sunk the submarines. One of these submarines was the one which we chased for 27 hours and finally captured 46 prisoners.

The way we tracked this thing was [sic] we used sonic buoys to locate his [the U-boat's] position and then vectored the destroyers in between the sonic buoys. After hammering on him for quite a while he began to leave an oil trail and then with a combination of the sonic buoys and the oil trail, well, it was pretty easy to keep the destroyers on them. When it got dark, due to the fact that the weather was pretty rough, why the destroyers were going to maintain contact at night and the planes were going to join them fueling at daybreak and they were going to continue the attack.

Around about 11:30 [1130 hrs] the sub came to the surface and the destroyers started shooting at him, and he submerged. They made a depth charge attack and they held contact until 2:30 [1430]. At that time we lost contact. Captain Dunn launched me [launched him in his aircraft] to go out and see if I could relocate the sub, or least keep him under the water until daybreak, when we could start a more thorough search for him. So I went out and threw an expanded square [search grid] around the place where he submerged after the destroyer attack and he was definitely under the water all night, and the next morning I found a lot of oil slicks in the area. So I started investigating all the likely looking ones with sonic buoys and then about 8:30 [0830 hours the following day] I found one that had a submarine under it, so

Depth charges and Mk-24 torpedoes sank type IXC *U-172* on 13 December 1943 after a 27-hour hunt by VC-19 based on USS *Bogue* and escorting American destroyers in which the latter dropped 200 depth charges. (National Archives)

I called for the destroyers. The destroyers came over and immediately made contact. About this time, I was about out of gas and had to land and get more gas, and Lieutenant Ogle relieved me [relief aircraft and pilot].

The destroyers attacked, continued depth charge attack until about 11:30 [1130 hrs] when the submarine gave up and came to the surface. We had two fighters that were flying over the ship just for such an occasion as that. They immediately attacked with all guns blazing, and the destroyers attacked with their gunfire, and the submarine [captain] gave up, abandoned ship and [the U-boat] sank.

In this particular attack, we got 46 prisoners, including the Captain, the Executive Officer, the Engineering Officer and one midshipman, and 42 ratings [enlisted submarine crewmen]. The morale of this crew seemed to be very high. The men were all young, healthy looking and after the battle they'd had they were pretty tired, but their morale was pretty high, they came up fighting. A very good indication of the fact that the morale in Germany is not killed [sic] yet.

The next attack was actually the most dramatic of any attack we made. It was interesting due to the fact that the boy [another pilot] who made the sighting did not realize that his transmission was going on the air. He was setting out there wondering what to do and didn't know that the ship knew that there [sic] was anything out there and he had expended his charge and he was in kind of a spot. We just sat there and let him keep shooting at them [the German U-boat] until the ship [approached], [and] the attack group finally got out there. Actually, what had happened was his transmitter [antenna,] which was struck down but was working fine, the ship got the report the first time he sent it and immediately launched an attack group, which consisted of myself, Lieutenant Kenneth Hance, who is now a squadron commander, and Ensign Goodwin and Lieutenant Cookroft.

We flew 70 miles [113 km] to the attack and attacked at 1330. We sent two fighters in with Goodwin, ahead of Goodwin, who had 4 depth charges in his plane's armament, and he went straight in and made a fore and aft attack. The submarine was heading just about directly towards him [Goodwin] and he made a perfect straddle, a beautiful straddle and I came around from 120 degrees [easterly direction] about on his starboard quarter and made my attack, and my first two depth charges dropped slightly over. I immediately went into a sharp turn and the submarine started to submerge, and so I came back and dropped the rest of my ordnance on it. At the same time, the pilot who made the original contact came in and dropped the ordnance he had left. The submarine came back to the surface, although he was hit pretty bad,, and the submarine came back to the surface. Both my second [ordnance] drop, LeRoy's second drop, hit right on his stern and completely broke him in two. The destroyers got into the area about two and half to three hours later. They found a shoe with a foot in it, and lung tissue and kidneys, life belt, a few and various and Sundry other things, pieces of wood with numbers on them, very definite evidence of a kill. That's about the sum and substance of the cruises made on the *Bogue*. Got back to Norfolk on the 29th of December. All in all, a very successful cruise.

Survivors of *U-172* (bottom left) await rescue by one of USS *Bogue*'s escorting destroyers after aircraft from the escort carrier sunk her on December 13, 1943. Forty-six of the 59 men aboard the U-boat survived their sixth and final patrol. *U-172* sank 26 merchant ships (152,000 tons) during the second through fifth patrols under the command of Kapitänleutnant Carl Emmermann between May 27, 1942 and Jul 24, 1943. Twenty-two-year-old Oberleutnant zur See Hermann Hoffmann assumed command on November 1, 1943 only to lose his boat six weeks later. He was one of the survivors. (Naval History and Heritage Command).

Interviewer:

That was the 29th of December 1943?

Lieutenant Bradshaw:

That's right, that is correct.

Interviewer:

Do you mind spelling us the name of this Fighter Director Officer, the one you said did a particularly good job of getting a man back to the ship?

Lieutenant Bradshaw:

Ben Fuqua.

Interviewer:

Not too sure?

Lieutenant Bradshaw:

No, I'm not exactly sure how he spells that. Fuqua, I think. I'm sure that's correct. From Tampa, Florida.

Interviewer:

Did you want to say something for the record about how ably Captain Dunn handles this CVE so that you think it is as good as a CV [large aircraft carrier] from the standpoint of a TBF man?

Lieutenant Bradshaw:

Definitely! Captain Dunn is one of the most aggressive Captains I've ever served under, and also one of the most able. He's absolutely not afraid of anything. He made a statement one time, that he'd take his ship within 8,000 yards [7,315 m] of any submarine and so help me, he'd do it. When this particular submarine came to the surface and started shooting it out, Captain Dunn was well in sight of it, steering the ship, heading for it full speed, standing on his bridge just pushing it. That kind of spirit in the captain goes all the way down through the ship. He has one of the finest fighting ships in the Navy, I think. Not a man that serves under Captain Dunn can't help but admire him. He's big bull but we all like him.

Interviewer:

Were any of those prisoners brought aboard the CVE or were all of them taken on the DD's [destroyers]?

Lieutenant Bradshaw:

They were all immediately taken aboard the DD's [destroyers], but they were picked up by the DD's and transferred to the CVE. We brought them all back on the CVE.

Interviewer:

From your experience, do you conclude that the Nazi subs are pretty toughly built and hard to sink?

Lieutenant Bradshaw:

Definitely. The experience with the one that we took so long on proves that depth charges are not too effective a weapon, when a sub is very deep. But[,] the other which we sank in such a short time, we sank in three minutes, proves that if you can catch them on the surface and hit him with depth charges and some other ordnance why they kill pretty easy.

Interviewer:

I'm not sure that it was recorded quite plainly on her how fast that last attack was.

Lieutenant Bradshaw:

The original contact was at 1305, the attack group was launched at 1309, he was sighted, and we commenced the attack at 1330 and I reported back to the ship that he was sunk at 1333. I think that is about the fastest a U-boat's ever been sunk. When the CVE's first came out, there seemed to be a lot of people afraid they couldn't operate in low wind conditions or bad weather conditions. Of course, they are not as good as the big carriers, but have seen some very bad weather, some very, very bad weather, and we've continued to operate with no trouble. I might take the statement that in the two cruises, totaling about 3,000 hours, we lost only one airplane and that was not due to bad weather, or operation of the ship, but was due to gasoline failure and the plane had to land away from the ship. We operated in some of the roughest weather you can find in the north Atlantic. We had 18 to 20 degrees pitch [tilt of the ship toward the bow or stern] and roll [tilt of the ship from side to side] and wind conditions anywhere from 30 to 50 knots down to zero wind. A lot of credit that we had such good luck is due to the fact that our Signal Officer is very capable and would give us a wave off if the ship was pitching too much. We would go around and make another approach. As far as bad weather conditions go, with the present radar and radio installations we had in the TBF, there's not too much danger from fog and such as that. The men have to be well trained. We have operated in weather so bad to make a real tight circle around the ship, we could not keep the ship in sight, [but] of course, all we could do was to make radar searches, but it may or may not prove very valuable. As far as night operations go, they are very, very feasible aboard these little ships because we made a total of 113 landings at night and we had two barrier crashes, neither of which were very serious. One barrier crash was due to the fact that the boy had the oil in his eyes, which I mentioned earlier, and the other was due to the general tough luck, I guess—come in high and held off and hit the barrier, but neither of them were serious. One hundred and thirteen landings, why, I think is impressive proof that night flying is feasible on small carrier. We'll further prove that in our future operations.[15]

U-850 under attack on 20 December 1943 by VC-19's Lieutenant (jg) Bradslan. The first image apparently shows that none of the vessel's anti-aircraft weaponry were manned at the time while the second image shows an explosion way off target. (National Archives)

A TBF/M Avenger skims over other Avengers parked on the deck of USS *Santee* (CVE 29), November 1943. The airborne Avenger has the ASW color scheme II while the others have scheme I. Lieutenant Commander Charles Jacobs via Emil Buehler Library-National Museum of Naval Aviation).

Wooden planking is torn from the deck of USS *Solomon* (CVE-67), while fuel from a Grumman TBF Avenger flown by Lieutenant William F. Chamberlin explodes as it strikes the carrier's ramp on 25 March 1944. The aft section of the aircraft broke away and fell into the sea with the radio operator and turret gunner; both survived and were picked up by a destroyer. The pilot survived as well. Chamberlin and his crew would perish three months later while attacking *U-860*. (Bob Lawson Collection via Emil Buehler Library-National Museum of Naval Aviation)

Type IXD2 *U-850* on 20 December 1943 as viewed from a TBF aircraft flown by Lieutenant (jg) La Fleur of VC-19. Depth charges and Mk-24 torpedoes sank her with its crew of 66. (National Archives)

The last U-boat lost through the actions of a composite squadron during 1943 occurred on December 20, with VC-19, after the destruction of *U-172*, with the sinking *U-850* off Madeira, Portugal from depth charges and Fido torpedoes. Kapitän zur See Klaus Ewerth, previously commander of *U-26*, and his crew of 65 perished. Composite squadrons would sink ten U-boats directly or indirectly during the course of 1944 beginning on January 16.

CHAPTER 10

Escort Carrier Operations
(January–August 1944)

"Oh, we got that son-of-a-bitch!"

LIEUTENANT COMMANDER JESSE D. TAYLOR

The escort carrier *Guadalcanal* set out upon its maiden operational voyage with escorts *Alden* (DD-211), *John D. Edwards* (DD-216), *John D. Ford* (DD-238, and *Whipple* (DD-217) from Norfolk on January 5, 1944. Captain Daniel V. Gallery Jr., commanding *Guadalcanal*, was a tough, no-nonsense leader who demanded the best out of the ship's complement including those with VC-13. The unit's first score occurred northwest of the Azores by sinking Korvettenkapitän Willy Mattke's Type IXC/40 *U-544* on its first patrol with depth charges and rockets, the first successful rocket attack on a German submarine by an Avenger.

Operations March–June 1944

Atlantic-based CEVs failed to sink a submarine during February, while 17 U-boats were lost to Allied surface and air forces during the month. March and April 1944 saw the loss of U-575, 801, U-1059, 515, and 68 by composite squadrons and warships. Fido torpedoes from two Avengers of VC-6 (*Block Island*) with depth charges and gunfire from the destroyer *Corry* (DD-463) and destroyer escort *Bronstein* (DE-189) sank Type IXC/40 *U-801* skippered by Kapitänleutnant Hans-Joachim Brans west of the Cape Verde Islands on March 17. *Block Island's* air contingent scored again two days later by sinking Type VIIF *U-1059* off the Cape Verde Islands. Twenty-three-year-old Oberleutnant zur See Günter Leupold took his first command out of Bergen, Norway on February 12, with the goal of reaching the Munson boats in the Far East where his crew would unload a supply of torpedoes. Unlike *U-801*, with the loss of all hands, eight men survived out of the *U-1059's* 55-man crew including Leupold.[1] The sinking of *U-515* and *U-68* followed in April from attacks by *Guadalcanal's* VC-58. Guadalcanal embarked on its second cruise on 7 March with nine FM-2 Wildcats, three TBF-1Cs, and nine TBM-1C Avengers with Escort Division 4, led *Forrest* (DD-461), *Chatelain* (DE-149), *Flaherty* (DE-135), *Pillsbury* (DE-133), and *Pope* (DE-134).

USS *Block Island* (CVE-21) originally commissioned as AVG-21, then ACV-21, before becoming the Bogue Class escort carrier CVE-21 in 1943. She made two transatlantic crossings to the UK transporting USAAF fighters during the summer of 1943 before becoming part of hunter-killer operations in the Atlantic. (National Archives)

U-758's conning tower awash shortly before the submarine submerged. A rocket attack was followed quickly by depth-bombs from Lieutenant (jg) Leonard L. McFord. Seeley then conducted another depth bomb attack. In March 1945, *U-758* was stricken from the German Navy after being damaged by British bombers at Kiel, Germany. Shown: Lieutenant Junior Grade Willis D. Seeley making rocket attack. (National Archives)

TBF Avengers of VC-58 from USS *Block Island* (CVE-21) made the first aircraft rocket attack on a German submarine on 11 January 1944 against *U-758*. The submarine survived the attack and returned to St. Nazaire, France on 20 January. Shown: Lieutenant (jg) Willis D. Seeley, USNR, making rocket attack. (National Archives)

Lieutenant (jg) Willis D. Seeley, USNR, of VC-58 and a TBF Avenger names *Len * Sharon* launched the first rocket attack against a German submarine. Photographed released on 25 May 1944. (National Archives)

The second TBF crew that attacked *U-758*. Shown: Lieutenant Junior Grade Leonard L. McFord, USN, (center) pilot, first sighted the enemy sub. His gunner was AMM2/C William H. Ryder, USN, (right) and his radiomen was ARM3/C Charles M. Gertsch, USN. Photographed released on 25 May 1944. (National Archives)

U-575 under attack by VC-95 from USS *Bogue* aircraft on 13 March 1944 north of the Azores. Pilot was Lieutenant (jg) D. A. Pattie. The submarin's sinking was a combined effort involving VC-95, Canadian frigate HMCS *Prince Rupert*, US destroyer *Hobson* (DD-464), US destroyer escort *Haverfield* (DE-393), an RAF Wellington bomber from 172 squadron and two RAF B-17 Flying Fortress bombers from 206 and 220 Squadrons. (National Archives)

U-801 was sunk on 17 March 1944, by a Fido homing torpedo from an Avenger flown by VC-6's Lieutenant (jg) Charles Woodell with suppressing strafing fire from a Wildcat piloted by Lieutenant (jg) Paul Sorenson and gunfire from the destroyer USS *Corry* (DD-463) and destroyer escort USS *Bronstein* (DE-189). (National Archives)

The U.S. Navy escort carrier USS *Guadalcanal* (CVE-60) photographed from a blimp of Airship Squadron 24 (ZP-24) while steaming off Hampton Roads, Virginia on 28 September 1944. Planes parked on her flight deck include twelve TBM/TBF Avenger torpedo bombers and nine Wildcat fighters. (National Archives)

Type IXC *U-515* left Lorient on 20 March on its seventh and final patrol, unde the command of Kapitänleutnant Werner Henke. Its previous patrols under Henke' command accounted for 22 ships sunk for a total tonnage of 140,000 tons earning him the Iron Cross First Class and the Knight's Cross with oak leaves. An Avenge spotted it on the evening of April 8, by an Avenger from *Guadalcanal* northwes of Madeira, Portugal and radioed the carrier. The carrier sent three FM-2s flown by Lieutenant (jg) Charles D. Hardesty Jr., Lieutenant (jg) William F. Pattison and Ensign Ellis R. Taylor that provided suppressing fire to clear the submarine' decks. TBM-1C, piloted by Lieutenant Helmuth E. Hoerner with Aviation Chie Radioman Richard T. Woodson and Aviation Ordnanceman Second class Raymond E. von Spreechen; a TBF-1C flown by Lieutenant Douglas W. Brooks with Aviation Ordananceman Second Class Leland F. Stone and Aviation Radioman Third Class Edward Browning Jr, conducted the attacks. The highly coordinated attacks with depth bomb and rockets forced *U-515* to submerge.

What followed was a series of depth charge attacks from *Pope, Pillsbury, Chatelain* and *Flaherty,* causing severe damage to the submarine. At 1505 hours, Henke ordered the boat surface at 1505 hours and ordered abandon ship upon seeing the warships coming in for the kill, with the *Chatelain* only 150 yards away. An Avenger and two Wildcats a minute later attacked, with the torpedo bomber releasing rockets while the fighters strafed the deck, now full of men attempting to escape the damaged vessel. Three minutes later, *Chatelain* scored a direct hit on the conning tower, starting a large fire. Henke and 43 men survived but 16 died, most from the strafing. Henke

Type XIC *U-515* Sunk at 1510hrs on 9 April 1944 in the North Atlantic north-west of Madeira, Portugal by rockets from two *Guadalcanal*-based Avengers of VC-58 and depth charges from destroyer escorts USS *Pope* (DE-134), USS *Pillsbury* (DE-133), USS *Chatelain* (DE-149), and USS *Flaherty* (DE-135). (National Archives)

U-515 sinks after American warships sank her on 9 April 1944. Note Depth Charges at bottom. (National Archives)

A group of survivors from *U-515* await rescue just after planes of VC-58 sank the submarine. (top left center) Forty-four of the 60-man complement survived but the boat's captain Korvettenkapitän Werner Henke was not among them. (National Archives)

Some of *U-515*'s survivors supported by a rubber life raft are towed towards a US Navy ship for rescue. Two Destroyer Escorts are standing by in background, the nearer of which appears to be the *Pope*. (National Archives)

and his men became prisoners of war and sent to the United States but, on June 15, 1944, a guard at the prison camp shot Henke dead while the intrepid submarine commander apparently tried to escape.

It was Type IXC *U-68*'s turn the following day, April 10, northwest of Maderia, Portugal. The U-boat was, like *U-515*, on its seventh patrol having previously sunk 33 ships for 197,400 tons. For Iron Cross recipient Kapitänleutnant Albert Lauzemis, it was his second patrol in command of *U-68*. At 0358 hours, VC-58 Avenger T-30 piloted by Lieutenant (jg) Eugene E. Wallace picked up the U-boat on radar at a distance of four-and-a-half miles, 78 miles from the carrier; breaking out of heavy overcast, he spotted the submarine and made two unsuccessful depth charge attacks.

At 0626 hours Wildcat F-4, flown by Lieutenant R. K. Gould and two Avengers VT-24 (Lieutenant Samuel G. Parsons) and VT-22 (Lieutenant H. E. Hoerner) broke out of the overcast with the fighter strafing and the Avengers conducting a depth charge and rocket attack. The lone survivor of *U-68* counted four attacks as he stood by his position at the 37-millimeter antiaircraft gun. Suddenly, the siren crash dive sounded. He helped secure the 37-millimeter gun and noticed a wounded gunner. He struggled forward with the wounded man to the conning tower, but the hatch slammed shut and the boat began to submerge, both men found themselves in the water.

Depth charges exploded and large bubbles appeared followed by debris, oil, battery acid. Several other men appeared but quickly drowned. The survivor, Hans Kastrup, his life jacket punctured by bullets held on to his dying comrade until rescued three hours later by one of the destroyer escorts. Kapitänleutnant Lauzemis and 54 men went down with the submarine.[2]

VC-55 participated in the sinking of *U-66* on 6 May 1944 west of the Cape Verde Islands. She finally sank when the destroyer escort USS *Buckley* (DE-51) rammed her. (National Archives)

Some of the 36 survivors of *U-66*'s 60-man crew. The boat's captain twenty-six-year-old Kapitänleutnant Gerhard Seehausen wasn't one of them. (National Archives)

Sometimes the contribution of an individual or unit during combat can be exaggerated, overstated or in the following event, a bit strange. One such event involved a pilot from *Block Island*'s VC-55 flying an unarmed aircraft during an early morning patrol on May 6, 1944 when he spotted *U-66* commanded by Kapitänleutnant Gerhard Seehausen, the vessel nearly sunk along with *U-117* the previous August. *U-66* was on its 112th day of the ninth patrol as it cruised on the surface at 0235 hours when Lieutenant J. J. Sellars' radar on Avenger T-12 picked up the U-boat twenty miles (20 kilometers) from the destroyer escort *Buckley* (DE-51). The intrepid pilot led the warship towards the quarry and, since his aircraft carried no ordnance, proceeded to fire his .45 caliber service pistol towards the enemy. This apparently had no effect, but *Buckley's* depth charges, guns, and ramming did. The *Buckley* rammed first enabled some of the Germans, ten in all, to climb aboard the American ship and a brief hand-to-hand battle ensued. Meanwhile, *U-66* broke free, turned around, and rammed the destroyer escort. The U-boat sank at 0341 hours and by 0900 hours, the warship had hauled aboard the last of 36 survivors, Seehausen was not among them.

The sinking of *U-66* became the *Block Island's* last successful hunt as on 29 May, *U-549* evaded the escorting screen and fired three torpedoes into the carrier, killing six men at 2013 hours. Screening escorts rescued 951 of the ship's complement. At the time of the sinking, the ship had six fighters in the air and fighter direction ordered the pilots to head for the Canary Islands. The aircraft ditched at night near the islands and two pilots, Lieutenant (jg) James G. McDaniel and Lieutenant (jg) John F. Carr survived but the rest consisting of Lieutenant Robert Buell, Lieutenant (jg) Julian Pitts, Lieutenant (jg) Robert Wyatt, and Ensign Robert E. Innis were lost.

USS *Block Island* sinking by the stern after *U-549* torpedoed her in the Eastern Atlantic on 29 May 1944. Six members of the crew were killed along with four fighter pilots who went missing attempting to reach and land in the Canary Islands.

Capture of *U-505*

The capture of *U-505* by American air and surface forces consisting of the *Guadalcanal* and escorts *Chatelain*, *Flaherty*, *Jenks*, and *Pope* of TG 22.3 off Mauritania, French West Africa on June 4, 1944 is a well-documented story in which Captain Gallery proposed to capture a U-boat. The operation was controversial as Admiral Ernest J. King would admonish Gallery after the event and thought of court martialing the *Guadalcanal's* skipper for jeopardizing Allied Intelligence if news of *U-505's* capture became public. Such a disclosure would have resulted in the Germans changing codes and change the Enigma's cipher wheels. Fortunately, those who participated in the operation kept it secret and the Germans never knew of *U-505's* capture. The Navy Department interviewed Captain Gallery on May 26, 1945 and he discussed his command of the *Guadalcanal* from commissioning to the capture of *U-505*. The capture became the first time the U.S. Navy had boarded and captured a foreign naval vessel on the high seas since 1815. The following are excerpts of that radio interview with corrections.[3]

We left on our first ASW cruise in January 1944 and operated in the vicinity of [near] the Azores on January 19. We got our first two U-boat kills when we surprised a refueling operation and depth charged and sank a big refueler [refueling submarine milch cow] and a small U-boat alongside of it. On our second cruise which began late in March, we got two more kills. We sank the *U-515* and picked up 40-some prisoners, including the captain, and sank the *U-68* the next day, getting one survivor and one dead man and a great deal of wreckage.

It was also during this cruise that we got the idea of trying to capture a U-boat. When we sank the *515*, we had been hunting her continuously for about 18 hours, making intermittent sound contacts, sightings by the planes at night and contacts by destroyers.

In other words, we'd been right on top of the *U-515* and had delivered several depth charge attacks, both from the air and surface vessels, which had damaged him until he got [to the] point where he had to come up…He suddenly popped up right in the middle of a group of three of our destroyers, which were only three to four hundred yards away from him [U-boat] and he was surrounded. We had three or four planes in the air at the time over this spot. As soon as he popped up everyone opened up on him in accordance with the usual accepted doctrine and hammered him to pieces, set fire to him and blew him up and he sank within a few minutes of the time that he had come up. He attempted to man his guns but the gunfire from our ships was so heavy that it drove the crew overboard.

In analyzing this attack afterwards, it occurred to us that if we had anticipated what was going to happen and had been ready for it with organized boarding parties, we might possibly have gotten aboard the *U-515* in time to save her. We were determined that on the next cruise we would anticipate such an event and be ready for it.

The next cruise started in May and at the departure conference attended by the representatives of Cinclant, ComAirLant, ComFairNorfolk, [and] DesDivLant. We discussed plans for boarding and capture and we agreed that if we encountered a submerged submarine and forced him to surface we should then assume that he had surfaced for only one reason, which was to try to save his hide, save the crew. And that as soon as he surfaced we would cease fire with any weapons that could inflict fatal damages on the submarine, that we would use only anti-personnel weapons from that point on, attempting to drive the crew overboard as rapidly as possible, meantime having our boarding parties already to go.

Each ship in the task force was ordered to organize and instruct boarding parties and to have all preparations ready for taking sub into tow on short notice. On 17th of May, approximately ten days after we had sailed…I told the group that we expected to be on a hot trail the next day and reminded them that our objective was to capture rather than sink, and said for all ships to have their boarding parties ready and be ready to tow. That was May 17th.

We went on and operated off Cape Verde Islands for approximately two weeks, operating continuously day and night and finally we were running short of fuel and had to head for Casablanca. However, on the way to Casablanca, we decided to run searches for a U-boat reported by Cominch to be home bound off the west coast of Africa.

We hunted for this fellow [U-boat] about four or five days and nights, had numerous indications that a submarine was nearby, such as disappearing radar contacts, noisy sonar buoys…We never did sight this fellow and we were finally about to give up the hunt. As a matter of fact, for all practical purposes, we had given it up and were on our way to Casablanca but were keeping fighter planes in the air to serve as escort and also on the outside chance we might still find the fellow…On June 4th, Sunday morning, at about 11:10 [1130 hrs], 150 miles [241m] west of Cape Blanco in French West Africa, the *Chatelain* reported that she had a possible sound contact.

Within a half-minute she reported contact evaluated as U-boat and she and the two destroyers nearest to her started the attach while, the *Guadalcanal* and my other two escorts turned away from the contact. The *Chatelain*, having the sound contact, was the attacking ship and the *Pillsbury* and *Jenks* were assisting ships. ComCortDivFour was in the tactical command at the scene of the attack. Lieutenant Commander Cassleman commanded the *Pillsbury*, Lieutenant Commander Dudley S. Know commanded the *Chatelain* and Lieutenant Commander Julius F. Way commanded the *Jenks*. As soon as the *Chatelain*'s report came into the combat information center on the *Guadalcanal* we vectored our fighting planes over to the *Chatelain*. All ships and aircraft guarded the same radio frequency so the fighters that heard the report were already on the way. The fighters sighted the sub running fully submerged.

The *Chatelain*'s first attack with hedgehogs apparently was ineffective and at this point the sub sighted the task force, fired one acoustic torpedo and reversed course. This temporarily shook off the *Chatelain*, but our fighters saw the sub reverse course, and being on the same radio frequency with the *Chatelain*, told her what was happening, coached her to reverse course too and then coached her on to a collision course with the sub.

She very soon picked up the sub again with her sound gear and following the indications of the sound gear and of the fighter planes in the air, she made a depth charge attack firing a full pattern, which rolled the sub on her beams and under the water. The fighter planes immediately reported, "*Chatelain* you struck oil, sub is surfacing." Then in a few seconds the sub broke surfaced and found herself practically in the center of a group consisting of the *Chatelain*, *Pillsbury*, and *Jenks*.

These ships and the two aircraft immediately opened fire on the submarine with anti-personnel ammunition. The planes fired 50 caliber guns; the destroyer fired 20 mm. and 40 mm. guns and some three-inch shells of high explosives rather than armor piercing. The Nazis scrambled overboard as fast as they could. They attempted to man the guns but there was just too much stuff flying and they went overboard pretty fast. As soon as it was apparent that most of them had gone overboard, Commander Hall, the Division Commander, issued the order, "Cease firing", "Away boarding parties."

The *Jenks*, *Pillsbury* and *Chatelain* all put boats in the water and Commander Hall then ordered the *Jenks* and the *Chatelain* to pick up survivors while the *Pillsbury* would board the sub. The sub was left running at about 10 knots with her rudder, hammed hard right and in just about full surface trim. The *Pillsbury*'s boat had to chase the sub and cut inside the circle to catch her, which she did, and the boarding party, consisting of eight enlisted men and Lieutenant (jg) Albert Leroy David, leaped from the boat to the circling sub and too possession of it.

U-505 under attack from VC-8 aircraft from the USS *Guadalcanal* on 4 June 1944. US Navy crews from the carrier and USS *Pillsbury* captured the submarine. One of the boat's 60-man complement was killed during the attack. (National Archives)

On deck, there was one dead man. They didn't know what was down below. They had every reason to believe, from the way the sub was still running, that there were still Nazis left below engaged in scuttling, setting booby traps and perhaps getting rid of confidential gear. At any rate David and two enlisted men, one named Knispel, the other Wdowiak [Torpedoman Third Class Arthur W. Knispel and Radioman Second Class Stanley E. Wdowiak], plunged down the conning tower hatch carrying hand grenades and machine guns ready to fight it out with anyone they found below. They very definitely put their lives on the line when they went down the hatch. However, they found no one below.

They did find that water was pouring into the U-boat through a bilge strainer about 8 inches in diameter which had the cover knocked off, and that all the vents were open, and the boat was rapidly flooding. When they found there was no one else below they called the other boarders below and went to work closing vents. They found the cover to the bilge strainer, slapped it back in place, screwed up the butterfly nuts on it and checked the flooding, just in the nick of time.

In the meantime another boarding party from the *Guadalcanal* arrived under the command of Commander Earl Trosino, Chief Engineer of the *Guadalcanal*, and took charge of the salvage operations. At this time the sub was so low in the water that to prevent the swells from washing down the conning tower hatch they had to close the hatch on the people who were working below. Those people down below wouldn't have had any chance whatsoever to escape in case the sub had gotten away from us.

The *Pillsbury* meanwhile was attempting to come alongside and take the sub in tow. She sent a message to the sub to stop the engines so she could get alongside. However, when they pulled the switches and it looked like she was going to up end and sink so they had to throw the switches to full speed ahead again to get the lift of the stern planes to keep the stern up, and the sub circled some more.

A boarding party from the USS *Pillsbury* works to secure a towline to the newly captured German U-boat *U-505* on Jun 4, 1944. Note the large U.S. flag flying from the periscope. (National Archives)

...Well, the *Pillsbury* finally had to back clear and sent a message saying that the sub had to be towed to remain afloat, but she didn't think a destroyer could do it... I told the destroyers to stand clear the I'd take her in tow myself.

So we maneuvered the *Guadalcanal* into position. I had them stop the engines on the sub and pulled up as quickly as we could, shoved our stern up against her nose, got a towline aboard and got her going again. Meantime the *Pillsbury* reported two compartments flooded to the waterline and they didn't know whether they could check the flooding or not. So we sent assistance to the *Pillsbury*.

About this time, or a little later, one of the destroyers, I think the *Chatelain*, reported that she had another possible sound contact and the *Flaherty* reported a disappearing radar pip. So I decided that was the nearest friendly port, which was Dakar.

We left the *Pillsbury* lying dead in the water with on destroyer standing by her and attempting to get her engines back in commission. At midnight the tow line broke as the first tow line we put out was only about an inch and a quarter wire. The towline broke and so we spent the rest of the night circling the sub and getting our big towline ready. We came alongside the sub again shortly after dawn and passed a big towline. Meanwhile I had instructed the boarding parties to try to get the rudder amidships. They signaled to me from the sub that the rudder was amidships, so when we then recovered our boarding parties and got underway again. However, it soon became apparent that the rudder was still not amidships. The sub rode the same way, about 20 degrees on our starboard quarter.

I found that the boarding parties had moved an electric indicator or had caused this indicator to move from the hard right to the amidships position but that they had no way of checking where the rudder actually was.

So, I had been just been looking for a good excuse to get over to the sub myself anyway and when the boarding parties reported this booby trap I figured I was as well qualified as anyone in the task group to open booby traps because I had an ordinance PG course and quite a lot of experience with ordnance. So we stopped and I went over with a selected party and we went aft to inspect the booby traps.

So we decided to assume that it was not a booby trap, close the fuse box cover and nothing happened. So, we then proceeded to open the watertight door very carefully so that if the after torpedo room was flooded we would be able to jam the thing closed in case water started squirting out around the edges. However, the after torpedo room was dry so we went aft and found the hand steering gear, rigged the clutches to engage it and moved the rudder amidships by hand, meantime determining that the pressure hull was intact and that there was no flooding in the after torpedo room. However, the boat at this time was riding with her stern well down and we found considerably later, in fact after we got in, that this was due to the fact that one of the after-ballast tanks had been ruptured by the depth charges.

We then fastened everything down and returned to the *Guadalcanal* and resumed the tow. In the meantime, the *Pillsbury* had gotten herself pumped out, got a patch over the hole and was able to rejoin. At this time, we got another message from Cinclant telling us that instead of going to Casablanca they wanted us for security reasons to go to Bermuda if the condition of the sub warranted it and telling us that we would be met by an oiler and a tug.

So we reversed course and headed for Bermuda. I was not too sure that we could make Bermuda or that the sub would remain afloat that long. However, I figured it would take us approximately three days to get to Casablanca and that if we were going to lose her at all, we'd lose her within three days. [T]herefore, I might just as well try for Bermuda as Casablanca because I could make Casablanca an keep her afloat three days, the chances were that we could keep her afloat longer.

In the meantime the Naval Operating Base, Casablanca, Moroccan Sea Frontier, was sending out the *Humboldt* [AVP-21, a seaplane tender] with Commander Rucker aboard, who is a qualified submarine commander. I figured that he would soon be there to give me advice and help. The next day, or rather on June 7th, we rendezvoused with the feet tug *Abnaki* [ATF-96] and transferred our tow.

A salvage party at work on *U-505*'s bow and conning tower as *Guadalcanal* approaches to take the German submarine in tow on June 1944. The submarine arrived at Bermuda on 19 June. (National Archives)

When we lost headway and transferred the tow to sub sank so far in the water that it looked like she was going all the way down. So we rushed our salvage parties back aboard, had the *Abnaki* heave her into short stay, tow as fast as she could and started lightening the sub. We removed all the loose gear that we could. We had electric submersible pumps which we sent over from the *Guadalcanal* and we rigged electric lines to the *Abnaki* and got these pumps running and pulled out probably some 30 or 40 tons of bilge water from the main control room. It was a very close thing that day as to whether she was going to go down or not.

As a matter of fact, while the issue was still in doubt, the *Guadalcanal* got ready to act as a pontoon and hold the sub up. We rigged a heavy wire from the forward starboard edge of our starboard corner of our flight deck, let it hang in a bite underwater and brought the other end in through our hawse pipe [pipe in which the anchor chain passes through] and over to our anchor windlass [a machine for lowering and raising an anchor]. We then cruised along very slowly with our bow about 40 feet [12 m] from the stern of wire hanging in the water so that if the sub started going down too far and heave around with our anchor windlass and try to hold the stern up until we got her lightened enough to save her.

After about an hour standing by to do this, it became apparent that it would not be necessary. We got the electric pumps going and got her up to manageable trim. When the salvage parties left that day, they to charge the batteries. They disconnected the diesel engines from the electric motor as that when the *Abnaki* towed at about nine knots the propellers turned over the electric motors which acted as generators and charged her batteries

The next day we were able to run some of the electric machinery on the boat, the pumps, the air compressors, to blow the tanks, pump the bilges and pull her up to full surface trim. We had to do all this without benefit of the expert advice I was hoping to get from Casablanca because we couldn't wait that long. The situation finally got desperate and we had to do this ourselves. The *Humboldt* arrived several hours after we had done this. The next day Commander Rucker inspected the sub, approved all of our salvage measures and assured us that she was in seaworthy condition for the tow home.

During all this time, that is the three days the *Guadalcanal* had her in tow herself, we conducted flight operations day and night because we were in submarine lanes. Other subs were supposed to be nearby and there was a full moon. So I thought it was necessary to keep our own air patrols up. At times we landed planes with only 15 knots of wind across the deck and got away with it.

After the *Abnaki* took over the tow we escorted her, well, first we refueled the task group from the [AO-36, oil tanker] and then we took all the confidential documents, secret codes, coding machines and a tremendous stack of dispatches, dumped them in ten mail bags and sent them over to the *Jenks*. We then sent the *Jenks* on ahead to Bermuda at full speed and this material was picked up at Bermuda the Naval Air Transport and flown to Washington.

Meantime, we proceeded in company with the *Abnaki*, which did the towing, and escorted her to Bermuda. On June 19th we turned the *U-505* over to the Commandant Naval Operating Base, Bermuda. Only one man in the submarine crew was killed [Oberfunkmaat Gottfried Fischer]. We buried him at sea while the capture was going on. The others were all rescued. I believe a total of 59 of them. The submarine skipper [Oberleutnant zur See Harald Lange] was pretty badly wounded and remained in the sick bay of the *Guadalcanal* throughout the trip back.

I want to mention the names of some individuals who did outstanding work in connection with this capture. They are: Commander Hall who commanded ComCortDiv 4; Lieutenant Commander Knox who commanded the *Chatelain*, which delivered the attack which brought the U-boat up; Lieutenant Commander Casslemon who was skipper of the *Pillsbury* that furnished the first boarding party and which attempted to get alongside the sub; Lieutenant Hodgson who commanded the aircraft squadron attached to the *Guadalcanal* and whose pilots rendered invaluable assistance to the *Pillsbury* in coaching her on and all members of his boarding party;

U-505 lies near the escort carrier *Guadalcanal* on 4 June 1944 after U.S. Navy salvage parties stoppe her from sinking and rigged a towline. This capture of an enemy vessel on the high seas was the fir since 1815. (National Archives)

the two who accompanied David down the hatch. The first ones to enter the sub were tw enlisted men named Knispel and Wdowiak.

Another officer who rendered outstanding service was Commander Trosinc of the *Guadalcan* He was in charge of all salvage operations and in my opinion is the officer who was principa responsible for getting the sub back to port. He spent many hours crawling around in th bilges, under the engines, into inaccessible places that he couldn't possibly have escaped fro if the sub got away from us, tracing out pipe lines, closing valves with his own hands, ar doing whatever was necessary to keep that submarine afloat. He definitely risked his lifetim and time again over a period of several days.

While these boarding parties were aboard the sub, there was constant danger that s would founder and take all hands with her and every valve, switch and push button in th U-boat was a possible booby trap. There were 13 demolition charges in the U-boat whi were later found and removed. I believe the first day we were able to find and pull the wir off only five or six of them. However, in spite of their inexperience and great danger their lives, all hands in the boarding parties did their stuff like veteran submarine sailo I consider it a great honor and a privilege to have commanded them and I'm very prou of their work indeed.[4]

Down South

While *Abnaki* towed *U-505* towards Bermuda, in the mid North Atlantic, VC-9 based on the escort carrier *Croatan* (CVE-25) aided in the destruction of Type XI *U-490* commanded by Oberleutnant zur See Wilhelm Gerlach. Further south i the Atlantic Admiral Jonas H. Ingram's Fourth Fleet acquired the services of th

Captain Daniel V. Gallery, Jr., USN and Lieutenant Junior Grade Albert L. David, USN. Photographed on board USS *Guadalcanal*. Lieutenant (jg) Albert Leroy David led a boarding party on board German submarine *U-505* on 4 June 1944. David was posthumously awarded the Medal of Honor, he passed away from a heart attack on 17 September 1945, for his leadership in the boarding the submarine and the initial salvage operations. (National Archives)

escort carrier *Solomons* (CVE-67), Carrier Task Group 41.6 (CTG 41.6). Assigned to the *Solomons* was VC-9 on its third tour, it was time for the unit's eighth and final U-boat victory. In the early evening of June 15, 1944, VC-9 scored its sixth and final kill. Aboard the *Solomons* on the morning of June 15, a TBF-1C Avenger torpedo bomber, piloted by Ensign George E. Edwards, took off from the carrier at 0709 hours on a routine anti-submarine patrol. The weather was clear, with scattered cumulus clouds at 2,000 feet (610 meters), and a moderate sea.

At 1021 hours, Edwards' radar operator picked up a target at a distance of 50 miles (80 kilometers) that turned out to be *U-860* commanded by Fregattenkapitän Paul Büchel. After leaving Kiel with another U-boat, *U-860* proceeded across the North and South Atlantic bound for Penang in the Indian Ocean. A few days before its sinking *U-860* proceeded on the surface day and night, which made it an easier target to pick up by patrolling Allied aircraft.

As Edwards approached, *U-860*'s G.S.R. set issued an aircraft-warning signal, and shortly thereafter, the plane appeared and began an attack. This plane delivered four attacks but scored no hits and on its fourth attack, rounds from one of the U-boat's 20-millimeter gun scored hits in the open bomb bay on Edwards's plane.

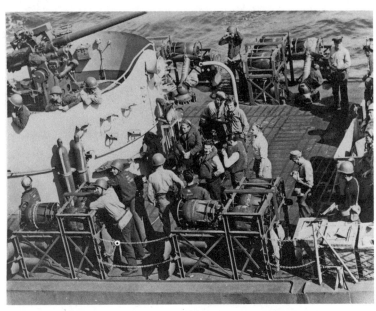

Destroyer escort *Inch* (DE-146) Prisoners from German submarine *U-490* (center, two wearing life vests, one in shirtsleeves) on Inch's quarterdeck, awaiting transfer to USS *Croatan* (CVE-25). Note the K-gun with fast-sinking streamlined depth charges mounted on the ship's side, 3/50 dual-purpose gun in upper left, photographer and guard with a Thompson submachine gun (both at right). (National Archives)

Survivors from *U-490* sunk on June 12 1944 north-west of the Azores by depth charges by aircraft from USS *Croatan* (CVE-25) and depth charges from the destroyer escorts USS *Frost* (DE-144), USS *Hus* (DE-145) and USS *Inch* (DE-146). The entire crew of 60 survived. (National Archives)

A fire broke out immediately inside the plane and it plunged out of control into the sea about a half-mile from the U-boat. Killed with Edwards were Aviation Radioman Second Class Albert D. Pacyna, and Aviation Machinist Mate Second Class Frank Kuczinski. Before submerging, *U-860* conducted an unsuccessful search for possible survivors from the torpedo bomber. VC-9 would lose and second plane and crew from the U-boat's accurate antiaircraft fire. Shortly before sunset, Buechel gave the order to surface. He was not satisfied with his crew's performance during the morning battle and wanted them to have additional antiaircraft gunnery practice.[5]

Back on the *Solomons*, Lieutenant Commander H. M. Avery, gunner C. D. Falwell (Aviation Machinist Mate First Class) and radioman W. J. Gorski (Aviation Radioman Second Class) took off in a TBM-1C Avenger at 1414 hours to conduct a square search gambit over the reported contact position. At 1722 hours, from a height of 1,500 feet (457 meters), the torpedo bomber's crew spotted the wake of a submarine from a distance of ten to 12 miles (19 kilometers). *U-860*'s bridge watch saw the Avenger approaching and immediately sounded the alarm.

The U-boat began circling as the Avenger approached and successfully kept the plane on its stern. The plane remained about 4,000 yards (3658 meters) away from the U-boat as Lieutenant Commander Avery radioed *Solomons* for assistance and dodged intense antiaircraft fire. For some twenty minutes, *U-860* kept circling keeping the plane on its stern and firing with its 37-millimeter guns.

A few minutes after Avery left the escort carrier, two FM-2 Wildcat fighters piloted by Ensigns T. J. Wadsworth, and R. E. McMahon and a TBF-1C piloted by Ensign M. J. Spear departed in search of Ensign Edwards. They returned to the carrier at 1720 hours without finding the missing plane or the U-boat and were about to land aboard when fighter direction vectored them to the area reported by Lieutenant Commander Avery. Ensigns Wadsworth and McMahon arriving over the target at 1743 hours and were directed by Lieutenant Commander Avery to conduct strafing attacks on the *U-860*'s starboard and port quarters while he coordinated a rocket attack with Ensign Spear. Three minutes later, eight minutes after sunset, the first coordinated attack consisting of 14 rocket and strafing runs began.

Ensign Wadsworth started a strafing attack from 2,000 feet (610 meters) on the U-boat's starboard quarter, pulling out at less than 100 feet (30 meters) directly over the conning tower through heavy antiaircraft fire. He effectively strafed the bandstand and the conning tower, expending 400 rounds of .50-caliber ammunition. However, the wing tank on Wadsworth's plane received hits from antiaircraft fire forcing him to return to the carrier. Due to the maneuvering of the submarine, Ensign McMahon had to begin his strafing run on the starboard bow in a steep dive from 3,000 feet (914 meters). He made a steep dive through heavy antiaircraft fire, peppering the deck and conning tower with 200 rounds of .50 caliber ammunition.

He then pulled out at 500 feet (152 meters) to clear the target as the first plane conducted a rocket attack.

Ensign Spear started his rocket attack simultaneously with the second strafing run. He attacked from the starboard beam of the U-boat and fired eight rockets in four pairs from a range of 800 yards (732 meters). Six rockets hit the water within lethal range slightly ahead of the conning tower while the other two landed beyond *U-860*. The pilot pulled out to his left after firing the last rocket, allowing his turret gunner to fire approximately 100 rounds at the U-boat. As Spear entered his dive Avery made a rocket attack from the U-boat's port beam. At a range of 600 yards (549 meters), he fired six projectiles, in three pairs, which hit the water within lethal range about 20 feet (6 meters) ahead of the conning tower.

During this first phase of the attack, all four planes passed over the U-boat within ten seconds. The submarine had straightened out at a slower speed, trailing oil with smoke streaming from the conning tower, and listing slightly to starboard. Effective strafing from the attacking planes reduced *U-860*'s defensive fire to short bursts which occurred about every ten seconds. The first attack scored hits in the forward part of the U-boat, and immediately after the attack, all telephone connections with the forward torpedo room were broken off.

At 1751 hours, a TBM-1C piloted by Lieutenant (jg) W. F. Chamberlain and a TBF-1C piloted by Lieutenant (jg) D. E. Weigle arrived on station to join the attack. This would become Chamberlain's second successful attack on a U-boat. A year earlier, on May 22, 1943, while serving with VC-9 on the escort carrier *Bogue*, Chamberlain participated in the sinking of *U-569* in the mid-Atlantic. As Chamberlain and Weigle arrived from the *Solomons*, Ensign McMahon conducted another strafing attack, in which he effectively expended the remainder of his ammunition, while Weigle attacked the U-boat's port beam, firing eight rockets in four pairs, at a range of 600 yards.

Within *U-860* (549 meters), the second attack scored hits in the warrant officers' room, in the bilges below the control room, and chlorine gas developed, which killed several men. The Avengers piloted by Avery and Chamberlain conducted a third and final attack on the port quarter of the U-boat. Avery flew his torpedo bomber in first strafing, followed by a depth charge run by Lieutenant (jg) Chamberlain.

Diving through bursts of antiaircraft fire, Chamberlain released two Mk-47 depth bombs from an altitude of 50 feet (15 meters). The bombs struck the deck of the submarine causing a violent explosion, which engulfed the plane and started a fire in the bomb bay and center cockpit. Chamberlain was apparently still able to maintain control of his plane, and after making a 180-degree turn, landed in the water about 500 yards (457 meters) on the port bow of the U-boat. The crew presumably went down with the plane. Killed with the pilot were Aviation Radioman First Class James. E. Finch and Aviation Machinist Mate Second Class Richard G. Hennick.

ome of the twenty survivors (center in underwear) of Type IXD2 *U-860* aboard onboard destroyer escort
JSS *Straub* (DE-181) or USS *Herzog* (DE-178) the morning after the vessel sank on 15 June 1944
fter attacks from VC-9 based on USS *Solomons* on 15 June 1944. (Captain Jerry Mason, USN, (RET))

On board *U-860*, the resulting pressure of the exploding depth charges dazed
verybody, many of them coming to only when the U-boat sank from beneath them
nd they found themselves in the water. With the exception of two men in the
onning tower at the start of the final attack, no other men escaped from within the
J-boat itself. At 1753 hours, the final phase of the attack began. However, before
he three American planes could get into position to make a final killing attack,
J-860 sank bow first. At 2330 hours, the destroyer escort *Straub* (DE-181) picked
ıp twenty-one survivors from *U-860* including the boat's Captain and Executive
)fficer.[6]

Hunting *I-52*

 German and Japanese submarines conducted special operations, codenamed in
apanese as *Yanagi* (willow) and *Kirschblüte* (cherry flower/cherry) in German, to
arry strategic war materials and technology between the two nations, beginning
n June 1942. Allied intelligence monitoring BdU communications alerted naval
orces in the Atlantic of a Japanese submarine attempting to make a journey to Japan
ia the South Atlantic. Approximately 870 miles south of the Cape Verde Islands

USS *Wake Island* (CVE-65). Underway in Hampton Roads, Virginia on 9 November 1944. The escort carrier with VC-58 conducted two unsuccessful ASW cruises between 17 June and 15 August 1944. (National Archives)

on June 24, 1944, the Japanese C-3 cargo submarine *I-52* was running such a mission, an Axis partnership to exchange strategic materials and technology, and heading for the U-boat base at Lorient, France. Five similar missions had ended previously with the sinking of *I-30*, *I-8*, *I-34*, *I-29*, U-boat *U-511*, and *RO-501* by Allied forces between April 30, 1942 and May 1944. It left Sasebo, Japan, with 11 tons of tungsten, 9.8 tons of molyb-denum, 2.2 tons of gold bars, 3 tons of opium, and 54 kilo grams of caffeine. In Singapore 120 tons of tin ingots, 59.8 tons of raw rubber, and 3.3 tons of quinine were loaded aboard, and the submarine headed to Lorient via the Indian Ocean. The Allies tracked its every movement as it sailed passed the Cape of Good Hope and into the South Atlantic.

Lieutenant Commander Jesse D. Taylor's radar operator, Ed Whitlock, aboard a TBM of VC-69 picked up *I-52* on his screen at 0039 hours, 55 miles (89 kilometers) from the *Bogue*. At 0044 hours, Taylor conducted a depth bomb attack on the submerging submarine. One was a near miss on the boat's starboard side. The pilot released a purple sonobuoy and the torpedo bomber's crew listened to the sonobuoy pinging on the intercom system. Taylor heard the submarine's propeller noise and released a Mk-24 Fido. A few seconds later the torpedo struck *I-52* aft of the conning tower. The sonobuoy recorded the explosion, followed by air escaping, and the vessel breaking up as it descended to its final resting place 17,000 feet (5,200 meters) below the Atlantic Ocean surface. Taylor, upon hearing the explosion, exclaimed over the intercom, "Oh, we got that son-of-a-bitch!"[7]

July and August 1944 saw the last two U-boats sunk by escort carrier aircraft in the Atlantic. The *Wake Island* scored one U-boat kill on July 2, when the Wildcat and Avengers of VC-58 caught *U-543* off Western Sahara, northeast of the Canary Islands. Nineteen-year-old Avenger pilot Lieutenant (jg) F. L. Moore, sighted the surfaced submarine at 2147 hours. 32 miles (51 kilometers) from the carrier, he briefly lost the contact before picking it up again on radar at a distance of two-and-a-half miles. He made his first run at 1,500 feet (457 meters) but broke off due to effective and thick anti-aircraft fire from the U-boat's 20-mm gun that punctured the left wing and fuselage. The Avenger circled and attacked again dropping two

Flight deck of USS *Bogue* flight of VC-42 Grumman TBMs painted in Atlantic paint scheme sometime between 1 August and 24 September 1944. Squadron aircraft sank Type IXC/40 *U-1229* on 20 August 1944. (USN via Bob Rocker)

AN-Mk-54 depth bombs that exploded near the vessel. He followed by dropping a Mk-24 Fido on the third run ahead of the submerging *U-543* before making a fourth run. By then, the boat had submerged. Either the depth bombs or the torpedo struck home Kapitänleutnant Hans-Jürgen Hellriegel, recipient of the Iron Cross First Class, and his 57-man crew perished.

Last Kill

In the North Atlantic Type IXC/40 *U-1229*, 26 days out on its first patrol and under the command of Kapitänleutnant Armin Zinke, it would become the last victim of escort carrier-based VC squadron. The After-Action Report and interrogation of survivors details the loss of *U-543*. Survivors of the sinking blamed Zinke for the loss and did not have anything positive to say about their captain. Crewmembers characterized him as, "the inepter German U-boat commander encountered in this war."[8]

During *U-1229*'s working up period and trials, Zinke was drunk a good deal of the time. At all times he was morose and uncommunicative with both the officers and the men, and it was seldom that he allowed anyone to address him, except in compliance with an order. The survivors held him directly responsible for the loss of their boat due to his practice during the last few days of the patrol of remaining continually on the surface during daylight.

Oberleutnant Willy Büttner, the engineer who would become the only officer to survive, was the opposite of Zinke, except for being a staunch Nazi, due to his competency, demeanor, and came from the ranks. In peacetime, he served on the Grille, Adolf Hitler's yacht. Although an ardent National Socialist, he readily admitted to the engineering crew that the war, and particularly the U-boat war, was lost. He further elaborated by calling the engine room ratings together in the diesel room.

He told them that the news from Germany was bad and that no one could tell what the future held in store for them. He stated that the boat was provisioned and fueled to stay at sea until November 1, and warned the men to save fuel at every opportunity. An officer questioned Zinke's tactic of staying surfaced during the daytime by stating it was suicidal to do so. Zinke responded by reminding him who was in command.⁹

The U-boat commander's tactic caught the attention of *Bogue's* VC-42 Lieutenant (jg) A. X. Brokas in TBM-1C Avenger of the *Bogue's* the surfaced vessel southeast of Newfoundland on August 20, 1944. Brokas took off from the *Bogue* at 1053 hours on August 20, 1944, in TBM-1C #19 on search for an enemy submarine sighted and attacked the previous day at 0040 hours by Lt. C. E. Lair, Jr., flying TBM-1D #11. At 1227 hours, the radar operator detected on his radar a small blip, bearing 227 degrees (south-southwest, distance five miles (8 kilometers). The plane was flying at an altitude of 1,500 feet (457 meters). Thirty seconds later the pilot visually sighted a fully surfaced submarine making ten knots, four miles away.

Brokas turned toward the sub and increased speed to full power. When about three miles distant, the submarine opened fire on the plane and continuing shooting until depth charges exploded nearby. The pilot circled and approached again launching a rocket attack from 1,200 yards (1097 meters). After releasing a salvo of two rockets he fired additional salvos at 1,000 yards (914 meters), 800 yards (1097 meters) and 600 yards (549 meters), respectively. Most of the salvos were short, but the last one hit. The submarine began an evasive turn to the left, causing it to present it starboard quarter to the airplane for a perfect depth bomb run. The pilot released two Mark 54 depth bombs at 160 feet (49 meters) by intervalometer. At the release point, the plane was at 100 feet (30 meters) altitude, making 230 knots. The bomb hit on the far side (port), one very close aboard just to port of the conning tower and the other about 40 feet (12 meters) from the bow.

As the plane pulled up and turned to port, the turret gunner fired at crewmember standing on conning tower. Debris flew off the conning tower from the depth bomb explosion, knocking off five men overboard and blowing off one of the antiaircraft guns.

U-1229 conducted two 360-degree turns, zigzagged, and then submerged. As the U-boat settled beneath the surface, Brokas flew down the sub's track, dropping a purple sonobuoy right on the swirl within 15 seconds of submergence. The boat descended to 197 feet (60 meters) when Zinke received news of serious damage to the boat' batteries; the attack damaged an estimated 35 cells. The motors began losing power rapidly as the boat took on a 17 to 20-meter downward angle. Zinke ordered the

U-1229 as viewed from the gunner's position of a VC-42 TBF Avenger flown by Lieutenant (jg) M.J. Sherbring. The submarine reportedly carried a Japanese spy and planned to land him on the coast of Maine. (National Archives)

Schnorchel raised in an attempt bring in fresh air to start the diesels. *U-1229*'s crew worked on the damaged batteries for the next two hours while American planes waited overhead.

Meanwhile, Brokas' radioman listened to a purple buoy released as *U-1229* disappeared and Avenger's crew listened to clear rhythmic sounds of the propeller beats lasting. The engine sounds abruptly ended and were replaced by metallic hammering and other loud noises made from the crew attempting repairs. Additional buoys in a standard pattern of four buoys dropped around the purple one as a center, the colors dropped being blue, red, yellow and green. Of these, only the red buoy functioned properly, but it gave no submarine indications. While laying this pattern, Brokas noticed the significant oil slick and marked it with a smoke float.

The *Bogue* organized an attack group upon receipt of Brokas' messages. All planes, which were in the air on other search sectors, namely, two pairs of Avengers and Wildcats arrived on scene. One plane served as a communications and navigational platform. The first plane on the scene was TBM-1C #12, flown by Lieutenant (jg) Mabry. At his arrival, 1336 hours, an hour had passed since *U-1229* submerged for an hour. Brokas continued seeking the target with sonobuoys. A second TBM-1C flown by Lieutenant (jg) Porter, was accompanied by FM-2 #9, Lieutenant (jg) Sulton. Porter assumed tactical command at the scene from Brokas so that the former might return to base due to low fuel.

The search was concentrated on the northwestern tip of the oil slick with Porter dropping four additional sonobuoys at this point. Meanwhile, additional aircraft arrived, Lieutenant Watson (FM-2 #7) and Lieutenant (jg) Sherbring (TBM-1C #21) at 1351 hours, and Lieutenant (jg) Sissler (TBM-1C #16) at 1410 hours. These three began searching at the other end of the slick, to the eastward. They soon noticed oil bubbling at that end of it. At 1419 hours, Watson picked out the dim outline of the U-boat under the surface at the eastern end and alerted the attack group. The sub evidently had submerged on a southerly, rather than a northerly, heading, had turned to the left under the surface, and emitted the tell-tail oil as it proceeded on a semi-circular course.

From the moment Watson located the U-boat beneath the surface, until it had been completely disposed of 24 minutes later, the killer group of three TBMs and two FMs was engaged in throwing everything they had at the undersea vessel. Porter made a special run and dropped a green sonobuoy. Five minutes later, at 1425 hours, two periscopes and Schnorchel appeared above the surface.

Lieutenant (jg) Sissler, the only pilot with rockets, immediately returned to attack at 1428 hours. The vessel began to surface, its deck's awash as the rockets struck. Sissler and his gunner, Demorest, were positive that seven rockets hit the hull at right angles about 12 inches (30 centimeters) below the waterline.

Two attempts to start *U-1229*'s engines moments earlier failed; Zinke ordered the tanks blown. The crew heard a sharp rapping sound in the boat as the periscopes and Schnorchel broached, which they accurately diagnosed as strafing fire. The captain considered the situation hopeless and he gave the order to abandon ship, some two hours after the first attack. As the crew emerged from the conning tower, they came under heavy strafing fire from the attacking aircraft and casualties were heavy. No attempt was made to man the guns and Zinke was last seen standing on the bridge apparently

Three images of Lieutenant (jg) B.C. Sissler's attack on *U-1229* with the first showing the splashes from an aircraft's machine gun fire while the second records a depth charge's near miss. Most of the submarine's aft section is covered in smoke and flame in the third image. *U-1229* submerged but had to resurface as poisonous gasses began building up inside due to damaged batteries. Forty-one of the boat's crew survived, but 18 died, many by strafing aircraft. (National Archives)

unwounded. Crewmembers began throwing life rafts and jumping into the water while Porter conducted the third and final depth bomb attack. He made a beam run from the port side, pressing his electrical release button at an altitude of 300 feet (91 meters). One bomb let go, hitting on the port side near the stern "right at the edge of the submarine," but it didn't explode. The other bomb hung up in the bomb bay. An examination later showed that the arming wire had caught in the shackle, thus jamming the bomb.[10]

The Avengers and Wildcats continued strafing attacks, seven or eight in total, from the moment the periscopes and Schnorchel appeared at 1425 hours, until they disappeared for good 18 minutes later. Half a dozen inert bodies remained on and around the bridge as *U-1229* sank by the bow, and at 1443 hours, the stern lifted above the surface again, the bow nosed over steeply, and the whole craft slid at a sharp angle, into the sea. Forty-one of the 59 men survived and were rescued seven hours later by a U.S. destroyer.

Escort carrier hunter-killer groups continued to make contacts with U-boats for the next eight months without a confirmed kill. Admiral Ingram's Fourth Fleet came close while positioned in the South Atlantic on September 8 to stop a rendezvous between the refueler *U-219* and cargo submarine *U-1062* outbound to Japan. Ingram had at his disposal escort carriers *Mission Bay* (CVE-59) and *Tripoli* (CVE-64). A TBM from *Tripoli* piloted by Lieutenant W.R. Gillespie found one of the U-boats, possibly *U-219*, and radioed, "I've got him! He's shooting at me, I'm going in to make a run!" There were no further reports, the U-boat shot down Gillespie and his crew—there were no survivors. *Tripoli* aircraft made two unsuccessful attacks later that day. A month later, 30 October, Tripoli aircraft made contact with *U-219* but failed to sink her. *U-1062* was not as fortunate as *Mission Bay's* destroyer screen sunk her two days after *Tripoli's* attacks on *U-219*.[11]

Captain Aurelius B. Vosseller (left) and an unidentified officer, possibly Lieutenant Commander Jesse D. Taylor commanding officer of VC-69 or Lieutenant Commander J.T. Yavsorsky commander of VC-42. (National Archives)

A TBF-1 Avenger silhouetted against at sunset as USS *Bogue* continues to hunt German U-boats. The escort carrier's last combat cruise of in the Atlantic ended on 11 May 1945. Thereafter, she operated in the Pacific beginning on 27 July. (National Archives)

A Grumman TBF Avenger of VC-9 launches from USS *Mission Bay* (CVE-59) in early 1944. The escort carrier began ASW operations beginning on 20 September to 16 October 1944 and a second from 27 March to 25 April 1945. (Bob Lawson Collection via Emil Buehler Library-National Museum of Naval Aviation)

Flight deck personnel on USS *Mission Bay* (CVE-59) make a final inspection of the 3.5-inch rockets on the underside of a VC-9 Grumman TBF-1C Avenger on 1 January 1944. VC-36 and VC-95 operated from the ship during two ASW cruises. (Bob Lawson Collection via Emil Buehler Library-National Museum of Naval Aviation)

TBF-1Cs of VC-6 pictured on the flight deck of USS *Tripoli* (CVE-64) during 15 March to 29 April 1944 when the squadron conducted an unsuccessful attack on *U-513* on 19 April. Three additional Atlantic cruises occurred from 24 May to 18 June, 1 August to 12 November 1944. *Tripoli* operating with TG 47.7 joined *Mission Bay* on a joint hunter-killer group and, on 28 September, a TBF flown by VC-6 pilot Lieutenant William R. Gillespie found Type XB *U-219* off the Cape Verde Islands. The submarine's anti-aircraft fire shot down the Avenger killing Gillespie and his crew. (Thomas Doll Collection via Captain Rich Dann, USNR (RET) and Emil Buehler Library-National Museum of Naval Aviation)

CHAPTER 11

They Were Dependable: USN Blimp Operations

"They Were Dependable"

FROM THE MAIN TITLE FOR THE PAMPHLET,
AIRSHIP OPERATIONS WORLD WAR II

This work on U.S. Navy's air campaign against the U-boat would not be complete without acknowledging the Navy's lighter-than-air blimp operations in the effort. Blimps, the term used interchangeably with airship, had been part of the Navy's inventory since the World War I and utilized in the World War II in anti-submarine operations, while flying over convoys or acting independently from bases that stretched from Newfoundland to Rio de Janeiro. The Navy had no definite blimp program until Congress authorized the construction of 48 non-rigid airships on June 15, 1940. However, the program by December 7, 1941 consisted of only 10 of them: four K-type patrol airships, three L-type trainers, one G-type trainer, and two ex-Army TC-type trainers. Personnel consisted of 100 pilots and 200 air crewmen. The program by 1945 had grown to 134 K-type, 22 L-type trainers, eight G type trainers, and four M-type patrol airships with a personnel level of approximately 706 pilots (down from 1,500 in 1944), and 7,200 air crewmen. Airship Squadron ZP-12 at Lakehurst, New Jersey and Airship Squadron ZP-32 were the first squadrons commissioned in January 1942. Six Fleet Air Wings and one Utility Squadron were in operation by the end of hostilities. Five wings operated from the United States, Caribbean and South America, while one blimp squadron operated from Port Lyautey, French Morocco, the latter being the first non-rigid blimps to make a transoceanic flight.

Naval Air Station Lakehurst, New Jersey during October 1942 of four Navy K-Type Blimps in a hangar. The presence of U.S. Navy blimps covering convoys may have kept U-boats from attacking, although a U-boat did sink one merchant ship while a blimp patrolled overhead. (Photographed by Lieutenant Commander Chas Kerlee. U.S. Navy, now in the collections of the National Archives)

U.S. Navy K-Type airship on an Atlantic Convoy, probably during 1942. Blimps did conduct several unsuccessful attacks against U-boats and their range along with slow speed allowed for prolonged coverage. (National Archives)

Fleet Airship Wing One (Headquarters, Lakehurst, New Jersey)

Squadron	Location
ZP-11	NAS South Weymouth, Massachusetts
ZP-12	NAS Lakehurst, New Jersey
ZP-15	NAS Glynco, Georgia
ZP-24	NAS Weeksville, North Carolina

Fleet Airship Wing Two (Headquarters, Richmond, Florida)

Squadron	Location
ZP-21	Richmond, Florida
ZP-22	Houma, Louisiana
ZP-23	Vernam Field, Jamaica

Fleet Airship Wing Three (Headquarters, Moffett Field, California)

Squadron	Location
ZP-31	Santa Ana, California
ZP-32	Moffett Field, California
ZP-33	Tillamook, Oregon

Fleet Airship Wing Four (Headquarters, Recife, Brazil)

Squadron	Location
ZP-41	São Luiz, Brazil
ZP-42	Maceió, Brazil

Fleet Airship Wing Five (Headquarters, Trinidad, British West Indies)

Squadron	Location
ZP-51	Trinidad, British West Indies

Airship Utility Squadron One (Headquarters, Meacham Field, Key West, Florida)

Squadron	Location
Detachment One	NAS Weymouth, Massachusetts
Detachment 1-1	Fisher's Island, New York
Detachment 1-3	Naval Mine Warfare Test Station, Solomons, Maryland

Squadron 14 (Headquarters, Port Lyautey, French Morocco)

Squadron	Location
ZP-14	Port Lyautey, French Morocco

The number of convoys escorted by naval airships grew in relation to the number of those available, conducting 35,600 operational flights (380,000 flying hours) in the Atlantic by May 1945.

The original caption for this image is "Sunset over the Atlantic" finds another Allied convoy moving peacefully towards its destination. A U.S. Navy K-class lighter-than-air aircraft hovers overhead watching for any sign of enemy submarines, June 1943. (Office of War Information Photograph from the National Archives)

PBY-5A 63-P-14 above a U.S. Navy K-Blimp flying over the Mediterranean. This blimp operated out of NAS Port Lyautey, French Morocco as part of Squadron K-14. (Mark Aldrich)

Atlantic Convoy Coverage

Year	Number of Vessels
1942	8,000
1943	27,000
1944	36,000
1945	6,500
Total	77,500

Only one airship was lost to enemy action, K-74 shot down by *U-134* in the Florida Straits on July 18, 1943. The blimp's crew of nine evacuated the ship and were rescued, except for Aviation Machinist Mate Second Class Isadore Stressel, who was attacked and killed by a shark minutes before rescue.[1]

Final Thoughts

Escort carrier hunter-killer groups continued patrols over the Atlantic until the end of the war, contacts with U-boats decreasing as the war drew to its final months. The BdU lost 231 U-boats during 1944 and another 124 the following year. The use of Ultra in locating enemy submarines, along with the technological innovations of hedgehog depth charges, radar, the Mk-24 acoustic torpedo, and the sonobuoy ended the U-boat's dominance and they, as the hunter, became the hunted. The BdU kept U-boat losses secret and crews venturing out into the Atlantic were unaware of such misfortune, and that the odds were against them in returning from a patrol. Would such young men have joined the U-boat service between 1944 and 1945 if they had known of the catastrophic losses? Those men mirrored those trying to kill them; they were young, in their teens and twenties, and for most, their lives cut short by a depth charge or torpedo dropped by U.S. naval aircraft. Only 10,000 men survived of the 40,000 who served aboard U-boats, a 75 percent fatality rate. It was in all intent and purpose a death sentence. Allied air and surface, forces by the beginning of 1944, knew a U-boat's position on any given day and by the use of anti-submarine technology, death was a near certainty.

It was a war of attrition and briefly, it appeared the U-boat would continue sinking Allied merchant ships faster than could be built, and Britain and Russia would ultimately fall, starved of food and armaments. Yet, the ability of the United States to rearm and out build ships, along with the development and sharing of anti-submarine warfare technology between the United States and Britain, meant that the near annihilation of U-boats was a forgone conclusion.

Allied air forces sank 48 percent of all U-boats (372) using the often quoted number of 783 lost by all causes. American air forces sank 159 U-boats. Most of those losses resulted from the strategic bombing of submarine bases and pins by the 8th 9th, and 15th Air Forces. Navy air forces (composite and patrol) destroyed or participated in half of that number alone or in conjunction with other Allied surface and air units. Additionally, Scouting Squadron Nine contributed to sinking *U-576*, while carrier-based aircraft sank a pair of Vichy French submarines in the Mediterranean during Operation *Torch*.[2]

Two naval air units, VB-112, and VS-62, while not determined as the primary agent in a U-boat's destruction, participated in the demise of a like number of German submarines. An aircraft of VS-62 on May 15, 1943 spotted Type IX/C *U-176*, commanded by Korvettenkapitän R. Dierksen, surfaced in the Atlantic north of Cuba. Cuban Patrol boat CS-1 arrived on the scene guided by smoke markers dropped from the aircraft. Subsequent depth charging by the boat sank the U-boat along with its 53-man crew. A PB4Y-1 Liberator piloted by Lieutenant L.T. Denison of VPB-112 participated with British warships in the sinking of Type VIIB *U-1279* on February 27, 1945 in the English Channel. Oberleutnant H. Falke and his crew perished.[3]

Glossary of German Navy Officer Rank and United States Navy Equivalent

KRIEGSMARINE	U.S.N.
Kapitän zur See	Captain
Fregattenkapitän	Commander
Korvettenkapitän	Lieutenant Commander
Kapitänleutnant	Lieutenant Commander
Oberleutnant zur See	Lieutenant (Senior Grade)
Leutnant zur See	Lieutenant (Junior Grade)

Appendices

Appendix A: Patrol Wings, Atlantic Fleet December 1941

Patrol Wing Three (PatWing Three)

Seaplane Tenders	Squadrons
Clemson (AVD-4)	VP-31
Osmond Ingram (AVD-9)	VP-32
Lapwing (AVP-1)	
Sandpiper (AVP-9)	

Patrol Wing Five (PatWing Five)

Seaplane Tenders	Squadrons
Chandeleur (AV-10)	VP-51
Thrush (AVP-3)	VP-52
Gannet (AVP-8)	
Greenee (AVD-13)	

Patrol Wing Seven (PatWing Seven)

Seaplane Tenders	Squadrons
Albemarle (AV-5)	VP-71
George E. Badger (AVD-3)	VP-72
Mackinac (AVP-13)	VP-73
Belknap (AVD-8)	VP-74

Patrol Wing Eight (PatWing Eight)

Seaplane Tenders	Squadrons
Pocomoke (AV-9)	VP-81
Goldsborough (AVD-5)	VP-82
Barnegat (AVP-10)	VP-83
Biscayne (AVP-11)	VP-84

Patrol Wing Nine (PatWing Nine)

Seaplane Tenders	Squadrons
Humbolt (AVP-21)	VP-91
Matagorda (AVP-22)	VP-92
Absecon (AVP-23)	VP-93
	VP-94

Appendix B: Fleet Air Wing Strength January 1943

Fleet Air Wing 3 (Coco Solo, Panama)

Squadron	Aircraft Assigned	Base
VP-33	PBY-5	Coco Solo

Fleet Air Wing 5 (Norfolk)

Squadron	Aircraft Assigned	Base
VP-31	PBY-5 (11)	(8) Quonset Point, Rhode Island
		(3) Elizabeth City, New Jersey
VP-52	PBY-5 (11)	(9) Bermuda
		(2) Norfolk
VP-94	PBY-5A (12)	(1) Jacksonville, Florida
		(11) Natal, Brazil
VP-201	PBM-3 (14)	(12) Banana River, Florida
		(2) Norfolk
VP-202	PBM-3 (12)	(10) Corpus Christi, Texas
		(2) Banana River
VP-203	PBM-3 (11)	(9) San Juan, Puerto Rico
		(2) Norfolk
VP-204	PBM-3 (8)	(6) San Juan
		(2) Norfolk
VP-205	PBM-3C (1)	Norfolk

Fleet Air Wing 5 (Norfolk)

Squadron	Aircraft Assigned	Base
VP-82	PV-3 (11)	Argentia
VP-84	PBY-5A (11)	Iceland
VP-93	PBY-5A	(3) Argentia
		(2) Greenland
		(1) Argentia
	PV-3 (7)	Argentia

Fleet Air Wing 11 (San Juan)

Squadron	Aircraft Assigned	Base
VP-32	PBY-3 (6)	(4) Guantanamo, Cuba
		(2) Great Exuma, Bahamas
VP-34	PBY-5 (12)	(4) Great Exuma
		(4) Trinidad
		(2) Guantanamo
		(2) San Juan
VP-53	PBY-5 (10)	Trinidad
VP-74	PBM-3 (14)	Natal
VP-81	PBY-5 (5)	Trinidad
VP-83	PBY-5A (11)	Natal

Fleet Air Wing 15 (Norfolk)

Squadron	Aircraft Assigned	Base
VP-73	PBY-5A (12)	Port Lyautey, French Morocco
VP-92	PBY-5A (10)	Casablanca, French Morocco

Appendix C: Fleet Air Wing Strength January 1944

Fleet Air Wing 3 (Coco Solo)

Squadron	Aircraft Assigned	Base
VP-1	PB2Y-3 (13)	(8) Coco Solo
		(5) San Diego, California
VP-206	PBM-3S (13)	Coco Solo
VP-207	PBM-3S (13)	Coco Solo

Fleet Air Wing 5 (Norfolk)

Squadron	Aircraft Assigned	Base
VP-16	PBM-3D (6)	Elizabeth City
VP-214	PBM-3S (12)	Harvey Point
VP-215	PBM-3S (12)	Harvey Point
VP-216	PBM-3D (4)	Harvey Point
	PBM-3S (4)	"
VB-113	PB4Y-1 (6)	Norfolk

Fleet Air Wing 7 (Plymouth, England)

Squadron	Aircraft Assigned	Base
VB-103	PB4Y-1 (12)	Dunkeswell, England
VB-105	PB4Y-1 (13)	"
VB-110	PB4Y-1 (12)	"

Fleet Air Wing 9 (New York)

Squadron	Aircraft Assigned	Base
VP-6	PBY-5A (7)	Greenland
VP-15	PB2Y-3 (13)	(9) Bermuda
		(3) Quonset
		(1) New York
VP-74	PBM-3S (13)	Elizabeth City
VP-84	PBY-5 (15)	(13) Quonset
		(2) Norfolk

Fleet Air Wing 11 (San Juan)

Squadron	Aircraft Assigned	Base
VP-32	PBM-3S (14)	Guantanamo
VP-204	PBM-3S (13)	Trinidad
VP-205	PBM-3S (12)	Trinidad
VP-210	PBM-3S (12)	(6) Great Exuma
		(6) Guantanamo
VP-212	PBM-3S (11)	San Juan
VB-128	PV-1 (13)	San Juan
VB-131	PV-1 (11)	Zandery, Suriname

VB-132	PV-1 (11)	(5) Trinidad
		(5) Curacao
		(10 San Juan
VB-141	PV-1 (11)	Curacao

Fleet Air Wing 12 (Miami)

Squadron	Aircraft Assigned	Base
VP-208	PBM-3S (12)	(9) Key West, Florida
		(2) Grand Cayman Island
		(1) Quonset
VP-216	PBM-3S (12)	Key West
VB-125	PV-1 (12)	(8) Key West
		(4) San Julian, Cuba

Fleet Air Wing 15 (Port Lyautey)

Squadron	Aircraft Assigned	Base
VP-63	PBY-5A (14)	Port Lyautey
VP-92	PBY-5A (12)	Agadir, French Morocco
VB-111	PB4Y-1 (13)	Port Lyautey
VB-112	PB4Y-1 (11)	"
VB-127	PV-1 (12)	(7) Port Lyautey
		(5) Agadir
VB-132	PV-1 (15)	Port Lyautey

Fleet Air Wing 16 (Recife, Brazil)

Squadron	Aircraft Assigned	Base
VP-94	PBY-5A (18)	(8) Belem, Brazil
		(4) Zandery
		(6) Norfolk
VP-203	PBM-3S (14)	(7) Natal
		(6) Aratu, Brazil
		(1) Belem
VP-211	PBM-3S (14)	(10) Rio de Janerio
		(4) Aratu

Squadron	Aircraft Assigned	Base
VB-107	PB4Y-1 (10)	(8) Ascension Island
		(2) Natal
VB-129	PV-1 (12)	(8) Ipitanga, Brazil
		(3) Recife
		(1) Quonset
VB-130	PV-1 (12)	Fortalleza, Brazil
VB-143	PV-1 (12)	(11) Recife
		(1) Quonset
VB-145	PV-1 (13)	(9) Natal
		(2) Fernando, Brazil
		(2) Quonset

Appendix D: U-boat Losses from Patrol Squadrons

1942

Date	Submarine	Unit(s)	Location
1 Mar	U-656	VP-82	46.15N, 53.15W
15 Mar	U-503	VP-82	45.50N, 48.50W
30 Jun	U-158	VP-74	32.50N, 67.28W
20 Aug	U-464		61.25N, 14.40W
5 Oct	U-582	VP-73	58.52N, 21.42W
5 Nov	U-408	VP-84	67.40N, 18.32W

1943

Date	Submarine	Unit(s)	Location
6 Jan	U-164	VP-83	01.58S, 39.22W
13 Jan	U-507	VP-83	01.38S, 39.52W
8 Mar	U-156	VP-53	12.38N, 54.39W
15 Apr	Archimede	VP-83	03.23S, 30.28N
27 Apr	U-174	VB-125	43.35N, 56.18W
14 May	U-640	VP-84	60.32N, 31.05W

17 May	*U-128*	VP-74	10.00N, 35.35W
		Moffett	
		Jouett	
25 May	*U-467*	VP-84	62.25N, 14.52W
20 Jun	*U-388*	VP-84	57.36N, 31.20W
24 Jun	*U-194*	VP-84	59.00N, 26.18W
9 Jul	*U-590*	VP-94	03.22N, 48.38W
15 Jul	*U-759*	VP-32	15.58N, 73.44W
15 Jul	*U-135*	VP-92	28.20N, 13.17W
19 Jul	*U-513*	VP-74	27.17S, 47.32W
21 Jul	*U-662*	VP-94	03.56N, 48.46N
23 Jul	*U-598*	VB-107	04.05S, 33.23W
26 Jul	*U-359*	VP-32	18.06N, 75.00W
28 Jul	*U-159*	VP-32	15.57N, 68.30W
30 Jul	*U-591*	VB-127	08.36S, 34.34W
31 Jul	*U-199*	VP-74	23.54S, 42.54W
3 Aug	*U-752*	VP-205	11.35N, 54.05W
7 Aug	*U-84*	VB-105	27.55N, 68.30W
7 Aug	*U-615*	VP-204	12.38N, 64.15W
		VP-205	
		VB-130	
11 Aug	*U-604*	VB-129	05.00' 20° 00' W
28 Aug	*U-94*	VP-92	17.40N, 74.30W
		HMCS *Oakville*	
27 Sep	*U-161*	VP-74	12.30S, 35.35W
4 Oct	*U-279*	VP-128	60.40N, 26.30W
5 Nov	*U-848*	VB-107	10.09'N, 18.00W
25 Nov	*U-849*	VB-107	06.30' 05° 40' W

1944

Date	Submarine	Unit(s)	Location
28 Jan	*U-271*	VB-103	53.15N, 15.52W
6 Feb	*U-177*	VB-107	10.35S, 23.15W
12 Feb	*U-761*	VP-63	35.55N, 05.45W
		HMS *Anthony*	
		HMS *Wishart*	
3 Mar	*U-392*	VP-63	35.55N, 05.41W
		HMS *Affleck*	
		HMS *Vanoc*	
15 May	*U-731*	VP-63	35.54N, 05.55W
		HMS *Kilmarnockc*	
		HMT *Blackfly*	
22 June	*U-988*	VB-110	50.13N, 02.59W
8 Jul	*U-243*	VB-103	47.06N, 06.40W
		RAAF 10 Squadron (credited for sinking)	
29 Sep	*U-863*	VB-107	10.45S, 25.30W

1945

Date	Submarine	Unit(s)	Location
20 Apr	*U-1107*	VPB-103	48.12N, 05.42W
25 Apr	*U-110*	VPB-107	48.12N, 05.42W
30 Apr	*U-326*	VPB-63	47.51N, 06.46W

Appendix E: U-boat Losses from Composite Squadrons
1943

Date	Submarine	Units	Location
22 May	*U-569*	VC-9 from *Bogue* (CVE-9)	50-40 N, 35-21 W
5 Jun	*U-217*	VC-9 from *Bogue* (CVE-9)	30-18 N, 42-50 W
12 Jun	*U-118*	VC-9 from *Bogue* (CVE-9)	30-49 N, 33-49 W
13 Jul	*U-487*	VC-13 from *Core* (CVE-13)	27-15 N, 34-18 W
14 Jul	*U-160*	VC-29 from *Santee* (CVE-29)	33-54 N, 27-13 W
15 Jul	*U-509*	VC-29 from *Santee* (CVE-29)	34-02 N, 26-02 W
16 Jul	*U-67*	VC-13 from *Core* (CVE-13)	30-05 N, 44-17 W
23 Jul	*U-527*	VC-9 from *Bogue* (CVE-9)	35-25 N, 27-56 W
30 Jul	*U-43*	VC-29 from *Santee* (CVE-29)	34-57 N, 35-11 W
7 Aug	*U-117*	VC-1 from *Card* (CVE-11)	39-32 N, 38-21 W
9 Aug	*U-664*	VC-1 from *Card* (CVE-11)	40-12 N, 37-29 W
11 Aug	*U-525*	VC-1 from *Card* (CVE-11)	41-29 N, 38-55 W
24 Aug	*U-185*	VC-13 from *Core* (CVE-13)	27-00 N, 37-06 W
27 Aug	*U-847*	VC-1 from *Card* (CVE-11)	28-19 N, 37-58 W
4 Oct	*U-422*	VC-9 from *Card* (CVE-11)	43-18 N, 28-58 W
4 Oct	*U-460*	VC-9 from *Card* (CVE-11)	43-13 N, 28-58 W
13 Oct	*U-402*	VC-9 from *Card* (CVE-11)	48-56 N, 29-41 W
20 Oct	*U-378*	VC-13 from *Core* (CVE-13)	47-40 N, 28-27 W
28 Oct	*U-220*	VC-1 from *Block Island* (CVE-21)	48-53 N, 33-30 W
31 Oct	*U-584*	VC-9 from *Card* (CVE-11)	49-14 N, 31-55 W
29 Nov	*U-86*	VC-19 from *Bogue* (CVE-9)	39-33 N, 19-01 W
		George E. Badger (AVD-3)	
		DuPont (DD-152)	
		Clemson (DD-186)	
		George W. Ingram (DE-62)	
13 Dec	*U-172*	VC-19	26.29N, 29.58W
20 Dec	*U-850*	VC-19 from *Bogue* (CVE-9)	32-54 N, 37-01 W

1944

Date	Submarine	Units	Location
16 Jan	*U-544*	VC-13 from *Guadalcanal* (CVE-60)	40-30 N, 37-20 W
13 Mar	*U-575*	VC-95 from *Bogue* (CVE-9)	46-18 N, 27-34 W
		Br. Sqdns. 172, 206 & 220	
		Haverfield (DE-393)	
		Hobson (DD-464)	
		HMCS *Prince Rupert*	
16 Mar	*U-801*	VC-6 from *Block Island* (CVE-21)	16-42 N, 30-28 W
		Carry (DD-463)	
		Bronstein (DE-189)	
19 Mar	*U-1059*	VC-6 from *Block Island* (CVE-21)	13-10 N, 33-44 W
9 Apr	*U-515*	VC-58 from *Guadalcanal* (CVE-60)	34-35 N, 19-18 W
		Pope (DD-225)	
		Pillsbury (DE-133)	
		Chatelain (DE-149)	
		Flaherty (DE-135)	
10 Apr	*U-68*	VC-58 from *Guadalcanal* (CVE-60)	33-25 N, 18-59 W
6 May	*U-66*	VC-55 from *Block Island* (CVE-106)	17-17 N, 32-29 W
		Buckley (DE-51)	
12 Jun	*U-490*	VC-95	42.47N, 40.08W
		Frost (DE-144)	
		Huse (DE-145)	
		Inch (DE-146)	
15 Jun	*U-860*	VC-9 from *Solomons* (CVE-67)	25-27 S, 05-30 W
24 Jun	*I-52*	VC-69 from *Bogue* (CVE-9)	15-16 N, 39-55 W
2 Jul	*U-543*	VC-58 from *Wake Island* (CVE-65)	25-34N, 21-36 W
20 Aug	*U-1229*	VC-42 from *Bogue* (CVE-9)	42-20 N, 51-39 W

Captured

Date	Submarine	Units	Location
4 Jun	*U-505*	VC-8 from *Guadalcanal* (CVE-60)	21-30 N, 19-20 W
		Chatelain (DE-149)	
		Jenks (DE-665)	
		Pillsbury (DE-133)	

Endnotes

Introduction

1   Actual total numbers of losses vary among sources in print and on the Internet. See Battle of the Atlantic: Countering the U-boat Threat and Supplying the Allies at https://www.history.navy.mil/browse-by-topicwars-conflicts-and-operations/world-war-ii/1942/atlantic.html.

2   Samuel Eliot Morison, *History of United States Naval Operations in WWII: The Battle of the Atlantic 1939–1943* (Edison, NJ: Castle Books, 2001), pp. 226–228.

3   Samuel Eliot Morison, *The Battle of the Atlantic 1939–1943*, pp. 224–226.

4   Gesellschaft für Elektroakustische und Mechanische Apparate translated is the Society for Electroacoustic and Mechanical Apparatus). The company, founded in 1930, originally produced radios for public use.

5   Metox did emit powerful radiation emissions and theoretically, the Allies could have tracked the device. See Navweapons at http://www.navweaps.com/Weapons/WINGER_Radar.php.

6   See Samuel Eliot Morison, *The Battle of the Atlantic: 1939–1943*, pp. 226–228 for additional information on high-frequency detection.

Chapter 1

1   Alan C. Carey, *U.S. Navy PB4Y-1 (B-24) Liberator Squadrons in Great Britain during World War II* (Atglen, PA: Schiffer Publishing, 2003), p. 24.

2   Carey, *U.S. Navy PB4Y-1 Liberator Squadrons in Great Britain*, p. 21. Generally, rhumbs are imaginary lines that cross all meridians and used for navigation.

3   See Bristol Operation Plan No. 1–41 (revised on October 23, 1941).

Chapter 2

1   Morison, *The Battle of the Atlantic 1939–1943*, p. 413. Losses occurring in the Eastern Sea Frontier, Canadian Coastal Zone, and North Atlantic Convoy areas.

2   See Gaylord T. M. Kelshall, *The U-boat War in the Caribbean* (Annapolis, Maryland: Naval Institute Press, 1994), pp. 8–9 and Morison, *The Battle of the Atlantic 1939–1943*, pp. 207–209.

3   CPO Mason's "Sighted Sub Sank Same' about the sinking is part of naval lore and is found in numerous sources. See Samuel Eliot Morison, *The Battle of the Atlantic 1939–1943*, p. 154.

4   USS Roper's sinking of U-85. Samuel Eliot Morison, *The Battle of the Atlantic 1939–1943*, p. 155.

5   It remains unknown whether the first or subsequent attacks by VP-82 caused the U-boat's loss. See VP-82 After Action Report.

6   Gaylord T. M. Kelshall, *The U-boat War in the Caribbean*, (Annapolis, Maryland: Naval Institute Press, 1994), pp. 110–111.
7   The sinking of U-576.The pilots were Ensign Frank C. Lewis and Ensign Charles D. Webb. See Samuel Eliot Morison, *The Battle of the Atlantic 1939–1943*, p. 249.
8   Lieutenant (jg) Robert Brown Hopgood's statement recorded in the After Action Report.
9   Lieutenant (jg) Hopgood's statement recorded in After Action Report.
10 VP-73 After Action Report and report on interrogation of U-158 survivors.
11 "Sank Sub, Open Club" found in the VP-73 After Action Report.
12 Samuel Eliot Morison, The Battle of The Atlantic 1939–1943, pp. 50–51.
13 Ibid.
14 VB-128's squadron history. For additional information on Battle Standing War Order 483, see Sebastien Roblin, *The Nazis Ordered Their U-Boats to Fight Airplanes. It was a Massive Mistake*, (The National Interest, August 28, 2018).
15 Alan C. Carey, *PV Ventura/Harpoon Units of World War 2*, (Osprey Publishing; Oxford, UK) p. 80.
16 See Samuel Eliot Morison, The *Atlantic Battle Won: May 1943–May 1945*, (Edison, NJ: Castle Books, 2001) pp. 21–26.
17 Morison, The Atlantic Battle Won, 28.
18 Gene McIntyre interview by the author.
19 Ibid.
20 Ibid.
21 Axel Niestlé, *German U-boat Losses During World War II: Details of Destruction*, (London: Frontline Books, 2014), p. 87.

Chapter 3

1   See Karl M. Hasslinger, Commander USN, *The U-Boat War in the Caribbean: Opportunities Lost*.
2   Karl M. Hasslinger, Commander USN, *The U-Boat War in the Caribbean*.
3   Gaylor T. M. Kelshall, *The U-boat War in the Caribbean*, p. 70.
4   Ibid., p. 85
5   The author chose not to include identifying information to protect the privacy of those involved and their descendants.
6   Office of the Chief of Naval Operations, O.N.I. G/Serial No. 5, Report on the Interrogation of Survivors from *U-94* Sunk on August 27, 1942.
7   Lieutenant Gordon R. Fiss' statement in VP-92 squadron After Action Report.
8   From VP-92's After Action Report of the attack.
9   See Gaylor T.M. Kelshall, *The U-boat War in the Caribbean*, pp. 155–159 on the sinking of U-94.
10 "The Fog of War," has its origin as, "a realm of uncertainty," by Carol von Claueswitz in his book *Vom Kriege* (1832). Claueswitz never used it: Colonel Hale is the originator and provided the specific meaning at the Aldershot Military Academy on March 24, 1896.
11 See Stetson Conn, *Guarding the United States and its Outposts,* Ch. XVI.
12 The ultimate fate of the survivors is not included in the squadron's report.
13 Pinholster's statements are from the VP-32 After Action Report.
14 Samuel Eliot Morison, *Atlantic Battle Won*, pp. 218–219.
15 Ibid., p.197.
16 Ibid., p. 195.

Chapter 4

1   "Ashore and afloat." Alan C. Carey, *Galloping Ghosts of the Brazilian Coast*, p. 9.
2   Alan C. Carey, *Galloping Ghosts of the Brazilian Coast.*
3   Morison Samuel Eliot, *Battle of the Atlantic Won*, p. 208.
4   Frank Burgess, e-mail to the author. Burgess was commissioned as an ensign in February 1945.
5   Richard A. Wilson, *History of VP-83, VB-107, and VPB-107 in the South Atlantic*, unpublished.
6   Ibid.
7   Ibid.
8   The *Archimede* left Le Verdon on 26 February 1943.
9   Alan C. Carey, *Galloping Ghosts.*
10 Letter written by Captain William J. Barnard, USN (RET) to Bill DeArmond.
11 Harold Carey's statements are part of the attack's After Action Report.
12 Davis' statements are part of the attack's After Action Report.
13 Harold Carey in After Action Report.
14 Office of Naval Intelligence, Op-16-Z, Report on the Iinterrogation of Survivors from *U-128.*
15 Davis in After Action Report.
16 Samuel Eliot Morison, *The Atlantic Battle Won*, p. 210.
17 Ibid., p. 214.

Chapter 5

1   Paul Richter, letter to the author.
2   Ibid.
3   Ibid.
4   Office of Naval Intelligence, Op-16-Z, Report on the Iinterrogation of Survivors from *U-591.*
5   Office of Naval Intelligence, Op-16-Z, Report on the Iinterrogation of Survivors from report *U-199.*
6   Samuel Eliot Morison, *The Atlantic Battle Won*, p. 214.
7   Letter from Captain William J. Barnard to Bill DeArmond.
8   Ibid.
9   Ibid.
10 Letters by Florence Carey from Bill DeArmond.
11 Office of Naval Intelligence, Op-16-Z, Preliminary Report on the Interrogation of Survivors from *U-604* and Office of Naval Intelligence, Op-16-Z, Report on the Interrogation of Survivors from *U-604* and *U-185.*
12 Lieutenant (jg) Harry Patterson's statements found in *U-74* After Action Report.

Chapter 6

1   Richard A. Wilson, *History of VP-83, VB-107, and VPB-107*, pp. 24–25.
2   Ibid., pp. 15–16.
3   Ibid., p. 16.
4   Ibid., p.16.
5   Ibid., p. 16.
6   Ibid., p.17.

7   Ibid., p. 17.
8   Ibid., p. 18.
9   Ibid., p. 18
10 Ibid., p. 19.
11 Ibid., p. 19.
12 Ibid., p. 20.
13 Ibid., P. 20.
14 Ibid., p. 22.
15 Ibid., pp. 25–26.
10 Office of Naval Intelligence, Op-16-Z, Report on the Interrogation of Survivors from *U-177*.

Chapter 7

1   VP-63 Squadron History.
2   Ibid.
3   Ibid.
4   Ibid.
5   Ibid.

Chapter 8

1   Alan C, Carey, *PB4Y-1 Liberator Squadrons in Great Britain*, p. 26.
2   Ibid., p. 29.
3   Lieutenant Brownell's loss originally recorded in the History of FAW-7 and referenced again in Alan C. Carey, *PB4Y-1 Liberator Squadrons in Great Britain*, p. 46.
4   Alan C. Carey, *PB4Y-1 Liberator Squadrons in Great Britain*, pp. 59–60.
5   Ibid., p. 60.
6   Ibid., p. 60.
7 ` Ibid., 81–82.
8   Alan C. Carey, *PB4Y-1 Liberator Squadrons in Great Britain*, pp. 80–81 and Axel Niestlé, *German U-boat Losses During World War II*, p.94.
9   Alan C. Carey, *PB4Y-1 Liberator Squadrons in Great Britain*, pp. 113–114.
10 Ibid., p. 114.

Chapter 9

1   The Japanese submarine I-175 sank *Liscome Bay* (CVE-56) off the Gilbert Islands on November 24, 1943.
2   Jeffrey G. Barlow, *The Navy's Escort Carrier Program*. Naval History Magazine, Volume 27, Number 6, December 2013.
3   Office of Naval Operations, O.N.I. 250-G/Serial 12. Report on the Interrorgation of Survivors from *U-569* Sunk on May 22, 1943 and VC-9 After Action Report for that date.
4   From Chief of Naval Operations, O.N.I. G/Serial No. 15, Report on the Interrogation of Survivors from *U-118* Sunk on 12 June 1943. Report of *U-118* survivors.
5   See VC-29 After Action Report.
6   Moroccan Sea Frontiers Forces, Preliminary Report, Interrogation of Survivors from *U-527* Sunk by A/C from USS Bogue on July 23, 1943.

7   See VC-29 After Action Report.
8   Ibid.
9   Lieutenant J. C. (jg) Forney's statement in After Action Report.
10   Lieutenant C. R. Staple's statement in After Action Report.
11   Lieutenant J. C. (jg) Forney's statement in After Action Report.
12   Office of Naval Operations Final Report G/Serial 27, Report of the Interrogation of Survivors from *U-664* Sunk on 9 August 1943 and VC-9 After Action Report.
13   Office of Naval Intelligence, Op-16-Z, Report on the Interrogation of Survivors from *U-185*.
14   Office of the Chief of Naval Operations, Final Report G/Serial 29, Report on the Interrogation of Survivors from *U-172* Sunk 13 December 1943.
15   Interview of Lieutenant (jg) Harold G. Bradshaw, US Navy Public Relations Department, 30 January 1944.

Chapter 10

1   Office of Naval Operations, Final Report G/Serial 37, Report on the Interrogation of Survivors from *U-1059* Sunk 19 March 1944.
2   Chief of Naval Operations, Final Report-G/Serial 36, Report on the Interrogation of Survivors from *U-68* Sunk on 6 May 1944.
3   The original written transcription contains numerous grammatical errors and has been corrected for clarity.
4   Interview of Captain Daniel V. Gallery on May 26, 1945
5   See VC-9 After Action Report.
6   Office of Naval Intelligence, Op-16-Z, Preliminary Report on the Interrogation of Survivors from *U-860*.
7   Excerpt from a wire recording of the attack recorded onboard the aircraft.
8   Office of Naval Operations Final Report G/Serial 46, Report on the Interrogation of Survivors from *U-1229* Sunk 20 August 1944.
9   Interrogation report of U-1229 survivors.
10   See VC-9 After Action Report.
11   Samuel Eliot Morison, *The Atlantic Battle Won*, pp. 295–296.

Chapter 11

1   The source on U.S. Navy Blimp Operations comes from, *They Were Dependable: Airship Operations World War II December 1941 to September 1945*, (United States Navy, 1946).
2   Army Air Force antisubmarine squadrons sank 13 U-boats while strategic bombings destroyed 68. See Axel Niestlé, *German U-boat Losses During World War II*, p. 304.
3   Axel Niestlé, *German U-boat Losses During World War II*, pp. 110, 122, 304–305.

Selected Bibliography

Government Sources

After Action Reports and War Diaries of selected squadrons, units, and ships of the U.S. Navy.

Anti-Submarine Development Detachment Air Force, U.S. Atlantic Fleet.

Commander Air Force, Atlantic Fleet. History of Air Force, Atlantic Fleet, Volume I, United States Atlantic Fleet, December 1945.

Conn, Stetson and Byron Fairchild. *The Western Hemisphere: The Framework of Hemisphere Defense* (Washington: Center of Military History, 1989).

Conn, Stetson, Rose C. Engleman and Byron Fairchild. *Guarding the United States and its Outposts* (Washington: Center of Military History, 2000).

Eastern Sea Frontier War Diary, Organizations of Air Forces, Chapter II, April 1943.

Eastern Sea Frontier War Diary, Organization of the Tenth Fleet. Chapter IV, April 1943.

King, Ernest J. Third and Final Report to the Secretary of the Navy Covering the period 1 March 1945 to 1 October 1945.

Moroccan Sea Frontiers Forces, Preliminary Report, Interrogation of Survivors from U-527 Sunk by A/C from USS *Bogue* on July 23, 1943.

Naval Airship Training and Experimental Command, U.S. Naval Air Station (Lakehurst: New Jersey, 1946). *"They Were Dependable": Airship Operations World War II December 1941 to September 1945*).

Office of Naval Intelligence, Op-16-Z, Report on the Interrogation of Survivors from *U-128*.

Office of Naval Intelligence, Op-16-Z, Report on the Interrogation of Survivors from *U-177*.

Office of Naval Intelligence, Op-16-Z, Report on the Interrogation of Survivors from *U-199*.

Office of Naval Intelligence, Op-16-Z, Report on the Interrogation of Survivors from *U-513*.

Office of Naval Intelligence, Op-16-Z, Report on the Interrogation of Survivors from *U-591*.

Office of Naval Intelligence, Op-16-Z, Preliminary Report on the Interrogation of Survivors from *U-604*.

Office of Naval Intelligence, Op-16-Z, Report on the Interrogation of Survivors from *U-604* AND *U-185*.

Office of Naval Intelligence, Op-16-Z, Report on the Interrogation of Survivors from *U-662*.

Office of Naval Intelligence, Op-16-Z, Preliminary Report on the Interrogation of Survivors from *U-848*.

Office of Naval Intelligence, Op-16-Z, Preliminary Report on the Interrogation of Survivors from *U-860*.

Office of the Chief of Naval Operations, Final Report-G/Serial 38. Report on the Survivors from *U-515* Sunk 9 April 1944 and U-66 Sunk on 6 May 1944.

Office of the Chief of Naval Operations, Final Report-G/Serial 36, Report on the Survivors from *U-68* Sunk on 6 May 1944.

Office of Naval Operations Final Report G/Serial 27. Report of the Interrogation of Survivors from *U-664* Sunk on 9 August 1943.

Office of Naval Operations Final Report G/Serial 28. Report of the Interrogation of Survivors from *U-841* Sunk 17 October 1943.

Office of the Chief of Naval Operations, Final Report G/Serial 29. Report on the Interrogation of Survivors from *U-172* Sunk 13 December 1943.

Office of Naval Operations Final Report G/Serial 31. Report of the Interrogation of Survivors from *U-761* on 24 February 1944.

Office of Naval Operations Final Report G/Serial 33. Report of the Interrogation of Survivors from *U-801* Sunk on 17 March 1944.

Office of Naval Operations Final Report G/Serial 37. Report of the Interrogation of Survivors from *U-1059* Sunk 19 March 1944.

Office of Naval Operations Final Report G/Serial 39. Report of the Interrogation of Survivors from *U-860* Sunk on 15 June 1944.

Office of Naval Operations Final Report G/Serial 46. Report of the Interrogation of Survivors from *U-1229* Sunk 20 August 1944.

Office of the Chief of Naval Operations, O.N.I G/Serial No. 5, Report on the Interrogation of Survivors from *U-94* Sunk on August 27, 1942.

Office of the Chief of Naval Operations, O.N.I. 250-G/Serial 12. Report on the Interrogation of Survivors from *U-569* Sunk on May 22, 1943.

Office of the Chief of Naval Operations, O.N.I G/Serial No. 15, Report on the Interrogation of Survivors from *U-118* Sunk on 12 June 1943.

Office of the Chief of Naval Operations, O.N.I G/Serial 17. Report on the Interrogation of Survivors from *U-598* Sunk on 23 July 1943.

Office of the Chief of Naval Operations, O.N.I G/Serial 20. Report on the Interrogation of Survivors from *U-487* Sunk on 13 July 1943.

Office of the Chief of Naval Operations, O.N.I G/Serial No 21. Report on the Interrogation of Survivors from *U-615* Sunk on 7 August 1943.

Roberts, Michael D. Dictionary of American Naval Aviation Squadrons, Vol. 2. The History of VP, VPB, VP (HL) and VP (AM) Squadrons (Washington: Naval Historical Center, 2000).

Sternhell, Charles M., and Alan M. Thorndike. *Antisubmarine Warfare in World War II*. Office of the Chief of Naval Operations, Operations and Evaluations Group (Washington, 1946).

United States Atlantic Fleet, Headquarters of the Commander Fourth Fleet. Preliminary Report on the Interrogation of Survivors of Submarine Sunk 30 July 1943 in 08-28S., 32-42W by 127-B-10.

U.S. Naval Department, Interview of Captain Daniel V. Gallery, May 26, 1945.

U.S. Navy Public Relations Department, Interview of Lieutenant (jg) Harold G. Bradshaw, 30 January 1944.

Published Sources

Carey, Alan C. *Galloping Ghosts of the Brazilian Coast: United States Naval Air Operations in the South Atlantic during World War II* (New York: iUniverse Inc., 2005).

Carey, Alan C. *PV Ventura/Harpoon Units of World War 2* (Oxford, England: Osprey Publishing, 2002).

Carey, Alan C. *U.S. Navy PB4Y-1 (B-24) Liberator Squadrons in Great Britain during World War I.* (Atglen, Pennsylvania: Schiffer Publishing Inc., 2003).

Kelshall, Gaylord T. M. *The U-boat War in the Caribbean* (Annapolis, Maryland: United States Naval Institute, 1994).

Kemp, Paul. *U-boats Destroyed: German Submarine Losses in the World Wars* (London: Arms & Armour, 1997).

Morison, Samuel Eliot. *History of United States Naval Operations in World War II. The Battle of the Atlantic 1939–1943*, Vol. I (Edison, New Jersey: Castle Books, 2001).

Morison, Samuel Eliot. *History of United States Naval Operations in World War II. The Atlantic Battle Won May 1943–May 1945*, Vol. X (Edison, New Jersey: Castle Books, 2001).

Atlantic Hunters (unknown author). Naval Aviation News, October 1950.

Niestlé, Axel. *German U-boat Losses During World War II: Details of Destruction* (London: Frontline Books, 2014).

Roblin, Sebastien, *The Nazis Ordered Their U-Boats to Fight Airplanes. It was a Massive Mistake* (The National Interest, August 28, 2018).

Rohwer, Jürgen. *Axis Submarine Successes: 1939–1945 (Annapolis, Maryland: Naval Institute Press, 1983).*

Smith, Bob. *PBM Mariner in Action* (Carrolton, Texas: Squadron/Signal Publications, 1986).

Unpublished Sources

Wilson, Richard A. History of VP 83 VB-107 VPB-107 in the South Atlantic WWII.

Index

Office of Scientific Research and Development
(OSRD), xviii

Panama Sea Frontier, 2, 12, 18, 40–41
Patrol Wings (PatWing)
    Patrol Wing 3, 1, 199
    Patrol Wing 5, 1–2, 6, 59, 194
    Patrol Wing 7, 5–6, 194
    Patrol Wing 8, 5, 8
    Patrol Wing 9, 6
    Patrol Wing 11, 6, 40–41, 59, 67
    Patrol Wing 6, 12, 40
Patrol Wing, Support Force, 2–3
Pinholster, D. C., 50–51, 134
Pinnell, C. I., 108–09
Prueher, Bertram J., 58, 62, 92–94, 149

Radar development, airborne, xv–xvi.
Retro-bombs, development, 113–14
Richter, Paul, 83–84
Robertson, Thurmond, 68–69
Roch, Helmut, 109–10
Roland, R. H., 80, 82
Rollmann, Wilhelm, 99, 101
Rostin, Erwin, 17–18

Sallenger, A. H., 145–46
Schacht, Harro, 61, 64–65
Schnoor, Sergio Candido, Brazilian pilot, 91
Schnorchel (Schnorkel)128, 133–35, 183–85
Schümann, Henning, 117, 120
Sea Frontiers, establishment, 16, 25, 30
Seehausen, Gerhard, 166–67
Sidi-Ferruch, French submarine, 133
Spears, R. C., 118–19
Stark, Admiral Harold, xv–xvi, 136

Taylor, Jesse D., 180–85
Tenth Naval District, 36–38
Tepuni, William, 16–17
The Spirit of 83, PB4Y-1, 92–94

U-boat bases, established in France, xii
U-boat operations (1939–1941), xi–xii, 8–9
U-boats
    U-43, 143, 202
    U-66, 39, 145–46, 166–67
    U-68, 168, 203

U-84, 9, 34–35, 200
U-85, 13–14
U-86, 152, 202
U-94, 42–43, 112, 200
U-103, 15, 57
U-108, 39–40
U-117, 117, 140, 144–47, 166, 202
U-118, 138–41, 202
U-124, 15, 57, 64–65
U-126, 60, 62
U-128, 15, 62, 69–75
U-129, 38, 58
U-130, 11, 39–40
U-135, 112, 200
U-153, 31, 40
U-154, 18, 39, 74
U-156, 37, 45–48, 199
U-157, 40, 44
U-158, 17–18, 199
U-159, 50, 200
U-160, 60, 62, 142, 202
U-161, 66–63, 95–98, 200
U-164, 63–68, 74, 199–200
U-172, 79, 91, 93–94, 152–57, 202
U-174, 26–29, 62, 199
U-177, 108–09, 201
U-185, 41, 47, 91–95, 149–50, 202
U-199, 74–75, 86–89, 92, 200
U-217, 138–40, 202
U-220, 140, 152, 202
U-243, 130–32, 201
U-271, 33, 128–30, 201
U-279, 30, 200
U-326, 133–34, 201
U-359, 134–35, 200
U-388, 27, 200
U-392, 117–20, 201
U-402, 117–20, 201
U-408, 22–24, 27, 199
U-460, 139, 150, 202
U-464, 20–23, 199
U-467, 27, 200
U-487, 142, 202
U-490, 174–76
U-503, 15–17, 199
U-505, 13, 168–74, 199
U-507, 61–67, 200